2ND EDITION

8-SECOND PR

New Public Relations
Crash Course

LIZ H. KELLY

8-Second PR
New Public Relations Crash Course - *2nd Edition*

LIZ H. KELLY

Published by *Goody PR Press*

Goody PR(part of *Sunrise Road Media Inc.*)
Santa Monica, CA 90403
https://goodypr.com
https://8secondpr.com

Paperback: ISBN: 978-0-578-34909-1
eBook ISBN: 978-0-578-34910-7

DEDICATION

8-Second PR is dedicated to the members of the Free Press who consistently focus their energy on reporting the truth and magnifying good.

And to thought leaders with a powerful story and message (authors, CEOs, entrepreneurs, historians, speakers, producers, brands and more), we are grateful for your positive impact with words. Your stories can change the world!

And lastly, this book is dedicated to my mother, Anne Heuisler, who taught English for thirty years (including having me as a student). She gave me writing genes, encouraged creative storytelling that started with home movies and puppet shows at an early age, and has been a role model for thousands of students for decades.

GIVING BACK

A portion of all book profits from *8-Second PR* will be donated to autism charities to help the 1 in 59 children on the autism spectrum, adults with autism and their loved ones.

We encourage all of our *Goody PR* clients to adopt a charity. If you don't already have one, brainstorm and research non-profits that have a personal meaning to you and/or your organization.

Journalism is the first rough draft of history.

Philip L. Graham,
President and CEO of
THE WASHINGTON POST

TABLE OF **CONTENTS**

FOREWORD

Foreword by **Jess Todtfeld,** CSP
Former TV Producer at *ABC, NBC,* and *FOX*
Media Trainer, Speaker, and Guinness Record-Setter for Publicity

You have in your hands a blueprint or framework to follow so you can get the attention you desire.

I know a thing or two about publicity. As a TV producer, I helped people share their messages with millions. As a media trainer and business owner, I found myself on the other side of the equation, seeking publicity to help promote my knowledge and services.

In promotion of one of my books on communication, friends in the public relations field jokingly suggested that I should run my campaign bigger than anyone else. What did that mean? Guinness record big. I accomplished it using the tactics you will learn in this book.

As I embarked on that PR journey, I looked back at my time as a producer, a "gate-keeper" to see what I had learned. As Liz Kelly will state here in this book, with eight-second attention spans, it is important for us to get our message (or pitches in this case) through—succinctly, quickly, and without any confusion. It takes years to figure out what works. After reading this book, you will learn how to work through this process, faster, easier, and with more results.

Marketing is about taking your message to the market. Publicity is powerful marketing as you are being presented to the masses by a third party. Publicity brings with it a third-party endorsement of you and what you are sharing with your audience. This endorsement is something you can use as promotion for years to come. This is one more reason why it is so valuable.

Some of the biggest secrets to breaking through and being successful in your media outreach are in the chapters of this book. You will quickly and easily learn how to grow your own PR superpowers. Figuring out your "wow" and being able to properly tell your story are some of the top strategies for connecting and winning over media gate-keepers. Surprisingly, most people pitching the media have trouble with both.

When I was on the receiving end of pitches, I booked and produced over 6,000 segments. In those 13 years, I can only imagine how many pitches were thrown out or deleted because they were confusing, did not match my outlet, or just could not communicate (quickly) why this was a story worth sharing.

Here is the good news. The media needs your help. They need it badly. And they really do want to hear from you. Why? Because they have an insatiable need for more content. That is where you come in. If you can stand out from the crowd and share stories that need to be told, many will give you the green light.

Follow the advice in this book. It will not only help you become better at the PR game, but become a better writer and better marketer, as well.

PREFACE

After doing marketing and PR for almost 20 years primarily for brands, corporations, small business owners, experts, authors and speakers, our goal is to give back by sharing our PR secrets in this revised *8-Second PR – New Public Relations Crash Course* (2nd Edition) to help you magnify your WOW Story! You will learn our updated publicity process, bonus tips and new case study examples in this updated version – that most Public Relations Agencies would never share with their clients.

To help you learn how to get more earned media (TV, print, radio and podcast interviews), you will find first-hand insights and examples so that you can get free publicity. If you are a CEO or marketing professional, my secondary goal is to help you better understand how PR works. If you hire a PR Agency or digital marketing service, you will learn how to work better together to get great media results.

Our *Goody PR* agency is grateful to have booked thousands of media interviews for clients on the *TODAY Show*, *CNN*, *HLN Weekend Express*, *BBC World News*, *PBS Postcards*, *The Chicago Tribune*, *Minneapolis Star-Tribune*, *NPR*, *710 WOR AM*, hundreds of local TV and podcast interviews, and many more outlets.

This marketing success story did not happen magically overnight. You will learn how we had to work for free for a year to get started and learn from mistakes. Our PR journey started after hiring two publicists for six months, and then booking 500+ media hits (print, radio, television and syndicated) for our first book: *Smart Man Hunting – A Fast Track Dating Guide to Finding Mr. Right* over a five year period. After this experience, we felt compelled to help others get their story in the headlines.

With the average attention span of an adult being eight seconds, *8-Second PR* will offer new tools and tips to help you get your brand in the news. Your biggest challenge is to tell a clear, concise, and compelling story. Great storytelling is a core skill you will learn in this book. And with a lot of practice and dedication, you can have immediate and long-term media success using our Story Energizer Process!

I first fell in love with brand story telling in a college marketing classes where we were asked to define the ice cream market segments as an extra credit project. After graduating, we helped define many corporate products and services as a training executive by partnering with marketing pros to define a powerful story and launch new products.

The most important skill I learned early in my career was to ask questions to define a moving story that emotionally connects to your target audience. By fine-tuning this discovery process, brand storytelling became one of my greatest strengths. This "magic" or WOW is what can move your brand forward with the same speed and force as a superhero like *Wonder Woman* (whose character was part of the inspiration for our book cover).

CASE STUDY EXAMPLE - FALL IN LOVE WITH BRAND STORYTELLING

While working for the first *Sprint PCS* office in the United States in the Washington D.C. area, I was fortunate to work with marketing pros who taught me how to tell great brand stories. Our company was called *Sprint Spectrum*. It was a "beta test" for *Sprint PCS* in the Baltimore-Washington area only. The best part was our team was 100 percent independent of

Sprint's Kansas City Headquarters for the first two years, so we could be creative and innovative with marketing and messaging.

When we launched *Sprint Spectrum* in 1995, no one predicted the company would sell 300 percent over forecast in the first year. As the first *GSM (Global System for Mobile)* network in the United States, we sold the first "affordable" cell phone ($99 Ericsson phones were the most popular, along with *Nokia* and *Motorola*). People could not get these phones fast enough, and we were in every major business news publication.

My job was to lead the corporate training team of seven professionals plus customer service interns, who trained 1,800 new employees in 18 months (100 people per month) how to sell and support our products and services. I sat in marketing meetings with promotional pros who previously worked for *Nike, Haagen Dazs*, and *Nestle* to determine the best way to train the front line employees (retail, sales, customer service, and retailers like *Best Buy*). This job is where I really fell in love with the whole brand storytelling and creative process. It was fun, and it worked!

To keep the product story simple, our team partnered across departments to develop three to eight key selling points for each launch. We then created PowerPoint "huddle packages" to train all customer-facing employees quickly – with pictures and bullet points that told a story. This process worked! And we were hooked!

When I later moved to Santa Monica, California, and worked for tech startups in the early 2000s, I always asked the team - on day one - what are the key selling points for the product? When there were blank stares, I drafted a bulleted list for the leadership team's review. Please do this exercise if you don't have them already.

My turning point into marketing and PR full-time started when I found myself laid-off after 9/11. No one was hiring, so I decided to write the book that I never had time to do. Drawing upon my corporate and startup experiences, I used the same discovery process to learn what it took to write a good book. I wrote about forty hours per week for nine months straight, and was laser-focused.

The result was a fun and practical how-to dating book, *Smart Man Hunting*, with multiple media hooks resulting in hundreds of interviews on *CNN, Lifetime*, many local TV stations, *The Chicago Tribune, The Washington Post, BBC Radio*, and more.

Honestly, I had no clue what I was doing writing my first book, except that I knew how to package a story. Many book marketing experts and media coaches taught me how to make the story media-friendly with great sound bites and fun examples. This creative storytelling process all started by defining the book's table of contents, secret sauce and key benefits for the reader. When brainstorming PR topics, think about what makes your story unique?

To make this *8-Second PR* marketing tips book simple and powerful, I have packaged everything in a fun, "how-to promote your business guide" with an eight-step Story Energizer Process, eight PR Superpowers, real-life case studies, and action items in each chapter to help you energize your story for Ultimate Media Success!

CASE STUDY EXAMPLE - HOW I LEARNED ABOUT PUBLISHING AND PR

For my first book, I approached the brand story development and publication process the same way you would approach a job you love or passion project. I was so dedicated that I would start editing some days at 6:00 a.m. (I am NOT a morning person and did not have a job at the time, so this early rising was really out of character). Our writing process included coffee meetings and conferences to ask authors and book marketing experts questions about these goals:

1. How to write a great book.
2. How to self-publish a book.

3. How to get a literary agent.
4. How to get a publisher.
5. How to write a great marketing plan.
6. How to pitch reporters with relevant media hooks.
7. How to write great talking points for an interview.
8. How to provide powerful content during interviews, and get invited back.

As a rough estimate, I probably invested over $100,000 in mostly my time, going to conferences, hiring PR firms, hiring media coaches, hiring a website developer, hiring a graphic artist, hiring a video reel editor, and more.

The good news is that the publishing and public relations process worked. As a result, I was fortunate to secure over 500 media hits (print, radio, TV and syndicated interviews) for three versions of the same book (more on this later). My first TV interview was on the local *ABC News WMAR* in my hometown of Baltimore, Maryland, at 5:50am EST the day after Thanksgiving (when no one was watching). The media magnification process grew from there (more about this later).

The Mission of this *8-Second PR* book is to empower at least 1 million people to both tell their WOW Story and Magnify their Positive Impact on the world. Are you in?

The reality is that the most important part of marketing anything is having a moving story that makes people cheer, cry, scream, stand up, smile or take action. You must immediately make an emotional connection with your audience (reporters, followers, readers, and influencers) to attract new fans, build loyal Brand Ambassadors who want to share your story, and increase your revenues.

To move your brand forward, you must become a "Word Artist" who loves to develop stories with meaning. If the message does not click immediately, keep reinventing the story until it generates your desired media results and fan cheers.

Marketing and public relations professionals make it all look so easy, but trust me, it is not. Pitching your story to reporters is like being a sales person for your brand. Be prepared for rejection and learning lessons as part of your everyday process. The key is to never give up! And our goal is to provide you with tips and tools to succeed!

Based on our experience, we will compare two night-and-day telecommunications company case studies in this book. Company A (*Sprint Spectrum*) sold 300 percent over forecast while Company B (*Motorola's Iridium*) filed bankruptcy after spending $7 billion—and these results were mostly due to the brand story!

If you take away anything from this book, remember this: A brand without a "Wow Story" will go nowhere fast.

Instead of your brand being a flop, we want your fans to be willing to sleep outside all night to get your book, services, or products - a scenario we witnessed at San Diego's *Comic-Con International* for eight years.

As a marketing foundation, getting to your WOW Story includes multiple elements. It is your personal and business brand, website, social media presence and digital assets (graphics, logo, photographs, videos, blogs, colors and more). It is your book, products and services, and business cards. It is what you wear, what you say, how you say it, and more that all contribute to the way the world views your brand.

With 4.55 billion or 57.6 of the world's total population being active on social media (as of October 2021, according to *DataPortal*, Kepios analysis), you can no longer rely on one-way marketing, which is posting an ad and not engaging with your fans. While working for *Fox Interactive Media/myspace* (2007-2008, when their business was booming), everyone focused on engaging fans in two-way conversations through compelling content, comments, contests, polls, events and more to increase Word-of-Mouth (WOM) Marketing for big brands such as *Toyota*, *Nike*, and *VO5*.

It's the same thing for creating public relations and marketing buzz for any brand! Relying solely on paid ads like they did during the *Mad Men* advertising agency days in New York City in the 1960s no longer works. Social Media Marketing is now a much faster way to reach your audience versus posting a billboard or magazine ad.

As a published author, I quickly learned about the power of EARNED MEDIA (where someone else vouches for your product or service) for building a brand. Some of our recent interviews for *Goody PR* clients have included *CNN International*, *CBS Health Watch*, *The Atlantic*, *Fast Company*, *ESPN Radio*, and many local TV news stories. You always want more reporters talking positively about you and your brand versus PAID MEDIA where you pay for ad space.

When you consider investing time and money in your public relations, remember, earned media is 3x more valuable than any paid advertisement because someone else is saying your book, product, or service are great. For example, you can pay $1,000 for a TV ad to be aired during a local news broadcast or have an interview that is worth $3,000 in Calculated Publicity Value during the same time on the same network (more on this later). Which option sounds better to you?

Once you have defined a Wow Story that connects with your target audience, you cannot stop there. It takes a lot of hard work, moving media hooks, good timing, follow-up, along with a lot of patience and a little luck to get into headline news stories.

Are you ready to learn how to energize your story with *8-Second PR?* You can have great media success and business results with the right tips, tools, focus and story!

Let's get started!

Reminder:

"EVERYTHING YOU DO OR SAY IS
PUBLIC RELATIONS."

– UNKNOWN

INTRODUCTION

> "IF I WAS DOWN TO THE LAST DOLLAR OF MY
> MARKETING BUDGET, I'D SPEND IT ON PR!"
>
> – BILL GATES

Are you struggling with how to get coverage in media outlets so people know your name? Do you want to learn how to book a TV interview with one email pitch or text? And would you like to increase your awareness, credibility, and sales by having other people recommend your brand in TV, print, radio and podcast interviews? If you answered yes to any of these questions, you are in the right place.

As a CEO/Founder, business owner, marketing manager, author, expert, speaker or brand expert, your challenge is telling a clear, concise, and compelling story in a way that immediately interests a reporter to tell your story. Remember, the average attention span of an adult is 8 seconds, so you've got to get to the point, IMMEDIATELY!

To fast-track your promotional journey, you'll learn a proven *8-Second PR* Story Energizer Process and eight new PR Superpowers to help you score more earned media, so your brand is found at the top of the page in *Google* search results.

In this "New Public Relations Crash Course" *8-Second PR – 2nd Edition*, it has been completely revised with new advice tips, national media case study examples and best practices for you. Here are 20 new things that can help you amplify your brand:

20 NEW STRATEGIES IN 8-SECOND PR - 2ND EDITION

1. New tips for navigating PR in a post-pandemic media world.
2. Many new case study examples added (especially national TV and radio interviews).
3. How to be a Great Media Guest who gets invited back.
4. How to build a Thought Leader Brand and get columns.
5. If you hire a PR agency, how to be a Great PR Collaborator to get great results.
6. How to better promote your book on *Amazon*.
7. What to say when you call a local TV newsroom.
8. How to get on the *TODAY Show* (see case study in Chapter 8).
9. How to get on *CNN* within 5 minutes via a text message (see case study).
10. How to measure the Calculated Publicity Value for TV interviews.
11. How to book 30+ podcasts for one book (see case study).
12. How to pitch podcasts to reach your niche audience.
13. How to Host a podcast (see case study on our New *8-Second Branding Podcast*.)
14. How to create a Digital Press Kit and *Google Docs* folders with visuals for reporters.
15. How to secure a column in a publication that reaches your target audience.
16. How to use Influencer Marketing – paid and unpaid.
17. Updated Digital PR statistics and social media tips to be more current.
18. How book awards can help promote your brand.
19. How to submit a book to our New *Goody Business Book Awards* whose mission is to "Uplift Author Voices" making a positive impact.
20. And many more surprises and Bonus Content.

If you have a personal or business brand to promote, you can amplify your story faster using our *8-Second PR* approach. You want to move millions the same way fans go wild at the *Super Bowl*, stand in line for hours to attend a concert, or anxiously await superhero movies. For example, you want your brand to be like a *Marvel* movie character (*Captain America, Hulk, Ant-Man,*

Scarlet Witch, Spider-Man, Iron Man and all *The Avengers*) that moves billions of fans worldwide!

To get booked on your top media picks, we will highlight how to pitch timely topics and use impactful messages that hammer home. Each of the eight chapters in this book includes a PR Superpower with action items to enhance your skills. For example, you will learn how to use your Media Hook Superpower to connect with reporters. With these new insights, you can secure more interviews on your favorite news programs, national magazines, or top radio shows.

By combining all eight PR Superpowers, tools and strategies in this book, your personal and/or business brand will become unstoppable. And in a digital world, everyone can benefit by reading the tips in this book for how to better present your personal brand online.

WHO SHOULD READ 8-SECOND PR TO PROMOTE A PERSONAL OR BUSINESS BRAND?

o Anyone who wants new ideas for how to better define a brand story for a business, product, service or book.
o Anyone who wants to have a personal or business brand get more recognition, and increase their SEO (Search Engine Optimization) so potential customers find you more easily online.
o Anyone who wants to get publicity, increase credibility, and/or increase sales for a brand.
o A business leader who wants to hire a marketing/PR agency, better understand the publicity process and/or be a supportive partner in the promotion process.
o Anyone who wants better control over a brand's reputation online and offline.
o Marketing and public relations professionals who want to hear another POV (point of view).
o College and graduate school students who are studying marketing, communications, public relations, and/or journalism.

> o Baby boomers who want a crash course on the power of digital marketing, branding and publicity.

While the majority think they can explain their story, many put people to sleep in less than eight seconds. We cannot stress enough the importance of IMMEDIATELY CONNECTING with your audience in a powerful way so that they remember you.

Great PR is about inspiring, connecting, and moving your desired audience to take action. The more entertaining and educational your story, the more the media, fans, and influencers will want to share it.

And while "Your WHY" is paramount, it is even more important to explain "WHY does it REALLY matter to your audience? And Why NOW?" A story pitch to a reporter or producer should never be "all about you." Instead, you should include how their audience can learn or benefit from your tips or insights.

Your brand message needs to be so compelling that people want to take a second look at what you are offering. While your delivery approach may be different for each marketing element (marketing, public relations, social media, events, books, promotions, seminars), a consistent message is a must for all branding elements.

You must be able to tell your brand story CONSISTENTLY in one sentence. Then, once you capture your audience's attention, you can expand on the topic.

CASE STUDY EXAMPLE - NO CLEAR MESSAGE WITH 14 MEDIA AGENCIES

As an example, let's take a look at a real story scenario where a major company did not have a consistent communications strategy. When I worked on the social media strategy as a marketing consultant for a major energy company in Southern California, I discovered they had already hired fourteen other marketing agencies. While developing digital marketing ideas for them, I uncovered that each agency was using a different brand message that created confusion.

As a result, the marketing team hosted an all-day marketing strategy meeting with these agencies in one room. The result was a complex summary chart to consolidate their story. It was a great first step towards getting everyone on the same page.

Our project ended shortly afterward because they did not want to add a fifteenth agency to the mix. We walked away with the satisfaction that our greatest gift was moving them toward one brand story.

WHAT IS THE WHY FOR THIS *8-SECOND PR* BOOK?

While many PR experts hold their secrets close, our Mission is to empower at least one million people and brands to magnify their positive impact through Wow Storytelling and media coverage. Honestly, I get a charge out of making others look good and want you to get more eyes on your brand. You can gain insights based on our unique 360-view as a former corporate executive, entrepreneur, published author, entertainment reporter, podcast host, and contributor to various publications. We know what many reporters are thinking as someone who's been a contributor to the *Huffington Post, The Examiner,* and *Red Carpet Report*. I have also ghostwritten columns for *Entrepreneur, Home Business Magazine, Inman News*, and many more outlets.

When I took a personality profile test designed by entrepreneur coach and author Roger Hamilton, it came back that my dominant personality trait was a "Star." Roger explained that a "Star" is like Oprah – it's someone who can look good on camera, but where they really shine is making others look good. So please let me help you look good!

After publishing and promoting my first book with success, I decided to use my marketing skills for good full-time at the end of 2008. I was no longer promoting my dating book and wanted to help others get their message heard by the masses.

SMART MAN HUNTING – 3 BOOK VERSION EVOLUTION

Below is a progression of our dating book to give you insights on how you can constantly re-invent your story to gain more interviews and reach a broader audience.

Each of our three book releases had a new marketing campaign based on new content (similar to this 2nd edition of *8-Second PR*.) The result was a solid five years of 500+ media interviews in national and local outlets, including *CNN, Lifetime, USA TODAY, Orlando Sentinel, Cosmopolitan, Marie Claire, BBC Radio,* and many more.

Book 2002 - *Smart Man Hunting* was originally self-published in 2002 through *iUniverse*. I hired a graphic artist to do the book cover, and it was available to purchase on *Amazon* and *Barnes and Noble* after only nine months. The version was a good start, and was updated in a major way for future editions.

Book 2nd Edition 2003 - Because the book was publicized on national TV in the first few months (*NBC's The Other Half* with Dick Clark), *Barnes and Noble* picked it up for a special program. They chose seven titles out of 12,000 self-published books in 2003. Fortunately, they assigned an experienced editor who worked with me collaboratively. The revised book featured new artwork, new content, and a book endorsement by John Gray Ph.D. (*Men Are from Venus, Women Are from Venus*) on the front cover. This 2nd edition was distributed online and in *Barnes and Noble* stores nationwide.

Book 3rd Edition 2006 - After more mega media hits in national and local outlets, I finally found a literary agent (through a friend, Vicki Winters, who met him on *Match.com*). Fortunately, he agreed to represent me within 24 hours of our first call. In addition, he secured a publishing deal within two weeks after sending the book out to publishers for an auction. *Kensington*

Books in New York published the 3rd edition with a new cover, new content, and the backing of a major publishing house. This book deal also came with a royalty advance at last!

Along with having a great brand story, media credibility, and household name testimonials, our dating book magic was 26 fun ABC Man Codes for the different personality types. These man codes (*Bachelor Available, Justifying Juggler, Confident Metro Male*) were the book's secret sauce because it provided unique, fun and relevant content that reporters loved (more on this later). What is the magic in your story? (We will talk more about this in Chapter 1: Wow Story.)

IMPORTANT AUTHOR TIP - If you ever publish a new edition of your book, you MUST edit and keep track of "What is New" so you have new content to pitch reporters and attract readers.

Because of the need to be relevant and timely with any media hook, I pitched dating stories based on holidays, current events (Valentine's Day, March Madness, Back-to-School), headline news, and evolving technologies (new dating sites, apps and more). We will talk more about this pitching process throughout the book, and especially in Chapter 8: Story Reinvention.

Most of my dating book interviews happened while I was working at corporate jobs. Juggling media requests with a full-time job can get a little crazy, but you will make it happen if it's a priority. You'll need to coordinate interviews, take time off, and be ready to apply TV makeup on the fly. While this balancing act sounds hard, if you are truly dedicated to your brand and mission, you will find the time for interviews.

For the best PR results, you ALWAYS want to be ready and flexible with great content when a reporter asks for an interview. Remember, the reporter is doing you a huge favor by interviewing you – for free – so drop everything to accommodate their schedule. While I do recognize that scheduling challenges can create some surreal circumstances, you must be really committed to your publicity.

CASE STUDY EXAMPLE - OUR ALMOST OPRAH MOMENT!

During the first week of working for a tech startup in Los Angeles, I was asked by an Oprah producer to confirm that I could fly to Chicago to be on *The Oprah Winfrey Show* "**if they needed me**." This request was a dream come true for any author, so despite the career risk of asking for time off at a new job, I took the gamble.

For this potential interview, the producer asked me to find a happy couple who I helped find love and confirm that they could also fly to Chicago. To be discreet, we made all our calls in the parking lot during breaks and after work. "If it happened" is the key phrase that was on my mind, which added stress to this juggling act.

The Oprah team ended up selecting Candace Bushnell (who wrote *Sex and the City*) for the segment instead of me. While most authors would scream out loud (okay, I did this too), this competition is what you will face when a reporter calls (especially for major media).

Millions of people with your area of expertise also want to share their story on TV. You must find ways to stand out to get any interview. I was not even close to Candace Bushnell's level as an author. Instead of getting upset, I celebrated coming so close to an Oprah interview with this level of competition.

Pitching your story to reporters and getting rejected are all part of this PR journey. When you get a media hit (story published), take time to do a dance. Every story (local TV, national TV, radio, podcast, blog and print outlets) adds up when building momentum and an online presence. You will have much better luck with smaller outlets at first. Don't discount a local reporter, blog or unknown outlet because with the reach of digital media, it may still get you great results.

Today, brands have new digital marketing tools to propel their story forward through social media, graphics, smartphone cameras, apps, email campaigns and more. We will talk more about building your Digital PR Superpower and lessons learned from teaching digital marketing at *UCLA Extension* in Chapter 2.

By now you might be asking, what is *8-Second PR*? Let's take a closer look. Here is a sneak-peek of the top eight things you will learn in this quick guide. You'll walk away with a plan for your Ultimate Media Success to raise brand awareness, increase sales, and change lives.

8-SECOND PR WILL TEACH YOU HOW TO:

1. Develop a memorable Wow Story that is authentic from the heart.
2. Get to the point immediately and create an emotional reaction.
3. Use attention-grabbing phrases in the first eight seconds of an interview.
4. Attract earned media interviews for free that are 5x more valuable than any paid ad with timely media hooks and powerful pitches.
5. Speak to your target audience at the right time using the right media.
6. Be entertaining and educational when presenting your brand.
7. Explain how your brand helps improve the lives of others.
8. Reinvent your story to consistently to score major media interviews.

8-Second PR will teach you a Story Energizer Process to propel your brand forward. Every chapter in this book includes a list of eight action items, relevant examples, and a PR Superpower that you can make your story even bigger than it is.

8-SECOND PR STORY ENERGIZER PROCESS

1. WOW STORY - Define Your Story Magic to Inspire Fans and Media.
2. DIGITAL PR - Dominate Your Digital Bank to Increase Word-of-Mouth Marketing.
3. CONTENT STRENGTH - Create Compelling Content that Emotionally Connects with Readers.

4. MEDIA HOOKS - Write Powerful Pitches to Move Reporters to Cover Your Story.
5. MEDIA VISION - Reach Your Target Audience by Laser Focusing on Niche Reporters.
6. MEDIA HITS - Make Your Interview Take Flight to Score Mega Media.
7. MESSAGE IMPACT - Magnify Your Interviews with Meaningful Soundbites.
8. STORY REINVENTION - Reposition Your Story and Extend Media Success.

Does this Story Energizer Process sound simple? Think again. It is really easy to say, and another thing to actually deliver during interviews. You must avoid rambling and get to the point with meaningful content. To enhance your media messages and results, you will learn how to tell a story that people want to share.

And now, can we have a DRUM ROLL, PLEASE? Are you ready for your *8-Second PR* Superpowers? Here is the magic in this book that will help you magnify your brand and reach the right audience at the right time.

8-SECOND PR SUPERPOWERS = ULTIMATE MEDIA SUCCESS

1. WOW Storytelling Superpower
2. Digital PR Superpower
3. Content Connector Superpower
4. Media Hook Superpower
5. Media Vision Superpower
6. Media Hits Superpower
7. Message Impact Superpower
8. Story Reinvention Superpower

Together, your *8-Second PR* Superpowers will make your brand unstoppable.

Your mission, if you choose to accept, is to protect, promote, and propel your brand story to new heights. And with your new *8-Second PR* Superpowers and mega media exposure, you will be able to amplify your positive impact on the world.

When developing your story, you must also think about your brand impact. How do you want to make a difference with your message?

According to *Inc. Magazine*, 85 percent of consumers have a better opinion of and prefer to work with businesses and brands that support a charity they also like.

Let's be real. No one wants to hear about you all the time. Your story will be much more meaningful if you can show how you and/or your brand can improve lives. It must be authentic and come from the heart. If a story does not align with your core, the audience will sense it immediately and go find another similar brand to support.

Everything in this guidebook is designed to help you attract hundreds of earned media interviews! We will talk about our baseball analogy for getting media interviews published later in Chapter 7 with your Media Hits Superpower.

To give you more ideas, you will find many case study examples in this book of what has worked and what did not fly. You can gain insights from our experience, and mega brand examples. We want to make it easier for you to get your story defined, shared, and magnified - quickly.

It is your time! Let's make it happen! Are you ready to take your New Public Relations Crash Course?

Don't procrastinate anymore. Keep reading, take notes, have fun brainstorming and develop your marketing and PR plan! You will also find a recap of each chapter's Action Items in the Conclusion of this book as your PR Success Roadmap.

Let's start building your Wow now!

Reminder:

"IT TAKES 20 YEARS TO BUILD A REPUTATION AND FIVE MINUTES TO RUIN IT. IF YOU THINK ABOUT THAT, YOU'LL DO THINGS DIFFERENTLY."

– WARREN BUFFET

STEP 1

WOW STORY

Define Your Story
Magic to Inspire Fans
and Media

> "PUBLICITY IS ABSOLUTELY CRITICAL.
> A GOOD PR STORY IS INFINITELY MORE
> EFFECTIVE THAN A FRONT-PAGE AD."
>
> — RICHARD BRANSON

Can you gain someone's attention in eight seconds? Honestly, how long does it take you to explain what you or your business does at a busy networking event? Can you explain your brand, book, or service with passion in one sentence? In today's fast-track world, you must be able to tell a powerful story with magic that moves people to want to know more.

With the average attention span of adult now being only 8.25 seconds (according to a *Microsoft Corp.* study), your job as a marketer just got a gazillion times harder.

This number dropped from twelve seconds in 2000 to eight seconds in 2015, and is probably lower now. In response to this study, *TIME* magazine reported this headline, "You Now Have a Shorter Attention Span Than a Goldfish" because the attention of goldfish is nine seconds.

The impacts of our decreasing attention spans in the digital age of smartphones, computers, tablets and smart watches have completely changed how you market and consume content. To get your point across, you must make an immediate connection with your audience, or they will move on without thinking about anything you just said!

To kick-off this *8-Second PR* book, we are going to dig deeper into developing your Wow Story. For marketing, public relations, and social media campaigns, you must have a clear, concise, and compelling story that gets both fans and the media excited.

AUTHOR PR CHALLENGE
IN A HIGHLY COMPETITIVE LANDSCAPE

As an author, your competition is off-the-charts! Did you know 4,600+ books are published EVERY DAY, and 1.7+ million books are published per year in the United States (according to the latest *ProQuest Bowker Report*, Oct 15, 2019)?

For your book to succeed, you must find ways to stand out with a unique POV (Point of View) and compelling content that inspires readers and reporters to share your work. And your marketing and PR success all starts with your story-behind-the-story.

Even though a Wow Story is the most important factor for your success, it always amazes us how many business leaders and CEOs skip this step. To help your brand succeed, here is your first, and probably most important, PR Superpower. If you can master this skill, you will be able to maximize your media exposure, brand awareness, and sales results.

Let's get started!

PR SUPERPOWER 1 - WOW STORYTELLING SUPERPOWER

You need to go way beyond telling a great brand story using the Wow Storytelling Superpower by defining your magic. By mastering your message, you can inspire fans, media and influencers to make your story go viral. You must make a lasting impression that moves the reader, reporter, or customer to share your brand story - over and over again.

Yes, you want to find an A-team, unique product, and powerful spokespeople, but ultimately, your media results go back to the brand story.

If you have the determination and dedication to edit your story more than 100 times to make it truly inspiring, you will have Ultimate Media Success. Use your first *8-Second PR* Superpower to stand out and be memorable. You've got this!

For this chapter, we will review how to build your brand story so it connects on many levels, provide insights from case study examples, and look at the details for two telecommunications companies with vastly different marketing results.

While reading this book, think about your personal and business brands. In many cases, there will be an overlap between the two. No one else has your personal story, and your WHY behind a product, service, or book, is how you can stand out.

As you go through the steps, take notes and start immediately applying these action items. Let's start making magic happen by reviewing the eight action items for this chapter.

STEP 1 ACTION ITEMS -
DEFINE YOUR STORY MAGIC TO INSPIRE FANS AND MEDIA

1. Identify three life changers that drive your personal/business brand story.
2. Pinpoint what work you/your company would do for free.
3. Define your personal brand using the power of threes.
4. Define your business brand wheel driving your story.
5. Identify three to seven Unique Selling Points your brand can offer others.
6. Define your brand mission, vision, and values.
7. Find three people positively impacted by your brand.
8. Share your story. Revise it. Share again.

PR SUPERPOWER 1 - WOW STORYTELLING SUPERPOWER

Successful marketing and PR is always driven by a powerful story. When I was recently with a *Goody PR* client at *FOX 11 Los Angeles* in the green room, someone asked me, "Why do you think they pick one person over another for a TV interview?" My reply was, "It's all about the story."

For this *FOX 11* interview, it was for a pre-election panel discussion with three guests on *The Issue Is* show hosted by Elex Michaelson. There are thousands of experts in Los Angeles who would have loved to be on this panel. The host chose our client Danny Zuker because he had a new and relevant political humor book, was an Executive Producer for *ABC's* hit TV Series *Modern Family*, and is a comedian. All of these things contribute to his "personal brand story" and why he was chosen for this special edition panel.

As a business brand example, let's look at the *Goody Awards* for Social Good. When developing this brand story, we met with over 20 CEOs of startups in the Los Angeles area to get their feedback on this online/offline awards program. Our pitch deck was on an *iPad*, and it illustrated the mission to inspire people to immediately recognize people, businesses, and brands doing good via social media. The lightning finally struck while I was having dinner with a CEO friend in Beverly Hills. He looked at me and said, "You are all about entertainment. We have the *Emmys, GRAMMYs*, and why not the *Goodys*?" And that was the magic moment for defining the *Goody Awards* brand story.

From that point forward, we changed our PR company name to *Goody PR*, and launched the *Goody Business Book Awards* in 2022 – all in sync with our personal and business brand and to "Magnify Good"!

Stories also have a HUGE impact on the success or failure of movies produced by the entertainment business. As I learned working for *Paramount Pictures*, it is a "business" because the primary goal is to make money. However, you are never guaranteed to make money on a film or book without great content and a marketing plan. How many times have you gone to a movie because of an awesome cast only to be disappointed by the story?

For example, here are three movie flops with bad scripts. Despite having incredible star power, these films got horrible ratings.

MOVIE STORY FLOPS – GREAT CAST, BAD SCRIPT

The Big Wedding - 7% rating on Rotten Tomatoes
Cast: Robert De Niro, Katherine Heigl, Diane Keaton, Amanda Seyfried, Topher Grace, Susan Sarandon, Robin Williams, Ben Barnes

Valentine's Day - 18% rating on Rotten Tomatoes
Cast: Bradley Cooper, Julia Roberts, Jessica Alba, Kathy Bates, Jessica Biel, Eric Dane, Jennifer Garner, Anne Hathaway, Ashton Kutcher, Jamie Foxx, Patrick Dempsey, Taylor Swift, Taylor Lautner, Queen Latifah, George Lopez, Hector Elizondo, Shirley MacLaine, Topher Grace

Grown Ups - 7% rating on Rotten Tomatoes
Cast: Adam Sandler, Kevin James, Chris Rock, David Spade, Salma Hayek, Taylor Lautner, Maya Rudolph, Mario Bello, Steve Buscemi, Tim Meadows, Shaquille O'Neal, Colin Quinn, Jon Lovitz,

I cannot stress enough the importance of defining your Wow Story in every marketing element. Your message should be the same across all marketing campaign tactics, which may include public relations, social media marketing, websites, blogs, videos, photographs, games, contests, apps, mobile marketing, ads, billboards, events, and more. Everything should revolve around a CONSISTENT clear, concise, and compelling story.

The messages should sync between your personal and business brand to make it even more genuine. For example, our *Goody PR* client *Warriors Heart* is the first and ONLY private and accredited residential treatment program in the U.S. exclusively for "warriors" (military, veterans, and first responders) struggling with addiction, PTSD and co-occurring issues. The WHY behind their team is what makes this program so authentic. The three founders are successful treatment providers, including two in long-term recovery. In addition, the founders include a *U.S. Army Special Forces* veteran, a former law enforcement officer (LEO) and a successful entrepreneur who has built social impact teams. In this case, the personal brands of the founders clearly represent their business brand.

And after the COVID-19 pandemic, people especially want to work with companies and individuals who "walk the talk" for whatever they represent.

WHY YOU MUST DEFINE YOUR BRAND'S SOCIAL IMPACT STORY!

Nearly two-thirds of US-based employees said that COVID-19 has caused them to reflect on their purpose in life. And nearly half said that they are reconsidering the kind of work they do because of the pandemic. Millennials were three times more likely than others to say that they were reevaluating work. - McKinsey & Company

Your brand story definition process may take months, or even years, to fine-tune. We urge you to start brainstorming and write down whatever comes to mind. Do not wait another minute. The first version is always horrible, but you will get nowhere if you do not JUST GET STARTED!

Test your brand story with friends, go on a walk to think about it, revise it, test it again, show it to people in the coffee shop, post ideas on social media, and ask for HONEST feedback. And then revise it again - until you get to a magic moment where you can actually see the desired emotional reaction on people's faces.

3 CS FOR WOW STORYTELLING

CLEAR - Your story must be clear in all your marketing communications so that the message is immediately obvious. Most media use sixth-grade vocabulary in order to reach a broad audience. While watching the news, I am always puzzled by guests who confuse the audience with graduate-school vocabulary. I dream about having a buzzer to hit every time someone uses a fancy word on the news. Instead, you need to go to the 30,000-foot level to tell your story clearly.

CONCISE - There is a delicate balance between being clear and concise. Your best bet is to use emphasis statements and the power of threes. When TV pundits say, "The top three things are . . ." or "The most important thing is . . .", they are the media pros to watch closely because they know how to keep the audience's attention. These pundits give you a focal point so you pay more attention. Listen carefully to what these storytelling experts say, and practice this emphasis statement approach.

COMPELLING - No matter how clear and concise you are, your words must make an emotional connection. Your message has to hit home to connect with your audience. It is never enough to just say "buy my new, cool, shiny object." You need to include the WHY behind it and HOW it can change lives. Having a compassionate spokesperson who can tell moving stories about how your product or service changed their life forever is the key to going from a sleeper to a WOW in all media!

DEFINING A NEW BRAND STORY

As a *UCLA Extension* instructor for digital marketing, my students define a new business idea and become CEO of their "new company" during the first week. This new product/service is the basis of all of their assignments during the 11-week class. Finding the right brand name and product in Week 1 is always the hardest part for my students.

Many students (and authors) come up with a brand name that is a cliché phrase or one-word that is already used by MANY others. The first step for defining ANY brand is to always Google the name, and see if you can buy the exact match URL.com on *GoDaddy* (or other service). Please – please – check this before deciding on your brand name!

Once our *UCLA Extension* students find a brand name that stands out, they are then challenged with defining their unique product, key selling points, competitive comparison, five-year budget, social media strategy, team, and more in a marketing plan. Their final exam is a 10-slide executive summary pitch deck that highlights their brand with charts, images, and visuals that would entice an investor to give them money.

For anyone thinking about starting a business or promoting a book, this pitch deck format is a great first step for defining your story versus writing an elaborate business plan. If people do not get excited about your idea immediately, you need to keep revising it until you find the WOW.

Similar to the media, a potential investor's time is very limited. Initially, a Venture Capitalist only wants to hear your story in a five-twenty minute pitch meeting. Your success with potential investors and the media is based on your ability to get to the point quickly and make a lasting impression!

If you are still defining your brand, consider creating a pitch deck to fine-tune your story using this format. It's a great exercise in branding!

DEFINE YOUR BRAND STORY USING A 10 SLIDE PITCH DECK*

- **Problem** – Describe the problem or issue that you are solving.
- **Solution** – How will your brand alleviate the pain?
- **Monetization** – How will you make money? (The more profit your brand can make, the bigger impact you can have on the world.)
- **Underlying Magic** – Describe 3-7 unique selling points/secret sauce.
- **Marketing and Sales** – Define your sales plan, digital marketing, and more.
- **Competition** – Describe the competitive landscape. Who else is doing this?
- **Management Team** – List the key players and core skills on your team.
- **Financial Budget and Projections** – Provide your five-year plan in Excel.
- **Project Timeline** – Define milestones for the first three months, one year, and five years.
  *Based on *The Art of the Start* by Guy Kawasaki

While working for a *Goody PR* client who was interested in investing in technology products to help the 1 in 59 children born on the autism spectrum, we met with over 25 startup CEOs before finding one with a clear, concise, and compelling story. In most cases, the pitch decks were either way too long (60-100 pages versus 10-20), too complex, and/or the CEO never got to the point after a one-to-two-hour meeting. In many cases, we would look at their leadership team after an hour and say, "So your product does this . . .?" And they would blush, and say, "Yes, that is it."

You must be able to get to the point IMMEDIATELY with fans and the media. If you see glazed over eyes while explaining your brand to anyone, hit the reset button and revise the story. Did you know Edison invented the lightbulb 1,000 times before success? You will not get it right quickly. Be resilient and bounce back from challenges when developing your brand.

Once you have a solid understanding of your brand story, it will be much easier to energize your story like a PR Superhero. Media, awareness, and sales can skyrocket if you get this part right, which is why we are spending so much time on it.

Are you ready to get started with your action items for this chapter? Let's do this!

8 STEPS TO DEFINE YOUR WOW STORY THAT INSPIRES

Step 1.1 Define Three Life Changers that Drive Your Personal Brand Story

To help you clearly define your story, go back to your personal core and think about what is most important to you. Think about life experiences and gamechangers that shaped your WHY. Reporters will want to know the story behind your story.

And if you are a marketing professional, you should do this exercise with all of your clients. Ready? Here we go.

WHAT IS YOUR STORY BEHIND THE STORY?

The first questions you need to ask yourself or a client include:

1. **What are the top three life-changing moments that drove you towards your personal mission?**

2. **What really inspired you to start your company, launch a product, write a book and/or choose your career?**

3. **What is the WHY behind your story?**

It does not matter if you are selling real estate, managing a CPA firm, teaching life skills, or an author, there is always a human story behind it that starts with your WHY. No one in the media wants to talk solely about your company, product or book – that is called an ad. Instead, reporters want to create an emotional connection with a person. You are much more likely to win over more media, fans and customers by speaking from the heart about why your product/service matters to you.

Did you know that Steve Jobs' backstory includes being adopted, taking calligraphy classes as a college dropout, being fired as CEO of *Apple*, starting *Pixar Animation*, and later being begged to return to *Apple* as CEO? All of these experiences led him to build a mega personal and business brand that has changed millions of lives around the world. What life experiences are your brand drivers?

We all have stories that have impacted our brand. What are the aha moments behind your WHY? Can you explain your personal story using three things?

For example, here are three defining moments for a former *Goody PR* client named Therese Allison, who wrote a self-help memoir called *Playing for Keeps – How a 21st century businesswoman beat the boys!* To better define her brand story for media interviews, we read her book and interviewed her to come up with a clear, concise and compelling story.

CASE STUDY EXAMPLE -
3 LIFE CHANGERS FOR AUTHOR THERESE ALLISON

As a Successful Businesswoman, Award-Winning Author, Mom and Mentor, Therese Allison's backstory included three pivotal moments about a personal tragedy, playing competitive sports, and career success that moved reporters to cover her story:

1. When Therese was only 15, her sister sadly committed suicide, which made her look at life very differently.
2. Afterwards, Therese put her energy into playing competitive sports in high school, where she learned how to WIN in both sports and the boardroom.
3. After college, Therese used her WINNING skills in Sales in the insurance industry, became financially independent at age 38, and retired early at age 43 when her company was sold to *AON* to spend quality time with her children (who then urged her to write a book to tell her story!).

Look back at your life and dig deep to define your WHY. What compelled you to start a business or write a book? Did you overcome a life challenge, develop a unique solution to a problem and/or found success in what you love doing most?

In our case, the three life changers driving our brand story as an entrepreneur, author and *Goody PR* Founder include:

1. A *Johns Hopkins University Carey School of Business* professor told us to "throw your textbook in the trash can", and think differently about how you really want to manage your life versus how you manage it today.
2. As a business traveler stranded during 9/11 in NYC, I wrote a diary that got us to start writing again, and think differently about our priorities.
3. After getting laid off a few months after 9/11 when no one was hiring, I put all of my energy into writing and promoting my first book. And after 500+ media hits and many lessons learned; I started our *Goody PR* agency.

All of these life changers led me toward my destiny to focus on making others look good! I just did not know it at the time.

So, what are three life-changing events that drive your personal brand and/or motivate your company? Everyone has a story, and the keywords in these moments will help you define your Wow.

Step 1.2 Pinpoint What Work You Would Do for Free

To find your authentic driver, think about what you would do for free. If your work is only about money, it will be much harder to have long-term success. Anyone can create a new brand, but to get to the Wow, you have to dig deeper into what motivates you.

When you are willing to work for free, your passion takes priority over profit. People can tell when you genuinely want to help them with whatever you are selling, so it cannot be all about the money. If you are testing a new program, software app, service or book, consider giving it away for free at first to build buzz.

AUTHOR PR TIP -
SET UP FREE BOOK GIVEAWAYS ON *AMAZON*

If you are an author, one of the best things you can do to promote your book is to give it away for free on *Amazon* as part of your publicity campaign! If you self-published with *Amazon,* you can schedule a book promotion to give away the *Kindle* eBook version in your *KDP* Author Central portal. You will need to set a time limit (2-4 days), and promote before, during and afterwards on social media!

While you may not get a royalty from these free books, you will get people talking about it, increase your book reviews – and maybe get a new client if your book is a sales lead tool for your business.

Every time a client or reader gets an interview or sales go up because of media exposure, I am genuinely happy for them. I cannot wait to share their story everywhere on social media. This feeling is real, and has nothing to do with money.

As a result of our passion to help others succeed, we often do extra work for free for our VIP clients who are on a monthly retainer contract. And to get our business started, I did free work for almost a year to develop a portfolio of case studies for our *Goody PR* agency. My initial "free" work has paid off 100 times over the past thirteen years with happy clients, steady referrals and positive impacts on the world.

My first pro bono work was PR for *Rich Dad Hawaii*. This group was working with Robert Kiyosaki's *Rich Dad* team to build a franchise. The founders hosted several *CASHFLOW ® Board Game* Clubs on the island of Oahu, Hawaii, along with entrepreneurial training events. For this initial marketing and PR job, I donated all of my time for free - including paying for travel and expenses to Honolulu from Los Angeles. When I secured media interviews for *Rich Dad Hawaii* on every local TV news station in Honolulu, the *Rich Dad* headquarters team in Scottsdale, Arizona, started paying attention.

For my second "partially free" job, I did a four-month integrated marketing, public relations, and social media campaign for the first *Rich Woman* Financial Education conference. This event promoted Kim Kiyosaki's new program and *Rich Woman* book. For this project, I worked with the *Rich Dad Hawaii* Project Director Lee Ann Del Carpio and her global team of entrepreneurial women. As a result, about 120 people from six countries attended. Once again, we got great media coverage from the local Honolulu TV news and a feature story in *Hawaii Business Magazine*. In this case, I was reimbursed for expenses, but that was it.

However, this *Rich Woman* marketing campaign led to securing one of our most loyal and long-term clients. Author, entrepreneur, social capitalist and *Warriors Heart* Co-Founder Lisa Lannon was on the *Rich Woman* event committee and saw my work. As a result of building a great client relationship and collaboration, Lisa has been a steady client for most of the past decade.

After securing 53 TV interviews for Lisa Lannon's business, *Journey Healing Centers*, over five years, the firm was sold to the most prominent company in their residential treatment niche, who wanted to keep their brand name. Lisa and her husband, Josh Lannon, then used the money to start *Warriors Heart*. I will cover more about their inspiring brand and PR success stories throughout this book.

In another case of working for a really low retainer, I managed clients for a successful PR agency in Beverly Hills, California. *LCO (Levine Communications Office)* had represented over 50 *Academy Award* winners and several U.S. Presidents for over 30 years. In this case, we worked for a much lower monthly fee. However, it was so worth it! As a result, I learned best practices and software tools that doubled our business.

As our company grew, *Goody PR* launched the *Goody Awards* for social good in 2012. As part of the program, we did pro bono integrated marketing campaigns for *Golden Goody Award* winners (our top humanitarian award) to raise awareness of people making a difference and their charities. This top award honored mostly celebrities, including Ian Somerhalder (*Vampire Diaries, Ian Somerhalder Foundation*) and Amma "The Hugging Saint" (who raised $60 million for charity through *Embracing The World*). At their peak, the *Goody Awards* had fans tweeting nominations using hashtags #HeroGoody #TeamGoody and more via Twitter from over 30 countries.

While you have to set boundaries on "free work" and "free giveaways", you should love what you do so much that you would do it all day long for no pay. What would you do for free?

Step 1.3 Define Your Personal Brand Using the Power of Threes

I cannot emphasize enough the power of clear, concise and compelling branding. When someone meets you at a networking event, how do you describe yourself by using only three key points? Remember, you only have eight seconds to grab their attention.

Getting to your point right away builds rapport much faster. Humor, tone of voice, and body language also play a critical role in making first impressions, especially when telling your story.

Think about what you might say, and practice it with enthusiasm and a smile until it gets the right response.

To give you more ideas, here are examples of brands developed with our clients. In all cases, you can also see how the personal and the business brands overlap.

2 PERSONAL BRAND EXAMPLES – WHAT DO YOU DO?

Realtor to the Stars and Philanthropist Debbi DiMaggio – They call me the "Realtor to the Stars" because I'm Joe DiMaggio's cousin and have a lot of celebrity clients. Joe's love for Marilyn Monroe is the same passion that I have as a top one percent Realtor in Beverly Hills and the Bay Area. My role model is Lady Diana, and I have adopted five charities. People say that I am a passionate **philanthropist, connector and luxury realtor**.

Autistic Animator and Advocate Dani Bowman – I want to be the Temple Grandin of my generation as an autism advocate. As an animator with autism, I empower others on the spectrum by teaching animation and entrepreneurial skills. We want to help them learn new skills and find jobs. People say that I'm a **business-savvy entrepreneur, autistic advocate and animator**.

Think about how these personal brands define their top three qualities. How would you describe your key strengths using the power of threes?

With the internet, you now have a brand online. Whether you are a celebrity, author, CEO, founder, leader, mom, dad, daughter, son, student or individual, you have a story to tell. It is what people think of first when they hear your name. Think about some of the mega brands you see , like Beyonce' and Richard Branson, and how their personal and business brands are in sync.

MEGA PERSONAL BRAND CASE STUDY 1 – BEYONCÉ

Beyonce's is a mega brand recognized worldwide as a **bold, confident, and empowering artist**.

As a well-known personal brand, Beyoncé is an American singer, songwriter, actress, and businesswoman. Did you also know that she grew up in Houston with parents who supported her journey? Her mother was a hairdresser, and her father was in sales.

Beyoncé started rapping and singing in a group called *Girls Thyme* at eight years old on the Houston talent-show circuit. Her brand story gained media attention as she became the lead singer of *Destiny's Child* in the 1990s (her sister Solange was a backup singer in this band).

Her father quit his job to help manage her career . Her brand name, Beyoncé, came from her mother's maiden name. The pressures from building Beyoncé's brand contributed to her parents' divorce. When *Destiny's Child* split up in 2006, Beyoncé released her second solo album *B'Day*, which included ten top singles such as "*Irreplaceable*" and "*Deja Vu.*"

After selling 100 million records and winning 28 GRAMMYs and 79 nominations, Beyoncé is now one of the most recognized global brands. (Source: *Wikipedia*).

Of course, there is a lot more to Beyoncé's Wow Story, and it did not happen overnight. Just like your personal brand, it can take decades to develop this magic.

Sir Richard Branson is another mega brand. As a business owner, investor, and philanthropist, he oversees his *Virgin Group*'s control over 400 companies.

MEGA PERSONAL BRAND CASE STUDY 2 – SIR RICHARD BRANSON

Sir Richard Branson's personal brand can be described as a mega businessman who is an **innovative, fearless, and social entrepreneur**.

Did you also know that Richard Branson was the oldest of three children? His mother was a former ballet dancer and airline hostess (Eve Branson), and his father (Edward James Branson) was a barrister.

As a student with dyslexia and poor grades, Richard told his teacher that he would "end up in prison or be a millionaire." Branson's first business venture occurred when he was 16 when he started a magazine called *Student*. In 1970, at the age of 20, Branson set up a mail-order record business, which later became *Virgin Records* and *Virgin Megastores*. He bought *Virgin Atlantic Airways* in the 1980s as his business grew at warp speed.

Sir Richard Branson was knighted in 2000 for his "services to entrepreneurship." Telling the rest of his entrepreneur story could take this entire book. Branson is also a humanitarian recognized for his environmental efforts. (Source: *Wikipedia*)

While anyone with a mega brand is under a microscope, Branson has kept mostly positive attributes in the headlines.

Now that we have looked at these personal brand examples, let's take a closer look at business brand examples.

Step 1.4 Define Your Business Brand Wheel Driving Your Story

Your personal brand should align with your business brand. If you are following your true WHY and would work for free, you will be able to propel your business forward. Look at all the drivers on your brand wheel as potential media stories.

When someone asks you to describe your business brand, find ways to make it fun and interesting. No matter what you say, add ENERGY and enthusiasm to your story. Speak with conviction and deliver the message with a smile. The minute you take yourself too seriously, you will lose your audience.

One of the many reasons this delivery is so important is because authors must OWN their brand story when talking to potential customers and the media. If you are not confident in your WHY, a producer will never risk having you on a radio or TV show.

Let's take a closer look at some case study examples of the power of compelling brand storytelling.

CASE STUDY EXAMPLE – PERSONAL AND BUSINESS BRAND MATCH

Tom Wheelwright, who is a CPA, CEO and Author of *Tax-Free Wealth* was a long-term *Goody PR* client. As a tax and wealth expert, Tom truly LOVES taxes more than anyone you will meet! His passion is to legally save people 10-40 percent permanently on their taxes, and it comes across in every media interview. This authenticity and enthusiasm are the foundation of his personal and business brands.

Tom Wheelwright's Personal Brand - While most people run the other direction when you say taxes, Tom's personal brand message is "I make taxes fun, easy, and understandable." This message is PR gold because it is clear, concise, and compelling - and will make you look twice. It also uses the power of threes to grab your attention.

Tom Wheelwright's Business Brand - After running a CPA firm for over twenty years, Tom created a new tax and wealth strategy and education company called *WealthAbility*. The company's motto is to help you to make "Way More Money" and pay "Way Less Taxes." For this business, Tom's team consults with clients to build tax and wealth strategies; provides educational tools; and is building a national network of CPAs. In support of this brand, he hosts two podcasts.

When we booked Tom on *FOX Business: Cavuto Coast-to-Coast*, his passion for taxes spoke volumes. How many CPAs do you know who can make taxes "fun, easy, and understandable"?

When we work with clients on their brand story, we always start with the big picture, key selling points and their WHY. Visuals can also help you see what a story may look like much faster with pictures, graphics, and videos.

Do not kid yourself into thinking this brand story process is easy - lightning will not hit overnight! You will need to have a lot of brainstorming meetings, walks, and meditations to get there.

Think about if you had to present your personal or business brand story in 30 seconds on the phone, in a meeting, or to the media. What would you say? How would you engage your audience to care?

If you work for a company, think about new PR ideas that you can propose to your team in your next marketing meeting. Keep in mind, there are hundreds, if not thousands, of experts who do what you do. And constantly ask yourself, how is your product and story different? Where is the magic?

WHY SHOULD A REPORTER INTERVIEW YOU?

In all cases, you always want to clearly define your personal story behind the story before approaching any media. When you talk to a producer or reporter, always provide a short bio with your WHY. Most reporters will want to know your story before scheduling an interview. People connect with stories first. You must be able to explain what makes you the best spokesperson with a unique product, service or result for them to put their reputation on the line by interviewing you.

Taking a brand story to Wow can require hard work, research, and interviews to get to the core. Let's take a closer look at a mega brand case study that frequently gets discussed in my digital marketing class. This campaign is a great example of how to take a non-emotional product and turn it into a moving story that inspires action.

WOW STORY CASE STUDY EXAMPLE - *DOVE REAL BEAUTY SKETCHES*

While *Dove* is a personal care brand owned by *Unilever*, their products are very boring in a crowded and competitive market. *Dove* sells antiperspirants, body washes, beauty bars, lotions, hair care, and facial products.

To bond emotionally with their target market (middle-aged women 35-55), they developed a BRILLIANT *Dove Real Beauty Sketches* marketing campaign that connected on many levels to millions of women.

For this campaign, women were asked to describe themselves to a sketch artist, who then drew what the individuals perceived as their own image, all while being videotaped.

The artist then asked a stranger to describe the same person. The artist did a second sketch of the individual based on the stranger's description and videotaped it.

When you compared the two sketches, the first sketch with the individual's perception was much less flattering than the second sketch based on a stranger's description.

The bottom line message to women from this campaign was You are More Beautiful Than You Think, and the videos were mega hits online!

This case study is a classic example of how you can take a really boring brand and turn it into a powerful Wow Story with magic! This story is relatable, timely, and compelling.

And for *Wonder Woman's* 80th Anniversary (October 21, 2021), *DC Comics* and *Dove* launched a new self-esteem project. Together, the two brands "are recognizing people who create real wonder and beauty" to "inspire new heroes that live authentically and confidently." (Google this campaign to learn more and watch the videos.)

To give you a closer look at the importance of defining a business brand, here is a marketing case study comparison of two companies in the wireless telecom industry where I worked early in my career. The two companies had night-and-day marketing results because of their brand stories.

BUSINESS BRAND STORYTELLING – 2 TELECOMMUNICATIONS CASE STUDIES

While there are many pieces to this business branding success story and tragedy, this comparison between the first *Sprint PCS* office in the United States and *Motorola's Iridium* Satellite company offers great learning lessons about why the brand story matters enormously. Both companies were located in the Washington D.C. area.

I was fortunate to work for the first *Sprint PCS* in Bethesda, Maryland, which was a huge marketing success that transformed lives and the wireless industry in 1995 forever. During this job, I learned invaluable skills for product storytelling.

At the time, only rich people and sales professionals could afford cell phones. This beta office was officially called *Sprint Spectrum*, and we had record-breaking sales. In comparison, *Motorola's Iridium* satellite phone company was also based in the Washington D.C. area and was a complete financial and marketing flop. The story behind these two brands provides key insights for anyone with a product to sell.

Sprint Spectrum Success versus Motorola's Iridium Flop

To get to the point, here is a big picture comparison snapshot with what happened in each case.

Marketing Element	Sprint Spectrum - first *Sprint PCS* in US, sold to *T-Mobile*	*Motorola's Iridium* Satellite Phones – filed bankruptcy, sold at a major loss
Brand Story	Clear, concise, and compelling message	Mixed messages developed by 16 regional gateway offices
Key Selling Points	5 key benefits on a wallet card given to every employee and retailer	No key selling points published
Pricing	Very affordable, $99 *Ericsson* phone	Way over-priced, $4,000
Overcame Objections	Yes – "First minute of incoming calls free" when there was a per minute cost	No – The majority don't need a brick-size phone that did not work in a city (urban canyon) & cost $11.00/minute

Team	50/50 telecom & non-telecom employees to inspire new products and ideas	Primarily telecom & government hires who went home at 5:00pm, and did not really care.
Corporate Culture	Product-driven, fun, teamwork, gratitude, fun quarterly staff meetings, big bonuses for employees	Bureaucratic, political BS!, horrible internal communications, no teamwork, VERY unhappy employees
Results	Sold 300 percent over forecast, Sold to Kansas City HQ, and later sold to *T-Mobile*	Filed bankruptcy, sold in desperation for $25 million with 77 satellites in sky, lost $7 billion

Sprint Spectrum in U.S. Triumph

This *Sprint Spectrum* product storytelling example has so many great learning lessons for marketers. The sales results were off the charts! The company's story was featured on the cover of major magazines as the fastest growing telecom company in the nation. This corporate experience was my all-time favorite job where I really saw the power of Wow Storytelling, marketing, and working with a passionate and talented team. Many of us worked 60 to 70 hours a week without a complaint. Once I even shared a hotel room with five people during a blizzard to meet our deadlines. And we loved it!

In comparison, working for *Motorola's Iridium* was a huge let down. Everyone was told to stay in their sandbox, and senior leadership was nowhere to be found at the Washington D.C. headquarters. I was truly saddened by the corporate culture in the U.S., but loved meeting the teams abroad in the regional gateway offices (who were happy, grateful, and the complete opposite of the HQ).

After finally being given the green light to work outside our department, we helped re-define the *Iridium* story by working closely with Marketing. Our Operations training team defined the new *Iridium* brand story as, "If you are working on an oil rig in the Indian Ocean and the power goes out for days, and you have no cell service, would you like to have a satellite phone with a solar charger that can save your life?" Sales went up 40 percent in six weeks, but it was not enough to save the company. It was mind-boggling that 120 people in Marketing missed the mark by never defining a Wow Story. It's always about the story!

Step 1.5 Identify Three to Seven Unique Selling Points Your Brand Can Offer Others

Most people skip the step of identifying the three to seven unique selling points for a brand. When you think about superheroes, they all have a few superpowers that make them unique. Think about your personal and business brand's superpowers. For example, can your brand save lives, find dream homes, make someone famous, help people lose weight, build wealth, save millions over a lifetime, teach something new and/or bring joy to your customer?

If you can clearly define and show how your product or service can improve lives, you will get many more earned media interviews, achieve your goals, and increase sales - and that is what we are here to help you do.

We consistently partner with clients to define their core messaging and brand story that can be turned into media hooks and pitches that are timely and relevant. For example, *Goody PR* recently worked with a retired surgeon, Dr. Richard S. Weeder, who started the *RW Cancer Education Foundation*. He's operated on 2,500+ cancer patients, and has seen many miracle remissions. Dr. Weeder started this foundation to give back. After meeting with Dr. Weeder and his team, we came up with these key selling points as a brand story foundation:

CASE STUDY - KEY SELLING POINTS - *RW CANCER EDUCATION FOUNDATION*

1. Provide wellness tools to prevent and overcome cancer through Immunity, Energy and Spirit, based on extensive experience as a doctor who's seen many miracle remissions.

2. Teach good health habits through seminars, books, podcasts, affiliates, partners and public awareness campaigns based on first-hand experience and research.

3. Educate everyone on how to unlock your body's healing ability by addressing your social, emotional and spiritual care needs.

4. Give hope to cancer patients with a proactive approach to wellness, developed by a team of medical professionals who've worked with thousands of cancer patients for decades.

For Dr. Weeder's new book, *The Key to Preventing and Overcoming Cancer – A Doctor's Guide to Unlocking Your Immunity, Energy and Spirit*, the book cover designer (Heidi North) and team came up with a blue butterfly graphic and messaging that is a perfect match for this brand. A blue butterfly is rare, and was chosen because it represents "life, endurance, change, rebirth, luck and hope" – which are all desired results from the book and foundation.

This brand definition process looks a lot easier than it is in reality. When defining your key selling points, always think about what makes your story different?

Step 1.6 Define Your Brand Mission, Vision, and Values

Mission, vision, and values are also major identifiers for your Wow Story. Many underestimate the importance of this step. Most business leaders are too busy building the details rather than looking at the big picture strategy, story, and marketing plan. These brand cornerstones can make or break your business, so do not pass "Go" until you've documented this core part of your brand identity.

If you do nothing else, define your brand's mission. Let's look at some of the biggest companies out there as examples:

MEGA BRAND MISSION STATEMENT EXAMPLES

Nike

Mission: To bring inspiration and innovation to every athlete in the world.

Oracle

Mission: We help you simplify your IT environment so that you can free up money, time, and resources to invest in innovation.

American Express

Mission: Become essential to our customers by providing differentiated products and services to help them achieve their aspirations.

MEGA BRAND MISSION AND VALUE STATEMENT EXAMPLES

Here are additional examples of Mission plus Vision statements to give you ideas:

Amazon

Mission Statement: We strive to offer our customers the lowest possible prices, the best available selection, and the utmost convenience. (2019)

Vision: Our vision is to be Earth's most customer-centric company, where customers can find and discover anything they might want to buy online. (2019)

Apple

Mission: Apple strives to bring the best personal computing experience to students, educators, creative professionals and consumers around the world through its innovative hardware, software and internet offerings. (2020)

Vision: We believe that we are on the face of the earth to make great products and that is not changing. (Tim Cook)

Walmart

Mission: To save people money so they can live better.

Vision: To become the worldwide leader in retailing.

SMALL BUSINESS MISSION, VISION, AND VALUES EXAMPLES

In addition, here are some small business examples:

Lyft

Mission: To improve people's lives with the world's best transportation.

Vision: Ride by ride, we are changing the way our world works. We imagine a world where cities feel small again. Where transportation and tech bring people together, instead of apart. We see the future as community-driven and it starts with you.

Uber

Mission: Make transportation as reliable as running water, everywhere, for everyone.

Vision: We ignite opportunity by setting the world in motion.

Goody PR

Our Mission: We seek to magnify the good in brands by defining and promoting a WOW Story that raises awareness, changes lives and ultimately increases sales.

Vision: We strive to amplify the good of at least one million social impact brands and influencers.

Values: Gratitude, Passion, Integrity, Innovation, Fun, and Balance

You can do this too! Start writing down ideas with your team and embrace being a Word Artist and/or hire someone to do it for you.

Step 1.7 Find Three People Positively Impacted by Your Brand

What most people do not understand is that your brand story is ten times more powerful if it includes how you helped someone else. Whether it is helping people overcome cancer, communicate better, build wealth, get healthy or rebuild lives, you should always be asking; "Why does my product or service matter to anyone?"

For example, when a reporter contacted us from *The Wall Street Journal,* she asked for insights from our tax expert client Tom Wheelwright about how the *Tax Cuts and Jobs Act of 2017* would impact small businesses. In addition, the reporter also wanted to highlight how one of Tom's clients used his advice.

In another scenario, successful businesswoman, mentor and author Therese Allison (*Playing for Keeps*) got an inspiring testimonial in a reader's review. The woman explained how she got two dream job offers after applying the career advice tips in Allison's self-help memoir. This type of feedback can be invaluable for your PR.

When *CBS Health Watch* wanted to do a feature story about *Warriors Heart* for Veterans Day, they wanted to feature a veteran who had been positively impacted by their residential treatment program. This media hit was one of our biggest success stories for a client that we will discuss in more detail in Chapter 8 (saving the best for last)!

Lastly, when I got this feedback about our *8-Second PR* book, we almost fell out of our chair!

PRICELESS TESTIMONIAL –
WHY WE WROTE THIS BOOK FOR YOU!

We can't thank Liz H Kelly enough for giving away her PR secrets in 8-Second PR. When we first started our new business Roma Leaf, my company could not afford to hire her PR agency, so Liz recommended reading her book instead. As a marketer, we knew the importance of PR, and went through it with highlighters and sticky notes. As a result of her 8-Second PR tips and examples of media pitches, we were able to land a feature *TV interview on FOX 11 Los Angeles* that was worth approximately $40,000 in Calculated Publicity Value, and contributed to an additional $10,000 in product sales. Trust me, read this book, take notes and share it with friends - because it is a gamechanger for brands!

–Mariya Palanjian, Founder/CEO, Roma Leaf and Globafly

Step 1.8 Share Your Story. Revise it. Share again.

Most importantly, your Wow Story must be constantly updated with new magic. As you get more feedback from your customers, clients, and the media, you will quickly learn what topics resonate with your audience, the best way to explain it, and how to show the positive impacts. This is one of the main reasons for this updated version of this *8-Second PR* book. Constantly listening to your customers, readers and media feedback are a must for any brand's long-term success.

8-SECOND BRANDING PODCAST: FORMER FORD BRAND VISIONARY SCOTT MONTY

To learn more about brand storytelling and reinvention from a pro, listen to our *8-Second Branding* Podcast interview with Brand Visionary Scott Monty who shares innovative ways that he transformed two underdog brands: *Ford* and *T-Mobile*.

As the Global Head of Social Media and Digital Communications for *Ford Motor Company* from 2008-2014, Monty used creative content, influencer partnerships and the *Escape Routes NBC* primetime TV series to fast forward the brand.

In this timely discussion, *Twitter* Rock Star @ScottMonty also shares how he uses "History, Literature and Philosophy" as the foundation of brand storytelling campaigns.

Listen on all major podcast platforms and/or visit our *8-Second Branding* Podcast page on *Goody PR's* website here: https://goodypr.com/8-second-branding

Once you have defined your story, the next step is to apply your unique story with compelling marketing campaigns, relevant media hooks, press releases with great SEO (Search Engine Optimization), engaging websites, moving photographs, professional graphics, viral videos, and social media content that moves people to take a second look, buy and/or share your story.

It is a constant writing and rewriting process. Eventually, you must let go of the revision process and publish your story to the world. Because this story reinvention process is paramount to your publicity success, we will keep talking about it throughout this book (and share how it helped score mega media in Chapter 8).

CHAPTER 1 RECAP

We hope you now have some new ideas for defining an inspiring brand story with a clear, concise, and compelling message. Are you ready to edit your story 100 times to define a Wow Story that inspires others to take action? You can brainstorm your brand's magic and make it happen!

Step 1 Action Items - Define Your Story Magic to Inspire Fans and Media

1. Identify three life changers that drive your personal/business brand story.
2. Pinpoint what work you/your company would do for free.
3. Define your personal brand using the power of threes.
4. Define your business brand wheel driving your story.
5. Identify three to seven unique selling points your brand can offer others.
6. Define your brand mission, vision, and values.

7. Find three people positively impacted by your brand.
8. Share your story. Revise it. Share again.

PR Superpower 1 - Wow Storytelling Superpower

Once you use these Wow Storytelling Superpower steps, you can pitch a brand that inspires others to write about you and/or buy your product.

Take a close look at how your personal and business brands are in sync. Do they complement each other? Can you explain your top three strengths? Can you explain your mission, vision and values? Do you know who you can help most? If you are not completely sure, keep working on it.

Never underestimate the power of a Wow Story that moves others to interview you, buy your book, refer customers to you and/or call your business for help. This magic is the main driver for your public relations and business success!

Once your brand story foundation is in place, you can go to the next level.

Chapter 1 - 8-Second PR Challenges

As we close Chapter 1, here are your *8-Second PR* Challenges:

1. How can you get someone's attention in eight seconds?
2. How can you tell your brand story in one to two sentences?
3. What were 3 game changers in your life that led you to your ideal job?
4. What work would you do for free?
5. What are three things that describe your brand in one sentence?
6. Do you have a powerful Mission and Vision that attracts fans?
7. What are your three to seven key selling points?

8. When are you going to schedule time to work on enhancing your Wow Story?

Before you go to the next chapter, take a walk. Absorb what you have read. Write some notes.

And then turn the page to learn more about dominating your digital domain.

Reminder:

"THE CATERPILLAR DOES ALL THE WORK, BUT THE BUTTERFLY GETS ALL THE PUBLICITY."

- GEORGE CARLIN

STEP 2

DIGITAL PR

Dominate Your
Digital Bank to Increase
Word-of-Mouth Marketing

> "IN THE DIGITAL SPACE, ATTENTION IS LIKE
> CURRENCY. WE EARN IT. WE SPEND IT."
>
> – BRIAN SOLIS,
>   digital analyst, speaker, and author (Engage!)

Do you own your brandname.com, and all the wrong spellings of this URL? In sync with defining a Wow Story, you must dominate the digital space for your brand to maximize Word-of-Mouth Marketing. If you cannot buy the .com and get the exact match name for your primary social media accounts, pick another name for your business, product, service or book title – because it's that important. This updated chapter can help you attract more brand advocates and influencers who share your story on the latest social media marketing platforms. A consistent name is just step one!

With 95 percent of people in North America using the Internet, and 4.66 billion people online on the planet (out of 7.9 billion, Source: *DataReportal*, 2021), you must make it as easy as possible for people to find your brand on all devices (computers, smartphones, tablets and more).

WHY WORD-OF-MOUTH MARKETING MUST BE A PRIORITY

People are 90% more likely to trust and buy from a brand recommended by a friend (*Invesprco*), and most of these recommendations take place online.

To amplify your marketing and public relations results, you must build a digital presence so raving fans become Brand Ambassadors online. Loyal customers will share your news and products with friends and family simply because they love it. This type of promotion is priceless.

Let's take a closer look at how you can own your digital bank and energize your brand story online.

PR SUPERPOWER 2 – DIGITAL PR SUPERPOWER

Once you have a brand name idea, the next thing you want to do is dominate your digital bank. For Ultimate Media Success, you must enhance your Digital PR Superpower to increase your Word-of- Mouth Marketing. You want to own your digital assets with the same superhuman strength as a superhero. Your digital bank includes a dot com URL, mobile-friendly websites, social media channels, blog names, videos, photographs, graphics, and more.

If you embrace digital marketing, your content will be listed all over the first page of *Google* results when someone searches on your product's name. To get everyone talking about you online and attract brand advocates, you must master this *8-Second PR* Superpower!

With almost everyone on social media in North America, you just cannot afford to ignore the need for digital marketing today. I get calls from potential and current clients in a panic because they have no social media presence. They are too busy, don't see the value and/or just don't want to do it. Please don't ignore digital! If you don't have the time or desire, hire a professional to do it for you. It's really a must-have versus an option for your brand promotions and reputation management!

Did you know that if *Facebook* were a country, "it would be the biggest nation on earth" (*Huffington Post*)? With approximately 1.9 billion daily active users on *Facebook* in Q2 2021 (*Statista*), sponsoring posts and ads on this platform is one of the most cost-effective ways to reach millions of potential customers and fans.

Here is why your Digital PR Superpower is beyond important for brand marketing!

TOP 5 BRAND BENEFITS OF SOCIAL MEDIA MARKETING

1. You can get immediate feedback from fans (it's the cheapest focus group out there).
2. You will increase your Word-of-Mouth Marketing (more people buy based on a friend's recommendation than anything else).

3. Reporters often check your social media before deciding whether to interview you. The bigger your fan base, the more likely you are to get the interview.

4. After every interview is published, you want to immediately share it on multiple social media platforms to increase your awareness, SEO, credibility, followers and sales.

5. You can also build media relations with reporters and podcast hosts by sharing their story and mentioning them in a post (they notice and care when you share!).

This digital marketing chapter could easily be an entire book. In this chapter, we will focus primarily on marketing strategy, features and content versus technical step-by-step processes. To learn more about the how to use specific features, use *Google* to find tutorial steps and videos posted by experts. You can easily find videos for how to set up a *Facebook* business account and use social media management tools to better manage *Facebook, Instagram, LinkedIn, Twitter* and more.

You can also take our *8-Second PR* classes (go to GoodyPR.com to learn about our Digital PR class on *Teachable*), sign up for my *UCLA Extension Digital Marketing* online course, attend *Social Media Club* educational events and/or read other books. (For more suggestions, see the "Resources" section in the back of this book.)

Ready to get started? Let's go through the eight Digital PR action items that can help your brand get more attention and reach millions online.

STEP 2 ACTION ITEMS - DOMINATE YOUR DIGITAL BANK TO INCREASE WORD-OF-MOUTH MARKETING

1. Buy the URL.com that is an exact match to your brand name FIRST.

2. Secure social media usernames for at least the top three channels with an exact match (if you cannot get the name, go back to Step 1).

3. Buy a mobile-friendly *WordPress* "Responsive" theme website template.

4. Post clear, concise, and compelling digital content with keyword hashtags.

5. Share high-quality photos that tell your brand story.

6. Create engaging videos that represent your brand.

7. Promote before, during, and after your brand launch.

8. Be active and current to engage your audience.

PR SUPERPOWER 2 - DIGITAL PR SUPERPOWER

First, let's emphasize why digital marketing is a must-have for every marketing professional and/or person promoting a business, book or cause. While digital does not replace the importance of traditional marketing (newspaper ads, billboards, TV placements, and brochures), your overall marketing strategy must include both earned media and Digital PR to get noticed.

Word-of-Mouth Marketing can result in 5x more sales than paid media (*Invesprco*), so you really cannot afford to skip this step.

Because most people do not go anywhere without their smartphones now, you cannot overlook mobile marketing campaigns either. To drive home this point, take a look at some fun facts about popular social media trends.

8 SOCIAL MEDIA MARKETING TRENDS

1. *Facebook, Instagram and Twitter are the most common social media platforms (Hubspot 2020).*

2. *The average American has access to more than 10 connected devices in their household (Statista 2021)*

3. *80% of video marketers claim that video has directly increased sales (Wyzowl, 2020).*

4. *79% of video marketers use Facebook as a video marketing channel (Wyzowl, 2019).*

5. *In 2023, Instagram is projected to reach 120.3 million monthly active users in the United States, up from 107.2 million users in 2019. (Statista 2020)*

6. *More women accounted for 56.4% of Instagram users (Statista 2020).*

7. *As of April 2020, LinkedIn's number of users in the U.S. reached 160 million, making it the country with the most LinkedIn users in the world (Statista 2020).*

8. *More men accounted for 57% of users on LinkedIn (Statista 2020).*

Because researchers have found about 65 percent of people are visual learners, your photographs, charts, and graphics are essential to your marketing success. If you do not have a good camera to take great photos and videos, it is time to invest in one and/or hire a professional photographer (more on photo tips later in this chapter).

Let's take a closer look at these digital marketing action items with case study examples.

Step 2.1 Buy the URL.com that is an Exact Match to Your Brand Name FIRST

Before you even finalize your brand name, you must go to *GoDaddy.com, Namecheckr.com, Namecheck.com*, or another company that sells domain names and purchase your brandname.com. If it is not for sale, pick another name.

We've seen SO many brands and clients use multiple names online, and it gets very confusing for potential customers and fans. Your job is to increase SEO (Search Engine Optimization) with a consistent name, so everyone can find you on the internet. Take the guesswork out of finding your brand online by using one name.

When I was thinking about this book, the first thing I did was a *Google* search for variations of "8-Second PR," and then I bought *8SecondPR.com*. I also purchased *8PRSecrets.com* and several other closely related URLs.

In another case, our *Goody PR* client *Warriors Heart*, discovered that WarriorsHeart.com was not available to purchase. However, the website was not live. As a result, I researched and connected them with the URL owner using the *WhoIs.com* directory. The *Warriors Heart* Founders asked the owner if they could purchase the URL from them. After several calls and meetings, the owner was so moved by their mission to heal military, veterans and first responders struggling with addition and PTSD that they gifted this .com domain to *Warriors Heart*.

For some more popular web addresses, you can often buy "premium domains" for a much higher price. While a URL at *GoDaddy* for one-year averages from $2 to $20, premium domains can cost thousands of dollars or more to acquire.

Some people even buy a bank of URLs for the sole purpose of making a profit by reselling them.

CASE STUDY EXAMPLE – BUSINESS.COM PURCHASED FOR $7.5 MILLION

In an extreme premium domain case, the *Business.com* URL was purchased in 1999 for $7.5 million by Jake Winebaum's *eCompanies* as a B2B (Business-to-Business) online destination. The site is still live and covers business trends and industry news for small-to-midsize growth companies. Around the time of this purchase, I worked for a startup owned by the *eCompanies* incubator (who also owned *Business.com*). This outrageous purchase price for the *Business.com* URL was always a frequent topic of conversation at our office.

In July 2007, *Business.com* was sold to RH Donnelley for $350 million, or 47 times the initial $7.5 million 1999 purchase price (*TechCrunch*). *Business.com* was later acquired by *Purch Group* in 2016. The terms of the deal for this Carlsbad, California, company were "not disclosed."

If you do not find a way to own your brand's exact match URL, there are much easier solutions versus spending outrageous amounts of money. Your best bet really is to change your name a little so it is unique and consistent. Bottom line, you must own your brandname.com, and there are no shortcuts.

To help you dominate your digital bank, here are our top tips:

8 TIPS FOR BRAND NAMES & EXACT MATCH URLS

1. Change your brand name to a two-to-three-word phrase until your exactname.com is available.

2. Avoid really long and complicated brand names (use sixth-grade vocabulary).

3. Add a number or color to the name with a meaning that adds to your story.

4. If it is for a non-profit, buy the .com and .org URLs if available.

5. Buy additional URLs with closely related spellings (example, I bought GoodyAwards.com and GoodieAwards.com).

6. Avoid using confusing spellings in your domain name.

7. Avoid dashes and punctuation in your URL name.

8. Make sure your brand URL is memorable with good SEO.

WHY YOUR NAME MATTERS FOR SEO
(Search Engine Optimization)!

One of the most important things to consider when selecting a brand name is great SEO. You want a unique name so your product or service is prominent in online search results. Please don't use a movie title, TV series, well-known brand name or over-used word.

What this means is that if you pick a brand name like "Celebrate" (no joke, someone in my marketing class chose "Celebrate" for their new company name), it will get totally lost in millions of search results for that one word.

I recommended the student change the brand name to a two-to-three-word phrase. By asking questions, I discovered that the student wanted to open a retail store with items to "Celebrate Big Birthdays", which is a much more unique name and better URL if it is available. In this case, you could be even more specific by adding geography such as "Celebrate Big Birthdays LA." While you want to keep your brand name simple, it also has to be unique so your fans can find you. Make sure you get this step right!

Step 2.2 Secure Social Media Usernames for at least the Top Three Channels with an Exact Match (if you cannot get the name, go back to Step 1)

SKIP AHEAD OPTION – IF 90% ENGAGEMENT RATE

If you have a 90% or higher engagement rate on your social media accounts already and don't need any new ideas or digital marketing insights, feel free to skip ahead to Chapter 3: CONTENT STRENGTH - Create Compelling Content that Emotionally Connects with Readers! If you don't know your engagement rate, you probably want to keep reading this chapter.

In sync with securing your brand's dot com and/or dot org space, you want to register the exact match usernames for at least your top three social media platforms.

With 97 percent of 16-to-64-year-olds logging into at least one social media platform per month (*Sprout Social*), you must prioritize digital marketing. **If you are not actively managing your social media, someone else will be talking about your brand online.** You want to be part of that conversation.

To stay focused, select the top three platforms that can best reach your target audience. If your social media efforts span too many sites, you will not be as effective. You want to consistently focus and post authentic content that inspires fans to engage online with your brand.

RESEARCH WHERE YOUR AUDIENCE LIVES ONLINE

Sure, you can set up more than three social media accounts. However, you want to develop a digital strategy that connects best with your target market and key influencers. Before you even start posting, research your options and secure your brand's usernames for the platforms who best reach your niche audience.

Social Media Channel	Marketing Benefits
1. Facebook	• *Facebook* is primarily for friends and family. • *Facebook* can be one of your best sources for Word-of-Mouth Marketing and sales leads. • *Facebook* has the largest number of users, so a business page and advertising budget are highly recommended. • On your personal page, be careful to balance promotional and personal posts to avoid sounding like spam. • Because *Facebook* competes with *YouTube* for video views, *Facebook* now promotes video content more. • 56% of users are males and 44% are females (2021). • 25.7% of users are 25-34 on Facebook (*Statista*, 2021). • 21.6% are 55+ with (11% 55-64) and (10.6% 65+). (*Statista*, 2021) • 82% of users are college graduates (*Omnicore*)
2. Instagram	• *Instagram* is the best channel for photo marketing and visual storytelling. • *Instagram* is great for brand promotions, and they are adding more ways to sell products on this platform. • 65% of people are visual learners with short attention spans, which makes visual marketing very effective here. • *Facebook* acquired *Instagram* for $1 billion, so businesses will need an ad budget as their "pay to play" algorithm dominates this platform. • *Instagram* has many features to engage fans (more on this later). • You can use up to 30 hashtags on a post, which is great cross-marketing.

Social Media Channel	Marketing Benefits
	• More visual brands best for *Instagram* include: Real Estate, Travel, Community, Animals, Art, Authors, Thought-Leaders, Causes, Awards, and many more. • The majority of *Instagram* users are 18 to 29, which is about 60% of adults online (*Sprout Social*). • In 2021, *Instagram*'s demographics include 18-24 years old: 67%, 25-34 years old: 60%, 35-44 years old: 49%, 45-54 years old: 43% and 55+ years old: 31% (*Hootsuite*).
3. Twitter	• *Twitter* is ideal for reaching people you do not know (influencers and reporters) using @username in a tweet that notifies the user of a mention. • You can easily cross-market using keyword #hashtags because it's like an instant chat group with people with common interests. • *Twitter* #hashtags are great for event marketing or disaster recovery because you can immediately reach people interested in a specific topic, issue, or geography. • Reporters use *Twitter* as a major source of news and trends. • When you get in a news story, blog on podcast, you should ALWAYS tweet it with the @username for the outlet and reporter. • *Twitter* has an advertising audience of 353 million (Hootsuite, 2021). • *Twitter* has 70% male versus 30% female users (Hootsuite, 2021). • 28.9% of their users are 25-34, followed by 28.2% are 35-49. • 82% of B2B Marketers use Twitter for organic content marketing (*Hootsuite*, 2021). • There was a 62% increase in video use on *Twitter* from 2019 to 2020.
4. YouTube	• As of 2020, there was an estimate of 2.1 billion *YouTube* users worldwide (*Statista*), so you can't afford to ignore it. • *YouTube* is one of the best ways to increase your brand's SEO (Search Engine Optimization) with videos showing up in *Google* search results. • *YouTube* is the second biggest search engine behind *Google* - and is owned by *Google*.

Social Media Channel	Marketing Benefits
	• To reach your target audience, create videos with titles and topics that solve problems, educate, and entertain ("How to" videos are great for marketing). • You can increase the video SEO if you use include keywords so people will find your videos (more about this later). • 400 hours of video are uploaded to *YouTube* per minute (*Google*). • 80% of 18-to-49-year-olds watch *YouTube*.
5. *LinkedIn*	• *LinkedIn* was acquired by *Microsoft* and has nearly 800 million users in 200+ countries and territories (*LinkedIn*). • *LinkedIn* is perfect for CEOs, small businesses and consultants who are marketing B2B (business-to-business). • 4 out of 5 B2B marketers use *LinkedIn*, compared to 91 percent of B2B marketers who use *Facebook* (*Oberlo*). • *LinkedIn* is great for networking with professionals in search of jobs, connections, and/or clients. • *LinkedIn* provides the ability for you to post blogs (great for SEO). • 28 percent of adults in the U.S. are on *LinkedIn* (*Pew Research Center* 2021). • The site attracts people with higher paying jobs with 45 percent earning over $75,000 (*Pew Research Center*). • 57 percent of *LinkedIn* users worldwide are male, compared to 43 percent of females (*Statista*, 2019)
6. *Snapchat*	• On average, 306 million people use *Snapchat* every day. • If you want to reach a younger demographic, *Snapchat* is great choice. • *Snapchat* users are more likely to discover new businesses. • *Snapchat* users are spending 35% more time in the Discover section every day (*Hootsuite*). • 60% are more likely to make an impulse purchase (*Snapchat*). • *Snapchat* reaches 75% of Millennials (ages 25-40 in 2021) and Gen Z (ages 6-24 in 2021). • Over 75% of the U.S. population aged 13-34 are on *Snapchat*. • Geofilters can help you reach a local audience faster.

Social Media Channel	Marketing Benefits
7. Pinterest	• The number of monthly active users on *Pinterest* has grown to 454 million in Q2 2021 (*Statista*). • 60% of *Pinterest* users are women (*Sprout Social*). • 80% of U.S. Millennial women and 40% of Millennial men are on *Pinterest* (*Sprout Social*). • 80% of U.S. moms are on Pinterest (*Sprout Social*). • The most popular pin/photo categories include art, art supplies, and hobbies followed by flowers, food, drinks, and gifts (*Statista*). • *Pinterest* is great for posting photos in albums with themes. For example, inspirational quotations and great Italian food can be album names. • *Pinterest* also lets you pin news stories with a link back to your website, which can drive traffic to your website. • 40 percent of *Pinterest* users have a household income of $100,000+ (*Pinterest*).
8. TikTok	• **TikTok is the 7th most-used social network**. • *TikTok* is the "leading short video entertainment platform" that reaches a younger demographic. • The majority of people use *TikTok* to find funny/entertaining content (entertainment, dance, pranks, fitness, beauty and pets are some of the most popular topics). • *TikTok* has nearly 100 million monthly active users in the United States • *TikTok* users are 60% are female, 40% are male. • 48% of U.S. adults between 18-29-years-old use *TikTok*. (*Pew Research*) • Teens account for 25 percent of *TikTok's* active user accounts in the United States. (*Statista*, March 2021) • The figure drops to 20% in the 30-49-year-old age group, 14% among 50-64-year-olds, and 4% for those 65 and up. • According to *Hootsuite*, "*TikTok* is still a bit of a wild west for brands. Case and point: *Ocean Spray*, a 90-year-old beverage company, nabbed 15 billion media impressions via *TikTok* in a month without doing a thing."

Now that you have reviewed your social media platform options and chosen your top three social media sites, go secure the username for each one. To make your marketing easier to manage, I recommend using **one consistent email** for all social media accounts connected to a brand.

Yes, this digital marketing setup process can take time, but it is really important for your brand strategy and Word-of-Mouth Marketing.

Bottom line, you always want to be smart and consistent in your digital marketing to make it really easy for customers to find you. If someone has a hard time finding your brand online, the majority will give up quickly (remember, the average attention span for adults is eight seconds).

Let's take a closer look now at some mega names and small business brand examples to see how well they dominate their digital banks. You will notice that the mega brands are much better at consistency compared to some small businesses who take shortcuts. Using different social media names to "make it work" rather than "make it easy for customers" is not a good idea.

MEGA BRAND EXAMPLES – DIGITAL BANK OWNERSHIP

Amazon – PERFECTLY CONSISTENT!

URL: *Amazon.com*
Facebook: facebook.com/amazon
Instagram: instagram.com/amazon
Twitter: twitter.com/amazon
YouTube: youtube.com/amazon

Sesame Street – MORE PERFECTION!

URL: *sesamestreet.org*
Facebook: facebook.com/SesameStreet
Instagram: instagram.com/sesamestreet
Twitter: twitter.com/seasamestreet
YouTube: youtube.com/sesamestreet

UGG – Not Exactly!

URL: *ugg.com*
Facebook: facebook.com/UGG
Instagram: instagram.com/ugg
Twitter: twitter.com/ugg
YouTube: youtube.com/user/uggaustralia — INCONSISTENT

SMALL BUSINESS EXAMPLES – DIGITAL BANK OWNERSHIP

Peet's Coffee

URL: *peets.com*
Facebook: facebook.com/peets
Instagram: instagram.com/peetscoffee — INCONSISTENT
Twitter: twitter.com/PeetsCoffee — INCONSISTENT
YouTube: youtube.com/channel/UChtMUHysfGfTPiWieYJY65g — INCONSISTENT
(NOTE: You need 100 subscribers now to own your *YouTube* URL.)

Fruit Bliss

URL: *fruitbliss.com*
Facebook: facebook.com/fruitbliss
Instagram: Instagram.com/fruit_bliss — AVOID UNDERSCORES in USERNAME
Twitter: twitter.com/fruit_bliss — AVOID UNDERSCORES in USERNAME
YouTube: youtube.com/channel/UCDTb_DphrOHGCS60joFEtgg (*Fruit Bliss Snacks*)

Step 2.3 Buy a Mobile-Friendly WordPress "Responsive"

Theme Website Template

When you build a website, we recommend using a "responsive" *WordPress* theme template that is mobile-ready for the best SEO. You may also try another option like *WIX Mobile Site Builder*. We prefer *WordPress* because it offers great SEO. Your job is to get as many eyeballs on your brand as possible so pay attention to what tools work best for optimizing your search results.

A "responsive" theme is a must because it is mobile-friendly, which means it adjusts to fit the user's device screen (computer, smartphone, and tablet). It's so important that *Google* will now lower your website in the search engines if you are not mobile-friendly. Search online for the themes that say "responsive" and pay the low fee and buy plug-ins when needed. It is so worth it!

For an example of a *WordPress* template, *Google* the Montana template by *ThemeForest* or "best *WordPress* responsive themes." You will pay a little for these templates, but it is usually a minimal one-time fee (around $17 to $59), plus you may opt-in for a support plan. The Montana template design is simple and has many customization options for the menu and layout. When you are reviewing options, look for the "Live Preview" button to view an actual website built using the template.

MOBILE WEBSITE CASE STUDY - THEMICHAELBLANK.COM

To see a really impressive mobile website for a small business owner, check out *themichaelblank.com*. As an author, mentor, coach, and real estate investor who specializes in apartment building investing, Michael Blank's website is easy to navigate, and the graphics, photographs, and videos speak volumes about his brand. The overall content conveys confidence in Blank as the author of *Financial Freedom with Real Estate Investing* and leading authority on apartment building investing. This digital presence has contributed to this CEO raising millions of dollars for multi-family investments.

For our *GoodyPR.com* website's most recent update, we chose the Noho template by *ThemeForest*. We like the clean design with video options. We are most proud of booking one of our clients on the *TODAY Show*, and share this video prominently on the home page (more on this story in Chapter 8). We also LOVE the Portfolio page in this template that showcases examples of our work with pictures, video, and descriptions. Each portfolio post also has great SEO for *Goody PR*.

However, once we bought the Noho theme template, it did not look exactly like the online "Live Preview" website. As a result, one of our *Goody PR* website developers customized it. As a team, we spent a few weeks going back and forth fine-tuning the format to tell a Wow Story for our "Magnify Good" brand and mission.

Even if you are very familiar with *WordPress*, we highly recommend hiring a developer to help you with the behind-the-scenes technical pieces. For example, our developer contacted the *WordPress* Noho template designer through online help to find ways to customize the website better and troubleshoot issues.

There are also *WordPress* plug-ins that you will need. Plug-ins are used for security, *Google Analytics*, connecting to your social media channels, social sharing, spam prevention, forms, ecommerce and other important features. Unless you are a developer, hire the pros to take care of these details. To be more efficient, we also highly recommend hiring a U.S.-based website developer for anything complicated so that you can regularly talk on the phone about details.

You can also use a project management software system to keep your website content and updates in a central place online for a team. For example, when working at *Fox Interactive Media/myspace*, we used *BaseCamp* to manage complex projects across departments. *Goody PR* has since used *BaseCamp* to manage big projects for clients with multiple team members in different locations.

Along with choosing a website template, here is a quick summary checklist of what you need to build your brand website.

Must-Haves for Websites	WHY you need it.
Buy URL from *GoDaddy* or Another Site	Buy your exact match dot com URL, and pay an annual fee before doing anything else when launching a new brand.

Must-Haves for Websites	WHY you need it.
Purchase your Responsive *WordPress* Theme or Template	Buy a responsive website theme that is mobile friendly. Buy a template as a starting point for a one-time fee of about $49 (average), and then hire a developer to help you with customizations.
Set up Hosting	You will need someone to host your website (*GoDaddy, HostGator*, and other sites). Hosting usually requires an annual fee and may include extra fees for custom emails (Example: yournameATwebsitename.com). Ask a lot of questions and get recommendations for the best hosting service.
SSL or Secure URL with https	Almost every website now uses an SSL (Secure Sockets Layer) with an https versus http address so it is more secure. *Google* started requiring SSL for online banking and shopping sites, and now all websites need it for good SEO and indexing. Remember, *Google* controls the Search results, so you want to play by their rules. Many hosting services now offer SSL as a free add-on as part of their service, so just ask – it's important.
Google Analytics	You should also set up *Google Analytics* for free so you can track your website traffic. (*Google* for the setup instructions online, and add to a plug-in.)
Plugins	*Plugins* are apps for websites (there are many). You want to add website plugins to your back-end administration portal for many reasons. Your best bet is to hire a developer who can recommend and install *plugins* based on your needs. Similar to any software program, plugins are also often updated, so you want to check them periodically.
Company Logo and Creative Assets	You will also need your company logo and creative assets (images and photos) ready for a website. If you do not have this creative, you can always hire a graphic designer. I recommend hiring a professional designer for logos. The cost can range anywhere from $1,000 to $20,000 for major brands. While we recommend investing in your logo and getting a referral from a trusted

Must-Haves for Websites	WHY you need it.
	source, *Upwork* and *Fiverr* are websites where contractors compete and may be cheaper. If you want to build a business around your brand, please invest and hire a professional for your logo! I hired Michele Weisbart (MicheleDesigns.com) for our *Goody Business Book Awards* logo, and it was so worth it! Check out https://GoodyBusinessBookAwards.com to see the hot air balloon logo!
Site Map and Content	You will also need to draft a site map that lists all the pages in your website Menu, along with your creative assets or content (text, images, video). Review the website's Navigation and processes. Make it easy for users to find and buy things. You can also hire professionals to help you design the site navigation for complex websites.

Now that you have purchased your dot com for your brand name, secured your top three social media site usernames, and launched your website, it is time to start posting compelling content online.

Step 2.4 Post Clear, Concise, and Compelling Digital Content with Keyword Hashtags

Similar to a great press release, media pitch, or keynote address, your online content must immediately grab the reader's attention. For branding, consistency is also essential in your digital marketing with your topics, tone, colors and keywords.

SEO STRATEGY IS YOUR NEXT PRE-LAUNCH STEP

When you prepare to post your content, plan a great SEO strategy first. Your digital marketing text and tags will determine whether people can find you online. For the best results, make sure you have a keyword strategy upfront.

You first want to identify keyword phrases that you will use over and over again to help direct traffic to your brand website and social media. This list of keywords should be used consistently in social media text posts, image names, photo names, video file names, and blogs to get the best results.

Choose 3-5 keywords or key phrases (long-tail and more specific to better reach your target audience). Use these keywords as hashtag phrases for your product, service, or book to use with every social media post. For example, for our *8-Second Branding Podcast*, we regularly use these hashtags:
#8SecondBrandingPodcast, #TopMarketingPodcast
#PublicRelationsPodcast, #AuthorMarketingTips and
#SmallBusinessMarketingTips.

We recommend using long tail keywords that have relatively low search volume and competition levels. For example, instead of using a single word like "restaurant" as the keyword, use a phrase like "best sushi restaurant Los Angeles." By adding the food type and geography, you can attract your target audience and sales faster.

Here are some more SEO keyword examples for businesses as a quick snapshot:

Mega Brand	Bad SEO Keywords	Much Better SEO Keywords
Airbnb	Vacation	"economy travel" "cheap hotel Los Angeles" "hotel alternatives Los Angeles"
Apartment Therapy	Apartments	"home décor and design" "how to update your home" and "New York"
Etsy	Jewelry	"handmade necklace" "custom jewelry designs Miami"
Wayfair	Homes	"home decorating design firm" "best home furnishings"
All Recipes	Recipes	"best low carb recipes" "best gluten free recipes"

We cannot emphasize enough the importance of using your SEO keywords everywhere in your digital assets, including blog posts, website URLs, press releases, columns, blogs, videos, image names, and social media posts.

To help you determine the best keywords for your brand, here are five tools:

5 Keyword Research Tools	Benefits
Google Keyword Planner	This tool is regularly used by advertisers on *Google*. It is one of the most accurate keyword tools.
Ubersuggest Discovery Tool	Ubersuggest is a free tool that specializes in generating new keyword ideas. It was recently acquired by Digital Marketing Expert and Bestselling Author Neil Patel.
Keywords Everywhere	This is a paid keyword research tool that displays keyword data on top of 10 websites ...including *Ebay, Amazon* and *Answer The Public*.
GetKeywords (one word)	A SEO tool that is focused on helping you find local SEO keywords. When you type in your target keyword, you can narrow results down by geography (country, state/province, or even city level.)
Google Trends	Use *Google Trends* to search keywords and find "related" terms. You can see if the keyword is growing in popularity.

Your brand's keywords are important for all digital content. How many times have you gone to *YouTube* to search for a video and could not find it? Chances are the person who posted the video forgot to put keywords in the title, description, and/or video tags in the back-end portal. People search YouTube for "How to" videos all the time, so use your keyword phrases in these five key areas to increase your chances of being found.

8-SECOND PR'S TOP 5 SEO TIPS FOR *YOUTUBE* VIDEOS

1. Use Keywords in the Video Title.
2. Use Keywords in the Video Description.
3. Use Keywords in the Video Tags (in the back-end administrative portal).
4. Use Keywords in the Main Image File that you select for the video (custom image).
5. Use Keywords in the 3 main hashtags for each video by placing them at the bottom of your video description.

As a brand owner, you put a lot of work into developing your content, so don't overlook the value of good SEO. And if you are a business, hire professionals to help you!

CASE STUDY EXAMPLE – *CAPTAIN AMERICA* VIDEO KEYWORDS

As a video success story example, we posted a video on our *Goody Awards YouTube Channel* of a popular *San Diego Comic-Con International* Panel. The video title was – "*Chris Evans Captain America* flexes muscles to Thor at *Comic Con 2014 Marvel* Panel."

As of 2021, this video has almost 1 million views! You're probably saying, well, yes people want to watch celebrity videos. However, there were 5,000+ fans in this Hall H convention center ballroom also posting videos of the same panel.

So how did this video get found so fast? Besides having a great camera with a zoom lens, the SEO keywords made a HUGE difference in getting discovered, including "Chris Evans Captain America", "The Avengers Panel", "Comic-Con Marvel", "Hall H" and "Comic-Con International 2014."

Now that you have more insights, start writing a list of everything you can do to improve your SEO! If people can't find your content, why bother doing marketing and PR?

WRITE CLEAR MESSAGES ON SOCIAL MEDIA POSTS

Once you have defined your keywords, your next step is to write clear messages on *Facebook, Twitter, Instagram, LinkedIn* and more, which is much easier said than done. No one wants to read a really long social media post or be left guessing what you meant. Your challenge is to make what you are saying obvious with as few words as possible.

If you are not sure if your content makes sense, ask a friend for HONEST feedback before posting. You can also do A/B testing. This content comparison approach is done all the time in advertising. Simply post two to three different versions of your message on social media to see which one gets the best response.

No matter what type of brand you are selling or promoting, you need to be clear in your first sentence. Remember, you have only eight seconds to get their attention!

To engage users, your posts should ask a question, take a poll, celebrate a milestone/recognition, announce a new product or even share a thought-provoking quote with keyword hashtags. To encourage engagement, add a "Call to Action" to guide readers towards what you want them to do (comment, share, donate, buy, vote, check it out).

CASE STUDY EXAMPLES – GREAT *INSTAGRAM* POSTS

@omarl.harris post – Good news! *The Servant Leader's Manifesto* is now officially an award-winning business and management book! #servantleadership #omarlharris

@monadelahooke post - The secret's out! Friends, due to the overwhelming support of *Beyond Behaviors*, we've created a Flipchart, a tool that you can use as a parent, teacher, or therapist to explain the basic principles of the *Beyond Behaviors* approach!....Follow the link in my bio to win a free copy! #BeyondBehaviors #BeyondBehaviorsFlipChart #paradigmshift

@lizhkelly post - LAST DAY! You can help heal our veterans & first responders by entering the RAFFLE & SILENT AUCTION by Sat, June 30 by 2pm CST for 2 handmade wooden American flags by #veterans & #firstresponders @WarriorsHeartHealing @WarriorsHeartFoundation as part of their #PayItForward Program (link in bio). #addictiontreatment #ptsdtreatment #warriorsheart #healveterans

WRITE CONCISE MESSAGES

While you may think it is easy to be clear and concise, it's not. For example, we consistently brainstorm potential media topics with new clients to learn about their products and services. In one case, a new client recommended, "Listen to my hundreds of podcasts (one hour each) to figure out which media topics to pitch about me." Really? No one has time to listen to hours of content to figure out what your brand means. If you cannot explain your brand story in a few sentences or a one-page summary with bullets and photos, you can forget about winning over the media, fans, and influencers!

To market your book, product, or service, you must grab your audience's attention immediately. If they are confused upfront, you may have lost them, and maybe forever!

Twitter is our favorite social media site for concise messages. Despite their 280-character limit per tweet, many posts could be much clearer and moving. Take a look at these tweet comparisons.

Original *Twitter* Message	Clearer *Twitter* Message
Increasingly, I have noticed entrepreneurs talking about "disrupting" industries as a primary objective and not just an effect of	Have you noticed many entrepreneurs talk more about "disrupting" industries versus

Original *Twitter* Message	Clearer *Twitter* Message
their innovation. Here is why I think it is time to start talking about solutions and building companies again.	actually taking action? Here is why I think we should focus on finding solutions.
An impressionistic artist who works mainly with a palette knife and oils. He has his own unique technique & style which is unmistakable & cannot be confused with other artists. His paintings usually reflect certain personal memories and emotions	Calling #ArtLovers! Check out this #ImpressionisticArtist who works mainly with a #paletteknife & oils. LOVE his unique technique & style that draws out so many emotions!
Are you heading to #advertisingweek #nyc? You won't want to miss this! Monday, 3:30pm et on the GREAT MINDS stage at #HudsonYards. Link below. #Advertising @NorthwellHealth @lifeaidhope @AnaNursingWorld @sjindavis #InternetEssentials #awnewyork #advertisingweeknow	No edits recommended! It's a clear, concise and compelling by @mrjonburk!

WRITE COMPELLING POSTS THAT EMOTIONALLY CONNECT

Compelling content is simply an authentic message from the heart that emotionally moves the reader. If you do not make people cheer, get excited, feel joy, cry or scream, you will get a low engagement (likes, shares, comments, shares, views, purchases, donations or more). As a marketing person, your goal should always be to move people to increase responses and revenue, and build a community of loyal fans and followers. If your audience is not thinking "wow, incredible, so inspiring, very helpful, fantastic, or how can I buy, donate or help," they are probably not spending a lot of time on your digital platforms.

In your social media posts, I highly recommend using emphasis phrases to focus your message on your one "most important thing" or "top three things." Apply it to every type of communication about your brand both online and offline (interviews, videos, photos, blogs, speaking events and more).

Liz H Kelly

Focus on sounding humble, grateful and balanced online. You want to avoid turning people off. People who only post long-winded text and photos of themselves online can get really boring fast. Remember, giving thanks, showing compassion and sharing helpful tips can go a long way in many facets of life, especially online.

Step 2.5 Share High-Quality Photos That Tell Your Brand Story

High-quality photos are one of the most important parts of any Digital PR strategy, and one of the easiest ways to tell a story in eight seconds. This topic is one of my favorites, and I could write a whole book about photo and video marketing. I am so passionate about photography that I had a dark room in our basement at age 17, own five cameras, and literally almost married someone because of the dark room in his home (no joke!).

According to *Forbes*, content with visuals receive 94 percent more views, so you should ALWAYS post online with photos or video.

While everyone has suddenly become a photographer with a smartphone, it is better to take important photos with a real digital camera. While smartphone photos continue to increase in quality, we prefer to use a camera for a website, marketing materials and media story images.

I had a debate on this smartphone versus digital camera topic with multi-media journalist Jefferson Graham on his *USA TODAY's Talking Tech Podcast.* He has very different opinions. *As a tech columnist for USA TODAY* for over two decades, Jefferson got to test every new smartphone camera. He now hosts and directs the travel photography series: *Photowalks with Jefferson Graham.*

While I love smartphone cameras (and they keep getting better), the *Chicago Tribune* chose an author photo that I took with a *Nikon COOLPIX P7700 Digital Camera* for client's book review story. The reporter was given ten photo options that included the book cover, author headshots, and photos taken backstage before a TV interview with an *iPhone* and camera. The major newspaper team probably chose the *Nikon* image because it was high quality (2MB), had good lighting, and the author was holding up their book.

Never underestimate the power of photos for energizing your brand story. If you think "everyone" can take great pictures and the camera does not matter, think again. Invest time and money in learning how to take great photos for your brand's success!

Let's dig deeper into how to take Wow Photos to capture your audience's attention. To learn more, I took a photography class at the *Corcoran School of Art* in Washington D.C. All of my photos were black and white for this class (love black and white, especially for texture!). I've also asked many professional photographers for their advice, and admit to having 40,000+ photos on our iPhone (practice and options help!).

To help you tell a more powerful brand story with photographs, below are our top eight for how to make people look twice:

8 WOW PHOTO TIPS

1. **BUY A GOOD CAMERA** - Quality photos matter on social media, so it is really worth buying a good camera. You do not have to spend a fortune, and the cost of many digital cameras is cheaper than an *iPhone*. Our favorite camera is a *Canon PowerShot* with a 60x zoom.

2. **TELL A STORY** - Take photos that tell a story that moves people. I learned this strategy listening to *National Geographic* photographer Dave Yoder speak at an event in Los Angeles. Yoder spent six months at the Vatican in Rome, Italy, to get the perfect photo of the Pope. Think about the story and details in each of your photos - expressions, colors, content, lighting, composition, and more.

3. **FIND GOOD LIGHTING** - Move around until you get the best lighting, inside and outside. Do not be afraid to ask people to shift places and/or even go to another location to get this right. Most people do not mind moving if you tell them it will make them look better! To see examples of good lighting, flip between cable news channels covering a live event at the same time and compare the quality.

4. **WATCH BACKGROUNDS** - Pay attention to the background so nothing odd is sticking out of someone's head! A tree or pole can be really distracting if it is in the wrong place. (So many people miss this detail!)

5. **USE THE RULE OF THIRDS** - Use the rule of thirds when taking photos. Line up the horizon and subject with the grid lines on your smartphone or camera. Avoid having your subject in the center. It is much better to place your subject to the right or left side as *60 Minutes* does in TV interviews. *Google* to find visual examples and videos that explain this rule.

6. **TRY DIFFERENT ANGLES** - Move your camera and body around to take different angles (above, below and to the side). We learned this tip from @MarcKarzen when we first moved to Los Angeles. Marc studied photography at the Sorbonne University in Paris, and later did graphics for *Saturday Night Live* and *Late Night with David Letterman* (Check out his new book: *Late Night Bumpers – 40th Anniversary Edition,* November 2021).

7. **LOOK FOR S-CURVES** - Photos with an S-Curve help draw attention and create a more positive visual. Pay attention to sidewalks, paths, streets, and buildings with curves. You can also direct someone's attention by slanting your camera when taking photos. We love to turn the camera to an unexpected angle.

8. **MAKE EVERYONE LOOK GOOD** - Our rule is to only post photos online that make everyone look good. You will win a lot more friends and fans by thinking about how everyone looks in a photo! Even if you look great, do not post a photo that makes others look really bad (unless it's your only photo of a monumental moment).

As a bonus tip, add energy to a photo with surprising expressions or motions. Try pointing up, jumping, and/or dramatically placing your arms to add emphasis.

In addition, photos with people get way more engagement than scenery photos. When we trained *Johns Hopkins University's Alumni Association* how to do social media, this was one of our top tips. Their posts were too focused on their historic buildings, and we encouraged them to start featuring their alumni instead.

By now, you should be inspired to take great photos and videos and/or know how to evaluate photographers you may hire.

If you are promoting a product (book, service, gadget, app, classes, store, etc.), the final step is to confirm your brand photo strategy on social media. What are your company's colors? What types of photos will convey your brand messages the best? How often, when, and where are you going to post photos? What is your keyword strategy?

Let's take a closer look at three examples of major brands recognized for posting rock star photos on *Instagram*:

Brand on *Instagram*	Why Brand Story Photos Stand Out
Instagram.com/*Adidas* 26 million followers "Impossible is Nothing"	*ADIDAS* posts moving photos of celebrities, artists, and their sports products. For example, they have a close-up photo of GRAMMY winner Pharrell performing live at a Los Angeles event wearing their gear. They also have a lot of outdoor action photos that are spectacular. You will find sunset shots with runner silhouettes, along with game-day photos. These photos support their brand tag line, "Impossible is Nothing."
Instagram.com/*Oreo* 3.2 million followers "Milk's Favorite Cookie"	*OREO's Instagram* has fun photos that tell a story. They consistently use their brand's blue and white colors and packaging. Every post includes an *Oreo cookie,* which is recognized worldwide. They also keep-it-simple, and post *Oreo* graphics and artwork. The photos all go with *Oreo's tag line, "Milk's Favorite Cookie."*
Instagram.com/ *LivingSpaces* 364,000+ followers "Invent Yourself, Reshape The World"	*LIVING SPACES* posts inviting photos of comfortable rooms filled with their furniture. These photos feature complementary products that can give their customers ideas on how to use multiple products, so it is great cross-marketing! All photos are high-quality with excellent lighting (so important!), and the photos all support their *Living Spaces* tag line, "Invent Yourself, Reshape The World."

My last photo tip for you is one that I learned at the *Corcoran School of Art*. My secret sauce for taking awesome photos is to take a TON of photos! The teacher taught us to take about 100 photos to get five great images. While I can now get about 30 great photos out of 100, this is after years of practice. (So if you don't want to take a ton of photos to get a few fantastic ones, hire a professional – seriously!)

Most people do not realize the time involved in editing photos either. Many times, I spend five hours editing a batch of 300 photos after a corporate event. Clients will often say, "Just send all the photos." Clearly, these comments suggest they do not understand the art of photography. And that is okay because marketing professionals and photographers are paid to tell a powerful visual story.

Recently, one of our Wisconsin author clients traveled to Hawaii for a Veterans Day Hawaii Tribute Trip to honor six WWII U.S. Marines who served with their father on Tarawa and Saipan, and who are buried at the National Cemetery of the Pacific (Punchbowl). Because photos are so important for media interviews, I recommended that the author Joseph Tachovsky (*40 Thieves on Saipan*) hire a local photographer to help capture the magic moments. After asking for recommendations on *Facebook* and friends from Hawaii, we found Kelli Bullock (*Kelli with an Eye on Photography*). Her photos told a powerful story, and some images were used on multiple TV interviews in Hawaii, Kansas City and on *PBS*.

We also prefer to hire professional photographers for client headshots. *Goody PR* has researched options, and highly recommends *Bader Howar Photography*.

PROFESSIONAL PHOTOGRAPHER RECOMMENDATION - *BADER HOWAR PHOTOGRAPHY*

We HIGHLY recommend investing in a professional photographer for your headshots and/or business photos – because you and your products deserve it!

If you live in the Los Angeles area and/or are visiting, we often refer clients to *Bader Howar Photography* in Santa Monica, California. A photo session with Bader is guaranteed to upgrade your brand!

https://www.baderhowarphotography.com

If you post someone else's photo on social media or a website, make sure to credit them properly and/or ask for permission. Some images are copyrighted and may require you to pay a fee to republish them. There are also websites where you can buy stock images (*Shutterstock*) and celebrity photos (*Getty Images*).

Along with professional photos, you can always post more casual smartphone photos because imperfect images can come across as more authentic marketing. However, for media interviews, reporters usually prefer a high quality headshot.

When posting photos, edit the images using apps and filters to make them stand out more online. You will find recommendations for photo apps in the "Resources" section in the back of this book.

For example, *Canva* and *Live Collage* are two photo apps that we use all the time. Both have free and paid options. Using their attractive templates can make you look like a pro! For more advanced branding, hire a graphic artist to help you develop unique templates for your personal or business brand.

Have a blast taking your brand story photos, post regularly on your top three social media platforms, use consistent keywords and hashtags, and/or hire a professional to enhance your visual storytelling.

8-SECOND PR REMINDER –
TAKE PHOTOS AT EVERY EVENT AND INTERVIEW

I scream inside when a client tells me they forgot to take a photo of a really important moment or event. It's too easy to get caught up in the emotions and forget, but you cannot afford to skip it. Some even say, "If you don't have a photo, it didn't happen."

For TV interviews especially, reporters want visuals. The better your visual images, you will increase your chance of getting an interview. Yes, I still want you to enjoy the moment, but don't forget to take photos for your social media and earned media.

You can tell a powerful story with a photograph in eight seconds – so make photographs one of your top priorities.

Pay careful attention to the strategy, story, and content.

BONUS CONTENT – *NETFLIX'S EMILY IN PARIS* PHOTOS AND VIDEOS STRATEGY

If you haven't watched *Emily in Paris* on *Netflix*, it's worth it just to be taken to "City of Light" and pick up a few social media strategy tips while being entertained! In this comedy-drama, Emily Cooper (Lily Collins) plays a twenty-something marketing manager at the high-end *Savoir* agency. When Emily is asked to revamp the social media marketing strategy, taking photos and videos on her "camera case" cellphone becomes a central part of her every day adventures.

To learn Digital PR from this show, check out the @EmilyInParis Instagram to see how the posts promote this *Sex and the City* type show. While Emily works on marketing campaigns for beauty and luxury brands (*Vespa, Peloton, Champere champagne* and *fashion icons*), 95% of the Instagram posts highlight the drama between the main characters.

People like photos and videos of people more, and most of the @EmilyinParis photos get 40,000+ likes and videos get 500,000 views. Yes, there is a powerhouse marketing team behind this *Netflix* hit, but you can still have fun checking out the photos and videos – and taking notes.

How can you add more people and emotion to your posts?

We are still talking about marketing here - right? Did you almost forget? It is easy to get side-tracked when you are having fun talking about photos!

Step 2.6 Create Engaging Videos That Represent Your Brand

Did you know that most people decide whether to continue watching a video within the first fifteen seconds? You must immediately capture your audience's attention based on the video's visual, sound and content quality.

Posting a great versus good video for your brand is an art. While some poor-quality videos taken with a smartphone go viral, your brand will be much better represented by a professionally made production. A great video can include many elements - a moving story, clear, consistent and compelling messaging, great lighting, great composition, graphics that complement the story, great editing, and background music - that are in sync with your brand message and mission.

To help you better manage your *YouTube* content, use their Analytics Reports to see what videos are getting the most views and comments. These *YouTube* reports provide great insights for marketers, including the traffic source (*Google, WhatsApp, Yahoo*, etc.), geography where people are watching and demographics. You can even see when viewers stop watching your videos.

For example, the *Goody Awards YouTube* Channel was started in 2012. In 2021, this channel has almost six million video views, 3,670 subscribers, and over 320 videos. Our biggest *Goody Awards YouTube* win is a *Hunger Games* cast video, which includes Jennifer Lawrence, Josh Hutcherson, Liam Hemsworth, and Lenny Kravitz at the *San Diego Comic-Con International*. There are several reasons why this *Goody Awards* video went viral and now has 1 MILLION+ VIEWS. Yes, it helped to have celebrities in it, but there were probably hundreds of other videos posted online of the exact same panel.

To help you create viral videos, below are the secrets for this blockbuster video:

BLOCKBUSTER VIDEO EXAMPLE - *HUNGER GAMES* CAST 1 MILLION+ VIEWS

1. **MATCH YOUR TARGET AUDIENCE** - Our *Goody Awards YouTube* Channel audience is mostly teens and people who want to change the world. In the *Hunger Games* movie series with Jennifer Lawrence as the lead protagonist, there are many women-empowerment messages that also matched the interests of our core demographic.

2. **EDIT TO TELL A STORY** - In this four-minute video, we pulled out the best stories from the 45-minute panel. When Josh Hutchinson and Jennifer Lawrence started describing the time they filmed their kissing scenes in bad weather and how snot was coming out of Jennifer's nose, all while laughing hysterically, we knew this moment was the video gold!

3. **FUNNY = MONEY** - Humor, of course, goes a long way with videos. I like to emphasize "Funny = Money" in my digital marketing classes. For this video, Jennifer and Josh were laughing so hard while describing their "Snot Kisses". You could also see the genuine audience reaction to this hilarious conversation.

4. **VIDEO QUALITY MATTERS** — My *Canon Powershot* 50x zoom camera made the video look almost like TV quality. Watching this video, you would never know the reality was that I was filming in a sea of 6,500 people crammed into the *San Diego Convention Center* Hall H. The video is far from perfect, but looks pretty good using this camera and a monopole to hold it steady.

5. **VIDEO COMPOSITION** - Where you place the camera angle also matters. For this viral video, I was fortunate to get an aisle seat in the center with friends. This center angle put me in the perfect location for video filming. I owe this placement to my unsung hero, Ting Lei, who literally slept outside the *San Diego Convention Center Hall H* - all night - with friends to get these great seats.

6. **LIGHTING MATTERS** - I was also fortunate that the lighting was good. My *Canon* camera is great for low light, which made a big difference in a darkened room. Similar to photographs, lighting is very important for video. Most movie productions spend a fortune on lighting for this reason.

7. **SEO, OF COURSE** - The SEO for this video post was a key factor in its success. We spent a lot of time getting it right - selecting the best photo for the main video image and including keywords in the video title, comprehensive description, and tags.
8. **VIDEO TITLE** - The video title also had great energy and stood out as different. The title for our top-ever video is "Jennifer Lawrence Kisses at *Comic-Con Hunger Games.*"

To see more examples of viral videos, Google and watch these favorites online:

WATCH THESE VIRAL VIDEO BRAND EXAMPLES

- The Late Late Show with James Corden – Carpool Karaoke (especially his video with Adele)
- BBC Dad – Children interrupt BBC News Interview
- GoPro's Fireman Saves a Kitten
- Dove Real Beauty Sketches | You're more beautiful than you think
- Always #LikeAGirl
- Nike Women

During my digital marketing class, students are also required to make a short video describing their new brand. The best videos include a story, many visuals (graphics, titles, photo images), and enthusiasm by the student (who is acting as a CEO of their new brand). It is a great exercise and much harder than you would think.

If you had to create a two-to-three-minute video about your brand, book, business or product, how would you tell the story?

ACTION ITEM: CREATE A VIDEO OF YOU TELLING YOUR BRAND STORY

For your business, it's best to create a short 2-3-minute video that tells your brand story in an educational and entertaining format. People fall in love with people versus products, so add an emotional connection. I created a short overview video to announce our new *8-Second Branding Podcast*, and have found it very helpful for inviting guests, promoting the show and attracting *Goody PR* clients.

And for media interviews, reporters want to see how you come across on camera before booking you or your brand spokesperson for TV, radio or podcasts. If you don't have a video of you speaking about your brand, add that to your action item list.

While video marketing and content keeps evolving on social media, here are some of the key features on five platforms. *Instagram* announced in 2021 that they are no longer a photo sharing app, and are now a video sharing app. To find out how to use the latest features, search for How-to videos on *YouTube*.

Social Media Platform	Video Marketing Features
Facebook	*Facebook Live, Facebook Watch*
Instagram	*Instagram Live, IGTV, Reels*, Stories with video, Short-Form
TikTok	Live Q&A, Picture-in-Picture, Top Streams, Short-Form
YouTube	*YouTube* Channels, Live Streaming
LinkedIn	*LinkedIn* Video, *LinkedIn Live*

Start brainstorming fun video ideas and a series to tell your brand story, similar to *Dove's Real Beauty Sketches* or the *Always #LikeAGirl* viral video examples.

If you don't have a big brand budget, that's ok. With creative ideas, the right setting, props, good camera, great lighting and the right spokesperson, you can still produce content that emotionally connects with your audience. The important thing is to just get started. With practice and the right tools, you can produce viral video content.

Sure, you can draft a script, but do not read it. You want the video to sound authentic, so an outline of key talking points works great for the filming preparation. You might need multiple takes, but that is okay.

GOODY PR CASE STUDY –
BOOK TRAILER VIDEO BETTER WITHOUT A SCRIPT

Many authors create a short Book Trailer video to promote new books. We highly encourage you to film product launch videos anytime you are marketing a new business, book or brand. And then continue to publish videos regularly as part of your overall marketing strategy.

When our bestselling author client Lynn Isenberg (*The Funeral Planner*, *Author Power*) asked for help filming a book promo video, we became the disruptor. Lynn is a recognized novelist, producer, and screenwriter, who is used to having a formal script. When we walked on the set, Lynn was prepared with cue cards for the talent to read for this video. After several disastrous takes, we recommended not using the cue cards to sound more natural. The results were 100 times better. It was still the same talking points, but the actor spoke more from the heart versus a script.

It's always good to have an outline of what you want to say, but avoid reading directly from a script to sound more genuine and authentic in all promotional videos.

Keep in mind that videos can be gamechangers for marketing, especially for authors, speakers and podcast hosts. What stories can you film to promote your personal or business brand?

GOODY PR CASE STUDY –
SPEAKER REEL VIDEO FOR TOM WHEELWRIGHT

As another case study example, I worked with a professional video editor to develop a speaker reel for CPA, CEO, and tax expert, Tom Wheelwright. He was speaking in Australia, and we found a video production team in Sydney to partner with us for this project. Tom spoke on six continents that year, and the video incorporated an interview with him, along with multiple clips of him speaking on stage in different cities. Everything from the composition, sound quality, order of the clips, banner text, main video image, title, description, and keywords resulted in a great response online with more speaking opportunities. You can watch this video on *Goody PR's YouTube Channel*: "Tax and Wealth Speaker Tom Wheelwright Puts Money in Your Pocket."

As we wrap up this section, here are some of the latest video marketing trends that emphasize the importance of this digital asset. Check out these statistics, and then get started with your video marketing plan.

WHY YOUR BRAND VIDEO MATTERS? – VIDEO MARKETING TRENDS

- 74% of adults in the US use *YouTube* (*Hootsuite*).
- 27.2% of online viewers watched 10+ hours of online video on a weekly basis. (*Statista* 2020 survey)
- 84% of people say that they've been convinced to buy a product or service by watching a brand's video. (*Wyzowl*, State of Video Marketing Report, 2021)
- Sequential storytelling is an effective tool for social media campaigns, such as *YouTube, Instagram, TikTok, or TV.*
- Short-form videos continue to trend in 2021. The increased popularity of *Instagram Reels* and *TikTok* support this growth.
- Worldwide spending on augmented reality and virtual reality (AR/VR) is forecast to accelerate out of the pandemic, growing from just over $12.0 billion this year to $72.8 billion in 2024. (*IDC*)

Step 2.7 Promote Before, During, and After Your Brand Launch

Once you have created a library of compelling content, you need to decide when and how you will share it online. While some people recommend waiting until the "official launch" to promote your book, product, service, or new movie, most marketing pros today will advise posting content before, during, and after a new product goes live. You can share the content in stages leading up to a launch and include teaser campaigns. Remember, anyone who thinks a marketing campaign should only be a three-month launch blitz is missing out on months of potential sales, brand awareness, and promotions.

Why do you think the summer blockbuster movies start marketing at *Comic-Con* a year in advance of the theatrical release? Producers often premiere "sneak preview" content that is exclusive for *Comic-Con* attendees just to wow the fans! The studios know the importance of building a fan base early. You always want to encourage Word-of-Mouth Marketing so that fans and influencers start building buzz for you.

PRODUCT LAUNCH CASE STUDY – *AUTISM GUARDIAN ANGELS*

When *Goody PR* built the branding and launch plan for *Autism Guardian Angels* (new *Venture Capitalist*) for autism products making an impact, aka *Shark Tank* for autism products/services), we developed an integrated marketing campaign with multiple elements, outlined here:

1. Developed a creative logo and powerful messaging with the founder and team.
2. Launched a mobile website before a major Autism Awareness Month launch campaign.
3. Posted consistent social media posts on *Facebook, Instagram, Twitter* and *YouTube before,* during, and after the launch.
4. Launched an *iPad* sweepstakes to enter on *Facebook* and *Twitter* during April's Autism Awareness Month.

5. Sponsored the first *Autfest Film Festival* hosted by the *Autism Society of America*, including films made by and about autistic people.

6. Cross-marketed with the *Autism Society* before, during and after *Autfest*.

7. Wrote blogs and press releases about *Autfest* and other autism events that we attended.

8. Honored autism advocate Matt Asner with a *Golden Goody Award* our top humanitarian *Goody Award*) "for dedicating over 20 years to expanding autism organizations.

9. Filmed red carpet interview videos at *Autfest* with autistic filmmakers, filmmakers, and stars (Ben Affleck after *The Accountant* screening, *ABCs' The Good Doctor* Cast and Academy Award Winner Pete Docter, *Inside Out*) to promote our new *YouTube* Channel.

This integrated marketing campaign "put *Autism Guardian Angels* on the map," according to our client who was thrilled to get so much attention within a short timeframe. This campaign not only connected with the millions impacted by autism, but it also raised awareness of this new investment fund within the tech community.

Step 2.8 Be Active and Current to Engage Your Audience

To keep your fans engaged with your content online, you want to regularly post and update your content with new themes, timely messages, and relevant campaigns. Similar to your media hooks, you want to adjust the story based on the season, trends, and campaigns. People like "new" things, so you cannot pick just one marketing theme, and let it go. We will talk more about reinventing your brand story throughout this book, and especially in Chapter 8.

The most important thing to remember about engaging fans on social media is it is a two-way conversation. It is a give-and-take. If you post all day long and never LIKE anyone else's posts in return, your fans and friends will get bored and go away. Unless you are a celebrity, well-known public figure, or influencer, your popularity will not last very long online with a one-way conversation.

Bonus Content	Best Times to Post on Social Media
Facebook	Tuesday, Wednesday, Friday between 9 a.m. – 1 p.m.
Instagram	Monday through Friday at 11 a.m.
Twitter	Tuesday from 9 a.m. – 3 p.m. and Wednesday from 9 – 11 a.m.
LinkedIn	Tuesday – Thursday from 9 a.m. – 12 p.m.

Source: *Best Times to Post on Social Media in 2021, Social Media Data*

Make it a priority to engage with your friends on social media. They are your best source of Word-of-Mouth Marketing. It's just polite to have a two-way conversation versus only talk about yourself online. Just like building any relationship, you have to work on it. And remember, your online conversations will impact your success.

ENGAGE FANS AND INFLUENCERS

Your digital marketing strategy is not complete unless it includes ways to engage your fans and influencers. While your friends are important, you have to go beyond their reach to expand your brand awareness.

People, especially influencers, often want something in return. You might offer an "exciting prize" for a sweepstakes, free products or services, and/or an experience (concert tickets, a trip, conference tickets) as a way to increase your fan engagement.

CASE STUDY EXAMPLE –
UNIVERSITY OF PHOENIX BACKSTAGE PASSES

While working for *Fox Interactive Media*/myspace, the *University of Phoenix* sponsored a "Back to School Campaign" that included a 35-city music tour with singer Kate Voegele *(One Tree Hill)*. Kate took classes on the bus on her laptop, and then perform at night at venues across the U.S. To keep fans engaged, Kate participated in a weekly online chat. Through a custom myspace page, fans could win backstage passes and be entered into a sweepstakes for an autographed guitar. This campaign was such a huge success that the *University of Phoenix* ran it three times.

In all digital marketing, you should always be listening to fans and engaging with them online (comment, like, re-tweet). You can do it yourself and/or hire a team of professionals so the brand is consistently present.

You should also invest in social media monitoring tools ranging from free to $5,000 or more per year (*Buffer, Hootsuite, HubSpot* and many more are options). Many of these online tools provide valuable reporting to help you identify trends. You can see what posts are working and what content does not connect to fans. (See the **"Resources"** section of this book for social media management tools.)

WHY MOBILE MARKETING MATTERS

MOBILE MARKETING CASE STUDY – *TAO NIGHTCLUB* CAMPAIGN

Mobile marketing is another digital marketing tool that is evolving, and cannot be overlooked as we close this chapter. With users spending an average of 69 percent of their media time on smartphones *(comScore)*, pay attention to this space.

As a case study example, check out this *TAO Nightclub* mobile promotion. Here's how this worked:

- 2,000 opt-in *TAO Nightclub* subscribers received an exclusive text message offer.
- 11 percent redeemed the offer.

- 220 additional attendees came to the event based on this offer.
- $1,770 revenue was generated in additional admission fees.
- $4,400 revenue was generated for additional drinks (two per person at $10 per drink).

What is consistent in mobile marketing case studies is that text message campaigns with a "special offer" work best. With over 40 percent of online transactions being made on smartphones from June to September 2017 (according to *Google Analytics)*, mobile marketing is gaining traction. With the right mobile campaign, it can add a significant return on investment (ROI).

Source: 30 Mobile Marketing Case Studies You Need to Know, Tatango.com blog

While many are still trying to figure out how to maximize mobile marketing, B2C (business-to-consumer) brands need to pay attention to this space. One simple solution for mobile marketing is to run a *Groupon* with a special discount offer to drive traffic to your store. You can set this up easily online and then watch your sales increase.

Engagement reports and ROI (Return on Investment) numbers should be evaluated whenever you are planning a social media marketing campaign. Once you have fine-tuned your digital marketing strategy, it will get easier.

BONUS CONTENT –
8 *AMAZON* MARKETING TIPS FOR AUTHORS

If you are an author, there are many digital marketing actions that you can take on *Amazon* to promote your book and increase sales, besides just publishing it. Below are our top 8 marketing tips on this platform:

1. **Research competitive books on *Amazon*** - See what is selling best in your niche, and develop your keywords connected to these books! (For example, to promote *8-Second PR*, we use the Keyword phrase "PR for Dummies".)

2. **Include keywords in your book sub-title** - For this new edition of *8-Second PR*, we included Public Relations in the updated sub-title. It was a huge mistake to leave these words out the title in our first edition.

3. **Select your book categories carefully on *Amazon*** – Categories matter! You can become an *Amazon* Bestseller faster by picking niche categories for your subject because they have less competition.

4. **Write a great book description using your keywords** – Take time to write a really solid description that includes reviews, a short book summary and bulleted items that outline the content versus one long, rambling paragraph.

5. **Include important Testimonials in your Amazon book description!** – You can include important book reviews and testimonials in your summary and/or Editorial Reviews on the *Amazon* book page to attract more readers.

6. **Use KDP Author Promotion Services** - If you self-publish your book using *KDP (Kindle Direct Publishing), use the Author* Promotion Services on the back-end. You can schedule a free or discounted book promotion to increase your sales and awareness for 2-5 days. Your additional downloads can help you become an *Amazon* Bestseller in the Top 100 Free Books section.

7. **Develop a Paid Advertising Campaign using your keywords** – Yes, paid ads are a must on Amazon for your book or brand! *Amazon* is a top search engine similar to Google. You must "pay to play" as an author or brand selling a product!

8. **Complete your *Amazon* Author Central Profile** - Include a short bio, headshot, photos and videos on your Amazon author page to increase your Amazon SEO and credibility as an author.

And P.S. – Reviews Matter - Of course, get friends, family and fans to write book reviews – they really impact whether your book shows up in *Amazon* search results! (If you like this book, we would be SO grateful if you write a review for *8-Second PR!*)

And because *Amazon* Marketing matters so much for books, we encourage you to listen to one of our most popular podcast interviews by an author who specializes in this topic:

8-SECOND BRANDING PODCAST –
AMAZON **BOOK MARKETING - PENNY SANSEVIERI**

We learned and applied many *Amazon* Book Marketing tips based on books by Penny Sansevieri, especially, *How to Sell Books by the Truckload on Amazon. I discussed these tips and book during an interview with the author on* our *8-Second Branding Podcast.*

If you are an author or selling a product on *Amazon,* you must listen or watch our interview called: How to Sell Tons of Books on *Amazon* with AME CEO Penny Sansevieri (June 10, 2021).

Visit *Goody PR's 8-Second Branding* Podcast page or just *Google* the show title because it is on all major podcast platforms (*Apple Podcasts, Spotify, Google Podcasts, iHeart Radio, Tune In, VoiceAmerica* and more): https://goodypr.com/8-second-branding

CHAPTER 2 RECAP

Are you now ready to dominate your digital footprint to increase the Word-of-Mouth Marketing for your brand? Do you have a content strategy to promote your brand, website and social media platforms so everyone instantly falls in love with your story? As a marketer, you must master your Digital PR Superpower to win loyal fans.

Step 2 Action Items - Dominate Your Digital Bank to Increase Word-of-Mouth Marketing

1. Buy the URL.com that is an exact match to your brand name FIRST.
2. Secure social media usernames for at least the top three channels with an exact match (if you cannot get the name, go back to Step 1).
3. Buy a mobile-friendly *WordPress* "Responsive" theme website template.

4. Post clear, concise, and compelling digital content with keyword hashtags.
5. Share high-quality photos that tell your brand story.
6. Create engaging videos that represent your brand.
7. Promote before, during, and after your brand launch.
8. Be active and current to engage your audience.

PR Superpower 2 - Digital PR Superpower

Your Digital PR Superpower strength will impact your ability to reach a mass audience way beyond your friends on *Facebook*. Using these tools and tips, you can increase your Word-of-Mouth Marketing and referrals. Your digital marketing elements must include a responsive website, compelling social media content, photographs that tell a story, viral videos and mobile marketing campaigns with a great ROI (Return on Investment).

To continually engage fans, your digital marketing campaigns need to be creative and current with a rock solid rollout plan. When a superhero puts on their gear or gadgets, do you think they leave anything to chance? No, they triple-check that the equipment, tools, and systems are flawless. So develop a solid Digital PR plan, and prepare to launch!

Chapter 2 - 8-Second PR Challenges

As we close Chapter 2, here are your *8-Second PR* Challenges:

1. Are you able to secure your exact match .com and top three social media usernames for your brand?
2. What is your SEO (Search Engine Optimization) keyword strategy for your content?
3. How is your website content going to wow a fan in eight seconds?
4. What is your visual marketing strategy for photos to tell a story in eight seconds?
5. What are you going to include in the first eight seconds of your videos to engage your audience?

6. What is your 2-3 minute brand story video going to include?
7. Can you tell a powerful story in a tweet that is clear, concise and compelling?
8. What marketing elements will be in one of your digital marketing campaigns?

You will naturally enhance your Digital PR Superpower with practice. Your best bet is to map out a calendar of digital marketing campaigns with different themes, dates and holidays to highlight throughout the year. Start brainstorming to identify new ideas to promote your brand. Do A/B testing for your content to see what works best! Based on the feedback, continually revise your strategy, launch new campaigns, and post new photos and videos until you get a high engagement (likes, comments, shares).

In the next chapter, we will take a closer look at writing compelling content that grabs the reader's attention through press releases, columns, blogs and more.

Reminder:

"THE PUBLIC IS THE ONLY CRITIC WHOSE OPINION IS WORTH ANYTHING AT ALL."

– MARK TWAIN

CONTENT STRENGTH

Create Compelling Content that Emotionally Connects with Readers

> "PEOPLE DO NOT BUY GOODS AND SERVICES. THEY BUY RELATIONS, STORIES AND MAGIC."
>
> – SETH GODIN

What is your favorite movie or TV show, and why? It doesn't matter if you're a Hollywood writer, CEO, or publicist, your marketing results depend on whether people are moved by your written story. Words can make or break your brand's public relations success. To gain more fans and interviews, you must develop exceptional brand content that emotionally connects on many levels. Creating content with unlimited strength is not easy, and will require you to be continually innovative.

Content is not King or Queen today. Content is the "Connector" to your audience for marketing! Most importantly, you want to write compelling stories that make people smile, scream, cry, cheer, and/or take action.

PR SUPERPOWER 3 – CONTENT CONNECTOR SUPERPOWER

Once you own your digital domain, it is time to magnify your brand story with clear, concise, and compelling content that will make a lasting impression. To move readers, use the Content Connector Superpower to write memorable story that is unstoppable. You can gain the undivided attention of your fans by creating press releases, columns, blogs, videos, emails and social media posts with timely, relevant, and/or evergreen content.

An evergreen story is a plus because it has a long shelf-life and can connect to your target market audience for years. Evergreen story examples include profile stories, how-to guides, product reviews, lists (top tips are always good), best practices, and success tips with case study examples. Get ready to dig deeper using this *8-Second PR* Superpower. You want to continually review your content strength by asking, does it work?

STEP 3 ACTION ITEMS — CREATE COMPELLING CONTENT THAT EMOTIONALLY CONNECTS WITH READERS

1. Define what you are announcing to the world.
2. Write a compelling headline with eight words or less.
3. Write a clear and concise one-sentence summary.

4. Add a quote from the heart to emphasize your message.
5. Tell a compelling story in 300 to 800 words.
6. Include credible references and statistics.
7. Choose the best press release distribution system.
8. Proofread. Test. Proofread.

PR SUPERPOWER 3 - CONTENT CONNECTOR SUPERPOWER

As I mentioned in the beginning of this book, one of our key strengths is a 360-degree perspective of what stories are most likely to attract earned media (TV, print, radio and podcast interviews). This chapter will include insights based on my personal experiences as a marketing professional, publicist, author, podcast host and entertainment contributor. As a way to give back and magnify good, I have written 600+ stories as a reporter and ghostwriter for various publications. The benefits of this 360-view is that I can share PR Secrets with you for what the media really wants and how to develop great content.

In addition, it's important to note that as a Public Relations professional and/or industry expert, one of the fastest ways to get media is to offer to write a story for a publication. As reporters and editors continue to move at warp speed, I've seen an increase in outlets asking for story submissions in response to media pitches. If the publication is a good match for your core audience, there are endless opportunities for good writers to get published and build a brand as a recognized thought leader in their industry. We will talk more about targeting the right media in Chapter 5: MEDIA VISION - Reach Your Target Audience by Laser Focusing on Niche Reporters.

> THE STRENGTH OF EVERY STORY IS HOW PEOPLE FEEL AFTER READING IT.

When you write a story for any publication or blog, you want to include emotion and relevance by incorporating moving insights and examples. For all media, it's also important to use sixth-grade vocabulary and KISS (keep it simple, stupid) as a guideline. The audience must get your point immediately and feel a connection!

To help you fine-tune your message, here are our best practice tips for building great content.

Step 3.1 Define What You are Announcing to the World

When you are writing a press release, story, newsletter or blog, the first thing you need to decide is what is your big announcement or headline? You then want to define your main message in ONE moving sentence. Remember, you must get to the point immediately in the first sentence to get their attention in eight seconds.

Before writing anything for a new client, I usually interview them for over an hour, review their website, read their book, and then brainstorm the best ways to share their message in different formats. During these client interviews, the goal is always to look for the content gold!

Most CEOs and experts do not know how to tell a good story in a clear, concise, and compelling way that moves people. Business leaders are very smart people, but their genius is not always in brand storytelling. They are usually so focused on building their organization that they have a hard time stepping back and defining their Wow Story for publicity campaigns.

To define your story more clearly to the media and fans, it's best to start with the five Ws: What, Who, When, Where and Why. When you are sending a pitch to a producer or writing a story, the reader is always looking for the answers to these five questions.

5Ws IN 8-SECOND PR CONTENT

WHAT – Your WHAT should be pretty obvious, but is not always easy to communicate. In all cases, your job is to get to the point in the first few sentences. If you are launching a new company or program, your brain is usually in overdrive thinking about 20 different qualities versus fine-tuning a one sentence explanation. If you are pitching a special segment to a reporter, your "what" is the potential headline or media hook that is timely and relevant. And anytime you are announcing a new program, product, service, study, book or event in a press release, blog, and social media posts, your content needs to go WAY BEYOND the What.

WHO – It is always best to include the WHO behind any announcement in your content. Ideally, the WHO is a spokesperson who can be interviewed by the media about whatever you are telling the world. To add context, emphasize the backstory of the author or founder with their personal story and WHY. You can also highlight a person who has been positively impacted by your brand, and is willing to share his or her experience. Having the WHO be someone whose life was changed forever by the WHAT is always best (This is how our client was featured on the *TODAY Show* – more on this in Chapter 8).

WHEN – You always want to clarify the timeframe of your announcement. Is it related to an event, campaign or contest? You also want to answer the question "Why Now?" to create a sense of urgency. If you write a social media post that says TOMORROW, your readers will definitely pay more attention. If you can associate your announcement with a current event, breaking news, holiday (there are so many now!), or season, it will give your content even more traction with reporters.

WHERE – When you pitch the media, you also want to include a WHERE. This information can add context that connects with the audience. Your WHERE could be your spokesperson's current or hometown city, business address, Amazon page and/or event location (physical address or online, which has been much more common during the pandemic). You want to be really specific with both reporters and readers so they can easily support whatever you are doing. The WHERE can also be a website page with a Call to Action such as donate to a charity, bid in an auction, buy a book, RSVP for a summit through *Eventbrite*, sign up for a program, or vote.

WHY – No matter what type of content you are sharing, you always want to be thinking "Why should anyone care?" and "How can this story help others?" If you post content that is "all about you," your audience will walk away in a split second. Alternatively, if you can clearly explain why this announcement impacts the reader and/or helps others have a better life, people will definitely pay more attention to your content.

When writing a press release, pitch or email, you always want to ask yourself, "Why would the reader care?" For the best response, present meaningful content with a personal impact story to connect to your audience.

You never want to sound like an advertisement when emailing or posting content. While PAID content is always an option at many TV stations, it is not nearly as valuable as someone else telling your story for free – because you earned their respect and interest.

IMPORTANT NOTE:
PUBLIC RELATIONS CONTENT IS NOT SALES COPY

It is very important to note that if your content objective is hardcore sales of a business, books or products, it will not work for public relations.

Sales copy is a separate art from writing compelling content with unlimited strength to engage fans and get booked for media interviews. Great PR content should always educate and entertain versus oversell. With powerful content, you can brand a company or an expert as the go-to source to solve a problem. As a result, sales will come more naturally by building your credibility. If you want direct sales copy for your website, hire a copywriting expert with that skillset for the best results.

When developing written content, your voice must be authentic and meaningful to connect to your core audience. Let's look at another example to illustrate this point.

CASE STUDY -
WARRIORS HEART FOUNDATION - FLAG ART FUNDRAISER

Goody PR recently worked on a *Warriors Heart Foundation* Awareness Campaign that was a Flag Art Fundraiser. The spokesperson and organizer was one of their Honorary Board of Advisors with an incredibly inspiring story. If you read the stories online, you would never know that it took several calls over three days to better define the campaign in a clear, concise, and compelling way.

As background, the spokesperson Chris Stricklin is a U.S. Air Force Colonel (Ret.) and Author (*Survivor's Obligation*) who purchased two wooden American flags made by veterans and first responders at *Warriors Heart* during their residential treatment program. Stricklin was planning a raffle and silent auction for these handmade American flags and wanted to draw as much publicity to *Warriors Heart* as possible.

Because Flag Day (June 14) was about ten days away, I recommended connecting the campaign launch to this holiday and continuing through July 4 (America's birthday). We also decided the best approach was to position these unique flags as "handmade art" versus something you would buy from an assembly line. As a connector, we decided to emphasize that the flags were hand-signed by the warrior who made them in their Wood and Metal Shop. These flags are donated by the warrior as part of their "Pay it Forward" program because the money raised helps provide hardship scholarships to those whose insurance does not fully cover their treatment costs.

When the campaign came together in one paragraph, it was very compelling and resulted in three powerful TV interviews in three weeks in three cities.

Here is the press release summary, plus a breakdown of the five Ws:

Press Release Headline and Opening Paragraph:

HEADLINE

U.S. Air Force Col (Ret.) Launches *Warriors Heart Foundation* Awareness Campaign on Flag Day

U.S. Air Force Colonel (Ret.) Chris R. Stricklin announces a *Warriors Heart Foundation* Awareness Campaign and Fundraiser from Flag Day (June 14) to Liberty Day (June 30). Anyone can support this effort and win one of two handcrafted flags by

Warriors Heart clients through Stricklin's Protecting Our Protectors *Facebook* event and donation pages. All proceeds from this flag artwork raffle and silent auction will help provide residential treatment for warriors (military, veterans, and first responders) overcoming their War at Home with chemical dependencies, PTSD (Post-Traumatic Stress Disorder), mild TBI (Traumatic Brain Injury), and other co-occurring symptoms.

In this press release example, the five Ws are all in this first paragraph to make it really easy for the reader to find. Let's take a closer look.

5 WS EXAMPLE - *WARRIORS HEART FOUNDATION* – FLAG ART FUNDRAISER

- **WHAT** – *Warriors Heart Foundation* Awareness Campaign and Flag Art Fundraiser
- **WHO** – The spokesperson was U.S. Air Force Colonel (Ret.) Chris R. Stricklin, who is a member of *Warriors Heart Foundation* Honorary Board of Advisors and served 23 years.
- **WHY** – All proceeds from this flag art raffle and silent auction will help provide residential treatment for warriors struggling with chemical dependencies, PTSD, mild TBI, and co-occurring issues.
- **WHEN** – The raffle ran from Flag Day (June 14) to the Liberty Day (June 30) event raffle. The PR campaign was extended to July 4 to cover stories about the results and winners.
- **WHERE** – Anyone can enter the raffle and silent auction for two flags handmade by *Warriors Heart* clients on Stricklin's Protecting Our Protectors *Facebook* fundraiser *page.*

Our main challenge for this campaign was juggling six potential website URLs because of everyone involved. The URLs included WarriorsHeart.com, *Warriors Heart Facebook*, WarriorsHeartFoundation.org, Operation *Warriors Heart Foundation Facebook*, and two *Facebook* pages created by Stricklin highlighting the fundraiser and Liberty Day Festival and Parade. The winners were to be selected at the Liberty Day Festival in Stricklin's hometown outside Birmingham, Alabama.

Even though the WarriorsHeartFoundation.org URL was featured in our media pitch as the main website, WarriorsHeart.com was referenced by all three TV stations as the place to get more information. Because the foundation was prominently placed on WarriorsHeart.com, this URL worked fine as the primary website. However, it's important to emphasize that the media is always looking for ONE website only (and sometimes, they don't even give a website). In this case, they selected the shortest URL in the pitches.

For this PR campaign, we were grateful to secure three TV interviews on very different topics on NBC Bay Area KNTV (Flag Day), CBS 46 Atlanta WGCL (Fundraiser and Veteran Healing), and CBS 42 Birmingham WIAT (July 4th Profile Story) local news. The interviews all coincided with Stricklin's travel schedule as a consultant at the time. And as a result of a team effort, Stricklin's campaign and fundraiser resulted in $10,000+ in donations to Warriors Heart Foundation.

Step 3.2 Write a Compelling Headline with Eight Words or Less

If you are writing a story, press release, media pitch, email newsletter or even a *YouTube* video title, the headline can mean the difference between the reader paying attention or completely ignoring your content. Focus on writing headlines that are an announcement with a verb, and emphasize "how the brand is helping others."

No one wants to be around people who only care about sharing their story. These megaphone hogs are a boring turn-off to all audiences (media, fans, and family). Avoid turning readers away, and instead, find ways to engage in two-way conversations by adding meaning - in eight words or less - to your inviting titles.

WRITE UNIQUE STORY HEADLINES

To attract readers, your title is probably the most important thing you will write. Use a unique and catchy phrase rather than what everyone else is saying about the same topic. Remember our viral video example with 1 million+ views? The "Jennifer Lawrence Kisses at *Comic-Con Hunger Games*" video title was a major part of the magic!

CASE STUDY EXAMPLES –
GREAT RESIGNATION TREND HEADLINES

Let's take a closer look at 2021 headline examples for the worldwide Great Resignation Trend about the record number of people quitting their jobs. Because "20 million U.S. workers left their jobs between April and August 2021" (*Fast Company*), many stories have been published about the causes and solutions. Take a close look to see how different reporters tried to grab your attention on the same topic.

Keep in mind that when you pitch an editor, they look at your email subject line as a potential headline. You can't underestimate the importance of unique titles for getting an interview or story published with your views. Be honest, as a business owner or employee, which one of these story headlines makes you want to read it first?

Ex.	Headline Example - Great Resignation Trend	Source	Headline Word Count
1	Who Is Driving the Great Resignation?	*Harvard Business Review*	6
2	5 Reasons Why Businesses Don't Need Bosses	*Real Leaders*	7
3	Mental Health Days Won't Solve The Great Resignation	*Forbes*	8
4	Why are so many Americans quitting their jobs?	*NPR*	8
5	The Great Resignation: How employers drove workers to quit	*BBC*	9
6	The real reason everyone is quitting their jobs right now	*Fortune*	10

| 7 | 'Micromanaged and disrespected': Top reasons workers are quitting their jobs in 'The Great Resignation' | The Washington Post | 14 |
| 8 | The 'Great Resignation' Is Finally Getting Companies to Take Burnout Seriously. Is It Enough? | TIME | 14 |

Some of these story headlines are more compelling than others. Headlines 2, 4, 6 and 7 are our favorites from this original list.

Ex.	Headline Example - Great Resignation Trend	Source	Headline Word Count
2	5 Reasons Why Businesses Don't Need Bosses	Real Leaders	7
4	Why are so many Americans quitting their jobs?	NPR	8
6	The real reason everyone is quitting their jobs right now	Fortune	10
7	'Micromanaged and disrespected': Top reasons workers are quitting their jobs in 'The Great Resignation'	The Washington Post	14

To make these headlines more inviting, here are our recommended revisions that are more clear and concise with attention grabbers.

Ex.	Revised Example - Great Resignation Trend	Source	Headline Word Count
2	5 Reasons Why Businesses Don't Need Bosses in 2021 (the year adds relevancy)	Real Leaders	10
4	Why are so many Americans quitting their jobs? (No edits)	NPR	8
6	5 real reasons everyone is quitting their jobs right now (adds a number with a list of reasons)	Fortune	10

| 7 | Top reasons workers are quitting in 'The Great Resignation' (removes first few words and gets to the point faster) | *The Washington Post* | 9 |

By removing excess words, you can make a headline stronger to entice your audience even more to read it.

It is also always best to include an action verb in story headlines, press releases, video titles and pitches. Below are original headlines from the above group that include action verbs.

Ex.	Headline VERBS - Great Resignation Trend	Source	Headline Word Count
1	Who Is Driving the Great Resignation?	*Harvard Business Review*	6
4	Why are so many Americans quitting their jobs?	*NPR*	8
6	The real reason everyone is quitting their jobs right now	*Fortune*	10
7	'Micromanaged and disrespected': Top reasons workers are quitting their jobs in 'The Great Resignation'	*The Washington Post*	14
8	The 'Great Resignation' Is Finally Getting Companies to Take Burnout Seriously. Is It Enough?	*TIME*	14

Our favorite Great Resignation headline by far would be this revision:

Ex.	Favorite Revision - Great Resignation Trend	Source	Headline Word Count
6	5 real reasons everyone is quitting their jobs right now	*Fortune*	10

This headline is clear, concise, and compelling, and creates an emotional response. Nine out of ten employees have thought about quitting a job during the pandemic (according to a *Monster.com* 2021 Survey).

For business readers, it also shows that the story is focused on five clear things versus a long analysis. The bottom line is that you need to get the reader or potential customer to click on your content or you will get nowhere with building your awareness, increasing sales, gaining fans, and/or securing media interviews.

As you know, we live in an information age where the majority of people are reading content on their smartphones. In the future, you will be even more challenged to get the attention of readers consuming your content via smart glasses or other objects. When I met a reporter from the *New York Times* at *CES* (*Consumer Electronics Show*) in Las Vegas, Nevada, he explained that his sole job was to prepare the paper for the future of reader consumption using new technologies. We have already seen live TV images on the mirror in luxury hotels. How can you quickly get someone's attention with a powerful headline if the story is posted on a mirror?

No matter what type of technology people use to consume their content, it all starts with a teaser headline that emotionally connects with readers.

Step 3.3 Write a Clear and Concise One-Sentence Summary

Once someone clicks on your headline, your next challenge is to grab their attention in the first sentence. While this might sound easy, it is not. You must write an opening that grabs the reader with a reason to continue consuming your content. To make this happen, be prepared to revise the first sentence ten times until it sounds compelling.

Let's look at the first sentence of the top Great Resignation Trend headline examples that include action verbs to see which one has the strongest opening.

Ex.	Headline	First Sentence
1	Who Is Driving the Great Resignation?	According to the *U.S. Bureau of Labor Statistics*, 4 million Americans quit their jobs in July 2021.
4	Why are so many Americans quitting their jobs?	Goodbye. Farewell. Adios. Sayonara. Workers have been giving their bosses an earful of such words as of late.
6	The real reason everyone is quitting their jobs right now	The Great Resignation has taken many by surprise: Nearly two-thirds of U.S. workers are looking for a new job.
7	'Micromanaged and disrespected': Top reasons workers are quitting their jobs in 'The Great Resignation'	Health concerns, increased workloads, unrealistic manager expectations are pushing many to the breaking point, readers tell me.
8	The 'Great Resignation' Is Finally Getting Companies to Take Burnout Seriously. Is It Enough?	Toward the end of last year, Anthony Klotz, a professor of business administration at Texas A&M University who studies workplace resignations, realized that a lot of people were about to quit their jobs.

If you read through the first sentence, our favorites continue to be stories 4, 6, and 7. And in our opinion Headline 7 is the best because it says; "readers tell me."

Ex.	Headline	FAVORITE - First Sentence
7	'Micromanaged and disrespected': Top reasons workers are quitting their jobs in 'The Great Resignation'	Health concerns, increased workloads, unrealistic manager expectations are pushing many to the breaking point, readers tell me.

In comparison, it is interesting to look at two different angles on the same topic in stories 4 and 6:

Ex.	Headline	First Sentence
4	Why are so many Americans quitting their jobs?	Goodbye. Farewell. Adios. Sayonara. Workers have been giving their bosses an earful of such words as of late.
6	The real reason everyone is quitting their jobs right now	The Great Resignation has taken many by surprise: Nearly two-thirds of U.S. workers are looking for a new job.

Without a doubt, the first sentence is ten times stronger in the Headline 7 story. This opening gets right to the pain points "of readers" versus statistics about what they are going to cover. The employee concerns listed (health, increased workloads, etc.) are relatable and create an emotional response - that makes you want to read more.

The first sentence for the Headline 4 story would be our second choice because employers want to avoid hearing "Goodbye. Farewell. Adios. Sayonara" from great employees. And because the target audience is business leaders, the element of "surprise" and "two-thirds" looking for a job, Headline 6 would be our third choice.

Step 3.4 Add a Quote from the Heart to Emphasize Your Message

It is also helpful to add a heartfelt quote to a story, press release, media pitch or website content for emphasis and meaning. Let's look at some of the quotes we found in these top 3 stories:

Ex.	Headline	Quote in Story
4	Why are so many Americans quitting their jobs?	"The pandemic and the rise of remote work have changed the way we view our lives and the world." - *in new working paper by UC Berkeley economist Ulrike Malmendier*

| 6 | The real reason everyone is quitting their jobs right now | "Most people don't evaluate their job satisfaction every one of 365 days in a year. Those shocks usually happen idiosyncratically for people. But with the pandemic, it's happened en masse." - Brooks Holtom, a professor of management and senior associate dean at *Georgetown University* |
| 7 | 'Micromanaged and disrespected': Top reasons workers are quitting their jobs in 'The Great Resignation' | After five weeks of working double shifts and weekends, Smith had had enough: "For the first time in my working life, I sent an email to my manager and informed her that I quit with no notice," he said in an email. |

In our opinion, the Headline 7 and story quote is still the most impactful because it's the most authentic and written by an actual employee who quit. In Headline 6, the reporter is directly quoting an expert, which is a great thing to include. And the "working paper" quote for Headline 4 also offers the pandemic impacts on people resigning.

When writing a press release, it is similar to developing a great story. As examples, check out these headlines, openings, and quotes for *Goody PR* press releases for different experts and industries. You can really turn almost any announcement into a compelling story with the right headline and genuine quotes. And yes, these are far from perfect. We could revise these releases for hours!

Case Study Examples - *Goody PR* Press Releases		
Headline	**First Sentence**	**Compelling Quote**
Leadership Author and Coach Omar L. Harris launches New Audiobook for '*Be a J.E.D.I. Leader Not a*	With new insights on modern leadership in 2021, Bestselling Author and Former GM	"There is new hope during this dark time for leadership in the form of an uprising of J.E.D.I. Servant Leaders joining forces to rebel against the top-down toxic

Boss' (16 words)	Omar L. Harris launches a new audiobook for his latest leadership book, "Be a J.E.D.I. Leader, Not a Boss".	forces of the ego-driven boss." - Omar L. Harris
Thousands of WWII Letters uncovered by '40 Thieves on Saipan' Co-Author Joseph Tachovsky *in New Book* *(15 words)*	*"40 Thieves on Saipan"* Co-Author Joseph Tachovsky announces that he uncovered thousands of WWII letters for his father's platoon and between his parents that are priceless.	"It truly was a gift, and how wonderful that they were diligent in saving this material...It certainly made my dad feel better." — WWII Author/Son Joseph Tachovsky

While we did not get these headlines to fit into eight words, the keywords are in the beginning. Always place the most important words in the front of a title because that is what people will see in *Google* search results. The quotes made these announcements even more real and explained the background and benefits.

BONUS CONTENT – Great Video Headlines and Descriptions

On a lighter note, let's switch to how to post videos with words that make them easier to find. Check out the different VIDEO titles below, first sentence and number of views for our *Goody Awards YouTube* Channel videos filmed at entertainment events. Look closely at how the title is very specific and unique. You'll also see that Chris Evans (*Captain America*) is clearly more popular than Chris Hemsworth (Thor) in these videos.

Keep in mind that all of these videos were taken in a packed room with thousands of fans and reporters posting the same video content. There are multiple reasons why our videos stood out and went viral that you can apply to your content too.

Notice how asking questions, describing a visual and talking about romance in the headlines and descriptions made these videos get more views. Yes, celebrities are in them – but look closely at how thinking differently about titles and descriptions can attract more eyeballs.

Ex.	Video Title	First sentence	Video Views
1	Claire Danes *Homeland* describes Carrie and Quinn Romance	*Watch this fun video of Claire Danes (Homeland)* describing the romance between Carrie Mathison and Peter Quinn (Rupert Friend) in *Homeland Season 4.*	116,916
2	Did Miles Teller play the drums in *Whiplash* Movie?	During this *Whiplash* movie Oscar Screening Series hosted by The Wrap, Director/Writer Damien Chazelle and Actor JK Simmons (*Spider-Man*) discuss whether Miles Teller *(Divergent)* played the drums in this film.	284,415
3	Chris Hemsworth Thor flexes muscles at *Comic-Con 2014 Marvel Panel*	Chris Hemsworth (Thor) flexes his muscles for 6,000+ Hall H fans during *Comic-Con 2014 Marvel* Panel for *The Avengers.*	243,704
4	Chris Evans Captain America compares muscles to Thor at *Comic-Con 2014 Marvel* Panel	*Captain America* Chris Evans compares his muscles to Chris Hemsworth as Thor during the *Comic-Con 2014 Marvel* Panel for *The Avengers* in Hall H with Moderator Chris Hardwick.	931,402
5	Ian Somerhalder and Nina Dobrev answer Delana Rain Kiss Question at *2014 Paley Fest*	*Vampire Diaries* stars Ian Somerhalder and Nina Dobrev answer *Twitter fan* questions during the *2014 Paley Fest* in Los Angeles, including will there be another Delana Rain Kiss and will Damon and Elena get back together?	1,319,169

Step 3.5 Tell a Compelling Story in 300 to 800 Words

Now that we have reviewed email subject lines, story headlines, press release titles, first sentences, and compelling quotes, let's look at how to put it all together. Telling a story in 300 to 800 words is the best length, but is not easy. We often work five to ten hours on a one-page press release or story to make it clear and a strong representation of the brand. It has to immediately answer the five Ws (What, Who, Where, When and Why) with meaning to capture the audience's attention.

Goody PR always sends a draft to the client for review and emphasizes that short is better. Inevitably, many clients expand an 800-word draft into a 1,200-word press release or column because they feel compelled to share more about their expertise. Because the majority of people do not want to read long stories, we work with them on multiple versions until the content is closer to 800 words or less. The final version is always a negotiation of words.

BE A 8-SECOND PR WORD ARTIST

To magnify your brand, the best thing to do is think of yourself as a "Word Artist." We can't emphasize enough the importance of getting to the point immediately in the age of short attention spans. Words mean everything in your PR, marketing and social media marketing.

When you write your first version of anything, recognize that it is a VERY rough draft. After you revise it several times, your story can have long-term durability. Sure, you can write it faster, but it will not be nearly as powerful.

One of my favorite classes EVER was a Business Writing class at the *University of Maryland*, College Park. The professor told us on the first day, "When you turn in your papers, you will automatically get a C. If you implement my feedback and turn it back in, you can earn a B. And if you take the feedback on the second version, and write a third version, you may get an A."

This professor changed my life and career significantly. While most people do not have the patience to write several drafts, it really makes a huge difference in the marketing profession. When you are writing content, it is so important to read it out loud to see if it makes sense. Then, test the message on others. This editing process will help you fine-tune your content, reach more people, and increase sales. Invest time in your content because it speaks volumes about your brand and builds your credibility as a thought leader.

The easiest way to start writing anything (book, blog, press release) is with an outline. Using this outline, your key points can become a subtitle, table of contents, chapters, bulleted lists, quotes, statistics, and case studies to keep the reader engaged. To avoid writer's block, start anything with a list of topics and then fill in the details.

HOW TO BE A THOUGHT LEADER – AUTHORITY MAGAZINE EDITOR - *8-SECOND BRANDING*

To help you better understand the importance of writing stories and books to build your thought leadership brand, listen to our *8-Second Branding* Podcast interview with *Authority Magazine* Editor Yitzi Weiner.

During this fun exchange, Yitzi explains how he started *Authority Magazine*, and the process his team has used to interview over 25,000 high-profile entrepreneurs, celebrities, public figures and authors in the past three years. Yitzi says his "secret sauce" for finding great stories is working primarily with publicists.

Listeners will hear his views on the importance of being an author, and the top three things needed to get a column in a major publication such as *Forbes* or *Inc* magazine. You'll also hear how Yitzi's *Authority Magazine* Thought Leader Incubator teaches people how to be the "Interviewer" and is a "bootcamp to become a correspondent" to increase your "authority." And then, Yitzi shares the one thing he wished he knew before becoming a writer and more fun facts. Follow @YitziWeiner.

To listen to this *8-Second Branding* Podcast interview, visit *Goody PR*'s page https://goodypr.com/8-second-branding

Once the big picture is clear, your topics can then provide a roadmap for your content. Always think about why should anyone care (remember, it's not about you, it's about the reader!). Always provide helpful tips for your audience. This information may include a top ten list, key resources, and/or a new product or service to enhance their lives or business.

Most people do not know how to summarize what they know. Your job is to find the story and write it in an executive summary format for a press release, column or blog. For example, one client told us to listen to their 20-minute podcast to get the key points for a press release. To do this, I ordered a transcript of the podcast, pulled out the key messages, and then wrote about five drafts before presenting it to them for review. The entire press release ended up being 776 words (just under the 800-word best practice guideline for press releases) and was picked up online by 213 media outlets, including *The Boston Globe, Los Angeles Business Journal, Markets Insider*, and many local TV stations.

To get this type of online pickup, you need to take time to write a great release that is both timely and helpful. Of course, there are other important factors to consider in terms of the press release newswire service, keywords, use of lists, and links.

For another *Goody PR* client, I wrote a press release with a list that has been great for both SEO (Search Engine Optimization) and pitching to the media as a recap.

PRESS RELEASE EXAMPLE – REAL ESTATE EDUCATOR EVIE BROOKS PANAMA

HEADLINE - Real Estate Educator Evie Brooks explains 11 Panama Investing Benefits on *ESPN Cover Your Assets radio show*

SUMMARY - For investors looking to diversify their portfolio and/or people interested in becoming an expat, Real Estate Educator and Investor Evie Brooks shared 11 reasons people are investing in real estate and organic farming on *ESPN Cover Your Assets radio show.*

Overall, the most important factors in any press release or story are the content, timeliness and message.

Step 3.6 Include Credible References and Statistics

Two other elements that can add a lot of value to a story on any platform are references with verifiable statistics. You can increase your content's value instantly by including numbers from credible sources. These numbers help explain the problem that you are trying to solve, and make a story pitch more relevant to a reporter.

We have spent hours searching for the health trend statistics to support *Warriors Heart* residential treatment program press releases, and are constantly looking for new studies and headlines to support their content. Statistics have included addiction rates for drugs and alcohol, opioid epidemic numbers, mental health studies, and suicide rates for military, veterans and first responders.

Numbers are always changing, and you want to find the most current and accurate information. When you search online, look for the most recent reference from major media outlets or well-known organizations. Share this information by linking to the exact website URL in your press releases, pitches and blogs. As an example, here are our research findings on the unacceptable veteran suicide rates that I have included in pitches for *Warriors Heart* because one of their primary goals is to reduce these numbers:

RESEARCH STATISTICS TO SUPPORT CONTENT - VETERAN SUICIDE RATES

Search Result 1 – June 2021:

Headline: *7,000 troops died in the Post-9/11 wars. A staggering 30,000 died by suicide*

"The number of veterans and service members who have died by suicide since Sept. 11, 2001 is more than quadruple the number who have died in Post-9/11 wars, according to a new study released on Monday by Brown University's Costs of War project. The study estimates that 7,057 service members have been killed in post-9/11 war operations, while 30,177 active duty service members and veterans have died by suicide."

Source: *Task and Purpose*

Search Result 2 – September 2021

Headline: *2021 National Veteran Suicide Prevention Annual Report Shows Decrease in Veteran Suicides*

"*VA's* latest data from 2019 shows a decrease in suicide among Veterans from the year prior. The decrease, reflecting the lowest number of Veteran suicides since 2007, provides hope and motivation for continued prevention efforts. This message is part of the new 2021 *National Veteran Suicide Prevention Annual Report*, which includes findings from our most recent analysis of Veteran suicide data from 2001-2019. The report contains the most comprehensive set of data about Veteran suicide mortality to date."

Source: Veterans Affairs (September 2021), Matthew Miller, Ph.D., is the director of VA's Suicide Prevention Program at the Office of Mental Health and Suicide Prevention

It is so important to take the time to find the best numbers for your content. And if you are pitching a reporter, he or she will be very grateful because you made their job easier. Of course, they may check another source, but sending numbers with good references will help you build long-term relationships with producers and writers. Your readers and reporters will also come back for more if they know you take time to find accurate statistics.

Step 3.7 Choose the Best Press Release Distribution System

Once your news announcement is written with optimal strength, including the headline, summary, opening, and five Ws, your next step is finding the right distribution platform. While many brands post their news as a blog on their website and/or email it to reporters, a press release distribution system can make your message travel much farther and faster.

The cost and methods for sending out a press release vary greatly. Many public relations professionals now question whether sending out a press release is even valuable. It is extremely rare today to get a call from a reporter in response to a press release.

While a press release often gets picked up online "as is," you still need to pitch individual reporters with a powerful media hook to get earned media (we will cover Media Hooks in the next chapter).

One of the biggest benefits of a press release is the SEO. As long as you write high-quality content and use a good distribution platform, the release will get picked up online by multiple outlets and show up in *Google* search results for years.

You can post a press release easily on a free service website. However, you really get what you pay for with press releases. Free releases will not get syndicated, and simply be posted as a page online. Sure, you can email the link to reporters. However, if someone is searching for your specific topic online, they will never find it.

When working with *Goody PR* clients, we have used three different press release services for various reasons. Here's a quick recap of options for you as a guide:

Press Release Distribution Service	Key Benefits	Limitations	Costs
PR Web* (now owned by PR Newswire)	Lower cost, good distribution, 24/7 customer service	No word limit. No limits on adding images. Additional	$389 for a national release with a video. Release is delivered directly to targeted

Press Release Distribution Service	Key Benefits	Limitations	Costs
		services available for a fee.	media lists based on the topics you select (Finance, Health, Military, Technology, etc.). Release includes a comprehensive report.
Business Wire*	Middle-of-the-road costs, you can go national or target delivery to a specific geographic area	400-word limit. Includes one logo image. Additional charges may apply.	Approximately $510 for a 400-word regional release or $940 for a national release. Release is delivered directly to targeted media lists. Additional charges for extra words, images, and social media report.
PR Newswire*	High-end release	400-word limit. Additional charges may apply and are the most costly.	Approximately $800 for a national release with 400 words. Release is delivered directly to targeted media list. Additional charges for extra words. PLUS $350 for any images. Release includes comprehensive report.

*NOTE: All press release prices and packaging are subject to change. You should contact the company directly for their current fee structure.

While we have spent many hours talking to all three press release services, we usually send out announcements via *PR Web* because the primary goal is SEO. For new clients, many send out monthly releases as part of an overall SEO strategy for the first six months or longer. Long-term clients often send out releases for big announcements only.

Alternatively, we used *Business Wire* for a client in Canada who wanted a hyper-local focus for their release. In this case, the release went to media in their province only.

For major news announcements, a few of our clients have used *PR Newswire*. The costs have ranged from $921 to $1,890. This high-end cost was off-the-charts because the client did not want to cut words. While *PR Newswire* is considered the best by far, it requires the biggest budget. It's probably worth the investment for a major launch announcement, but you don't need this top-of-the-line service for monthly releases.

It's also important to keep in mind that the best days to send out press releases are Tuesdays, Wednesdays and Thursdays. Most reporters are overwhelmed on Mondays, and are wrapping up stories on Fridays for the week.

Each press release distribution service will send you a detailed summary report, and the majority of the online pickups and engagements happen in the first 24 to 48 hours. The numbers may change within the first thirty days, but the initial response is really the most important.

You can also send a pre-release notice out to a specific group of reporters before the content is sent out via a news wire. Some reporters prefer to break the story first, and advance notice gives them this opportunity.

Another option is to send out a pre-release Media Alert to a specific reporter and offer an "EXCLUSIVE" interview. This exclusive story pitch email should include a deadline for a yes or no answer, and is usually offered only to major media competing for the same story.

Step 3.8 Proofread. Test. Proofread.

Your final step in creating compelling content that emotionally connects to readers is to proofread, test, and proofread again. Here are some steps you can take during this review process:

8-SECOND PR PROOFREADING PROCESS

1. **Use Spellcheck** – Yes, spellcheck should be an obvious step, but many of my *UCLA Extension* digital marketing students do not use it, and it drives me bonkers! Spellcheck will not catch everything such as missing words or the wrong version of a word, but is very helpful.

2. **Read It Out Loud** – It can help to read your content out loud before sharing it to see if the story flows and is conversational.

3. **Send Draft to a Colleague with No Background** – You can also send your draft to a co-worker or even a friend without explaining it. Ask them to proofread and provide honest feedback. It may surprise you what new eyes will find.

4. **Email Draft to Your Phone** – You can always email a draft to yourself and then read it on your phone. The majority of reporters open emails on their smartphone, so that's another great to test it there.

5. **Send It to Your Client** – After you complete steps one through four, you may want to send drafts to your client and ask for their feedback and edits. We send press release and column drafts to clients for review. However, most PR agencies do not share pitches for many reasons.

6. **Use Track Changes** – When reviewing documents with other parties, always ask them to use Track Changes in a *Word* doc so you can see exactly what they changed. You can also use *Google Docs* or *Dropbox* to track edits.

7. **Use Version Control for All Documents** – Version control management of documents is very important to save everyone time and preserve accuracy. We give documents a version number (example v1) plus the date in the file name. If you use something like *Google Docs*, it will track edits and timestamp it.

8. **Repeat Proofreading Process** – Once you make changes, go back to Step 1 and repeat this *8-Second PR* proofreading process. Always go through the content a few times carefully.

Once your content is triple-checked on multiple devices, then it's time to publish and share your story with the world! It is best to avoid making changes after a press release or story is published. However, we all make mistakes. If there are any typos or incorrect facts, it is important to update the content ASAP.

CHAPTER 3 RECAP

Are you ready now to write compelling content that captivates readers, fans and reporters? With the new tools and tips in this chapter for writing catchy subject lines, teaser headlines, press releases, blogs, quotes, first paragraphs, solid statistics, and video descriptions, you can publish compelling content with the same durability of a superhero.

Here is a recap of the action items we have covered, your new Content Connector Superpower, and challenges.

Step 3 Action Items — Create Compelling Content That Emotionally Connects With Readers

1. Define what you are announcing to the world.
2. Write a compelling headline with eight words or less.
3. Write a clear and concise one-sentence summary.
4. Add a quote from the heart to emphasize your message.
5. Tell a compelling story in 300 to 800 words.
6. Include credible references and statistics.
7. Choose the best press release distribution system.
8. Proofread. Test. Proofread.

PR Superpower 3 – Content Connector Superpower

With the average adult attention span being shorter than a goldfish, getting to the point right away is one of the most important skills for all marketing professionals. You cannot afford to take chances with sloppy or lengthy content that has no connection to the reader.

To get new ideas, *Google* your topic, then click "News" to see what headlines already exist. For your email, pitch, blog or video, choose a different 8-10 word title with a verb to pique more interest.

Your Content Connector Superpower can help you get the undivided attention of readers. All of these superhero writing skills can add to your marketing and public relations success!

Chapter 3 - 8-Second PR Challenges

As we close Chapter 3, here are your *8-Second PR* Challenges:

1. What are five compelling headlines that you can write in eight words or less about your brand or advice tips?
2. What are 3 evergreen stories that you can pitch?
3. How will the first sentence for each story compel the reader to continue?
4. Whom can you quote to add value to the content?
5. What statistics can add strength to your story?
6. What is the high-level outline for your content?
7. Are you going to send out press releases, and which service will you use?
8. Who is going to proofread your content and/or provide feedback?

You can now give any story more energy with your new *8-Second* PR Superpowers. You know how to be a Word Artist, so just start writing your first draft. With these advanced content writing skills, you can emotionally connect with your audience and reporters at warp speed. Remember, write at least three versions. The sooner you get started, the faster you can release your message and get media interviews.

In the next chapter, we will take a closer look at writing a compelling media hook or story angle to get reporters even more interested in covering your personal or business brand story. Are you having fun now with this creative storytelling process? Let's keep moving forward by building upon your story.

Reminder:

"SAY WHAT YOU MEAN, AND MEAN WHAT YOU SAY."

– GEORGE S. PATTON

MEDIA HOOKS

Write Powerful Pitches to Move Reporters to Cover Your Story

> "WHY FIT IN WHEN YOU WERE BORN TO STAND OUT?"
>
> – DR. SEUSS

Do you have ten media hooks with a moving story that you can pitch reporters about your brand, business or book? While you can always write a great column or press release, remember it is way more valuable to get reporters to cover your story as earned media (TV, print, radio and podcasts). When you pitch the media, a unique story "hook" or angle is what immediately grabs the media's attention, or not.

A MEDIA HOOK IS A UNIQUE WAY OF PRESENTING YOUR NEWSWORTHY STORY TO A REPORTER THAT INTERESTS BOTH THE NEWS OUTLET AND THEIR AUDIENCE.

Remember, it's not about your "cool company" or product, it's about "What's in it for them?" (WIIFT).

To get an earned media interview, you need 3 Whys. You need a powerful Personal Why, Why Now and Why will their audience care?

You will significantly increase your chances of an interview by connecting your media hook to the news or timely topic. For example, do you have a new launch announcement and/or do you have an expert who can provide unique insights and tips connected to a current headline news story? Most people approach public relations by thinking, "We just want people to know about what we do." While you may have an inspiring business, a media hook will never stick without a powerful backstory. Without a newsworthy story, you might as well pay for an ad.

PR SUPERPOWER 4 – MEDIA HOOK SUPERPOWER

To help you get more earned media (TV, radio, print or digital stories – for free), use your Media Hook Superpower. You always want to pitch a timely topic that uniquely connects your brand to an event, launch, milestone, or headline news story in a way that moves the reporter to cover your it.

With an eight-second adult attention span, you need to immediately grab the reporter's interest in your email subject line, topic headline and/or first sentence. Once you have sold the right reporter on your story idea, their media coverage can give your brand way more credibility than any paid advertisement.

If you build a good relationship with the reporter and have a reputation that you are "easy to work with and provide great story ideas," they will keep coming back for more. Use this *8-Second PR* Superpower to make lasting impressions, and secure hundreds of media interviews!

To get the media's attention, you must pitch a great media hook that can both entertain and educate their audience. While interviewing Former TV Anchor, Radio Show Host and Realtor Traci Baldwin Mahone on our *8-Second Branding Podcast*, she explained, **"You want to have a teaser that a TV anchor or reporter can say about an upcoming story that gets them so interested that they don't change the channel."** (This teaser is your media hook or story headline!).

In all cases, it is best to pitch how your company, product, book, or service is improving lives or making a difference in the world. If you have a "spokesperson" who is willing to share their personal story about how your business helped them, that can also significantly increase your chances of coverage. If a reporter is not immediately sold on your media hook, you can always go back and try again later with a different angle for the same client. Pitching the media is a delicate dance where you have to learn when to push and when to back off.

Let's go through how you can improve your chances of media coverage.

STEP 4 ACTION ITEMS:
WRITE POWERFUL PITCHES TO MOVE REPORTERS TO COVER YOUR STORY

1. Write a timely and specific email subject with a moving story hook.
2. Define a clear and compelling hook in the first sentence of every pitch.
3. Define the star(s) in each story pitch.
4. Define why the story is relevant and timely.
5. Define HOW you are helping others improve their lives.
6. Define three to eight talking points to support your story hook.
7. Provide supporting media for your story pitch.
8. Test Media Hooks A, B, C and repeat.

PR SUPERPOWER 4 - MEDIA HOOK SUPERPOWER

Develop your story options, and then pitch the right media hook to targeted media outlets who cover this topic at the right time. Think about the type of media (TV, print, radio or podcast), and emphasize what is most important to them in your email or call. For TV news, the producers are primarily looking for stories within a 7-day window, but for a daytime talk show, print or podcast interview, many reporters plan their calendar months in advance.

If a pitch is customized for a specific media outlet, it will always get the best response. For example, you should pitch very different interview topics to *TMZ Live* versus *CNN* about the same book (more on this later).

Step 4.1 Write a Timely and Specific Email Subject Line with Moving Media Hook

In this chapter, you will learn some of our email subject line secrets with examples. When you are pitching the media, you can send a customized email to a "warm contact" or "cold contact".

Your subject line should always be unique, specific and timely to get the best results.

A warm contact is a reporter who you have an established relationship with based on a previous story, personal connection or maybe you met them in person. In this case, you should send an individual email with a very personalized subject line. For example, your subject line might say "Referred to you by X" or "Great to meet you at X" – and a short summary of your timely topic.

You can also pitch "cold contacts" who you do not know. To be more efficient, we recommend using targeted lists based on specific topics the reporter covers (health, wealth, history and more). You can also use marketing automation platforms (*Mailchimp, Constant Contact* or *Sales Force*) that provide tools to create lists, customize messages and schedule emails.

Whether the reader actually opens your message, often depends on the subject line. To improve your results, here are our tips for email pitches:

8 PR TIPS FOR GREAT EMAIL PITCH SUBJECT LINES

1. **Add Personalization** – Your best bet is to send one email at a time with a very personalized subject line and message that mentions why the story is perfect for them. Because this process can be very time consuming, you can also use marketing automation tools that let you add the reporter's first name and/or the name of the outlet in a subject line or body to improve your response rate.

2. **Add Urgency** – Give a date or time in your subject line. Writing "Today" or "Wednesday" will get more reporters to open your email.

3. **Add Relevancy** – If you are emailing a specific audience, then add relevancy to the subject line. For example, if you are pitching reporters from Austin, and you have a local spokesperson, write "Austin CEO" in the subject line.

4. **Keep It Short with Keywords** – Use keywords with meaning and dashes to highlight WHY they should care about your content using the fewest words possible.

5. **Add Exclusive Offers** – For the media, you can offer an "exclusive story" in the subject line to increase your chances of a response.

6. **Add Numbers** – Many reporters like seeing numbers in a subject line because it shows that the content has focus (example: 5 Ways, 7 Tips, etc.).

7. **Limit Punctuation** – Always try to limit punctuation in email subject lines to a maximum of 3 to avoid being flagged as spam that goes into a junk mail folder.

8. **Do A/B Testing on Subject Lines** – Lastly, you always want to test different email subject lines and the timing. Send out at least two unique messages to see what is generating the most click-throughs and replies.

Once a reporter opens your email, a unique media hook is a must to grab their interest. There is a reason why people hire public relations pros to get more eyeballs on their story. You can do it too with creativity, practice and persistence. However, if you are really busy and have a budget, hiring a PR agency is always a good option.

GOODY PR CASE STUDY – UNIQUE MEDIA HOOK FOR *FAST COMPANY* FEATURE STORY

To make your story more newsworthy, your best bet is to tie the subject line and pitch to current headlines or timely events. For example, we were grateful to have a *Fast Company* reporter do a feature story on one of our clients. This is a VERY competitive outlet for business leaders. To stand out, I provided a personalized email subject line with the outlet name and a specific topic based on the client's book, work experience and reporter's area of expertise that clicked.

Email Subject Line: Timely Pitch for *Fast Company* - Great Rehiring Surge Solution - Hiring based on Behaviors vs Resume

The keywords in this email subject line pitch included:

- Timely (immediately grabs their attention)
- *For Fast Company (personalizes it)*
- *Great Rehiring Surge (timely topic for 2021/2022)*
- Solution (offers a solution to a problem)

Hiring based on Behaviors vs Resume (specific and unique media hook)

To find creative ways to present your story hook, you can *Google* keywords and click the "News" tab to see what is already out there. Reporters are always looking for a new way to present a hot topic, so it's important to do your homework to stand out. In this case, other stories talked about how employers were having a hard time finding talent post-pandemic, but no one was talking about this unique POV (Point of View) for hiring based on behaviors versus a resume.

If you Google "Great Rehiring Surge", here are some of the headlines compared to this *Fast Company* feature story.

Headline	Outlet	Media Hook / Topics
Here's where the jobs are — in one chart	*CNBC*	*Unique data can show trends visually on a chart based on solid resources.*
Uber Reaches Income Milestone as Rides Recover, Delivery Grows	*The Wall Street Journal*	*New signs of hope that the pandemic is over with Uber recording its first-ever adjusted profit last quarter.*
How to Hire Employees Using an Applicant Tracking System	*Entrepreneur*	*How to save time and reduce stress using an ATS (Applicant Tracking System).*
Leveraging Employee Communications in a Post Pandemic Hiring Surge	*Forbes*	*With more remote workers and record rehiring, why is it so important to have great communications strategy.*

Headline	Outlet	Media Hook / Topics
Hiring based on behavior, not resume	*Fast Company*	Why Former GM, Author and Executive Coach recommends hiring based on behaviors versus well-known schools and job titles to find great talent.

As you become a stronger *8-Second PR* Word Artist, you will learn how to fine-tune your email subject lines and media hooks to get a higher percentage of reporters interested. Asking a question (Who, What, and Why) is also a great subject line strategy because it says your pitch is more than just an announcement.

Let's look at a few examples for a hypothetical Boston Real Estate CEO named "Paul". For his company's holiday campaign to help the homeless, below are potential media hooks in subject lines. Which email would you open?

EMAIL SUBJECT EXAMPLES – HELP THE HOMELESS HOLIDAY CAMPAIGN

- How Former Homeless CEO is Rebuilding Lives this Holiday
- Why Boston Founder is Rebuilding Lives for Homeless This Holiday
- Local Story - How New Homeless Assistance Program teaches Job Skills
- Tomorrow – Boston CEO Thanksgiving Campaign for Homeless Kicks Off
- 3 Ways Boston can Help Homeless Assistance Program This Holiday

For all media pitches, you must get creative and try a variety of subject lines to see what works best. To learn from experience, marketing automation tools (*Constant Contact, MailChimp, Sales Force*) can tell you the percent of reporters who opened your email, who opened it, when they read it and what links they clicked. Anything over a 10% open rate is considered a good email pitch.

Step 4.2 Define a Clear and Compelling Hook in the First Sentence of Every Pitch

Once you have attracted the right media to open your pitch email, the first sentence is by far the most important line. It's like any content, the first impression matters. If they do not understand what you are saying in the opening paragraph, you can forget about them covering your story.

You always want to think "Why would anyone care?" You also want to pitch differently to TV, print, radio and podcast media. Writing different hooks based on the media format, reporter's topic and geography (national or local) will get better results.

Print can cover more detail in longer stories. TV loves visuals (photos, videos and the location), and the length usually ranges from 30 seconds to six minutes. A TV interview or news story with experts is usually three to five minutes, and must be tied to a current event topic. Sadly, a social good story about a charity event tends to get the least amount of time on TV.

Media Type	Most Common Format	Tips for Pitching	Audience
TV	2-3 minute interview (usually LIVE)	Emphasize visuals (photos, videos, book)	Very broad
Print/ Online Story	800 words (may be a feature story, column or expert quotes)	Emphasize unique expertise to increase credibility	Broad or niche
Radio	1 – 60 minutes (recorded or LIVE)	Emphasize expertise and unique story	Broad or niche
Podcasts	10 minutes – 2 hours (usually recorded)	Emphasize niche expertise and story	Very focused on niche audience

For Paul, the Boston Real Estate CEO with a cause, you could pitch reporters who cover real estate, social good, business leaders, and entrepreneurs. Depending on Paul's media experience and profile, you can pitch national and local TV, radio, podcasts and print outlets. If Paul has no experience on TV, it's best to pitch the local news before a national program.

Let's take a closer look at three examples of what we wrote in the first sentence of media pitches for *Goody PR* client Debbi DiMaggio that resulted in earned media for print, radio, and TV. As we've discussed previously, Debbi is a "Top 1 Percent Realtor," author, and philanthropist in the San Francisco Bay Area. She's written several books about real estate and has adopted five charities.

Publication	First Sentence in Email	Media Result
Unique Homes	As a potential real estate story on luxury home trends for *Unique Homes*, luxury home Realtor and author Debbi DiMaggio can discuss the latest trends that she will be sharing at the *Inman Luxury Connect* conference in Beverly Hills tomorrow.	National profile with feature story (one-page) that included a large photo of the author, book cover image, and great quotes.
KGO-AM 810 Talk Radio in Bay Area	As a potential Consumer Talk with Michael Finney on *KGO-AM* story, San Francisco Realtors Debbi DiMaggio and Adam Betta can share business and real estate success tips based on their VIP Philosophy and DiMaggio charisma that is highlighted in their new book, *The Art of Real Estate*.	A 10-minute live talk radio interview with Debbi DiMaggio and her husband/co-author Adam Betta on a top radio station in the San Francisco Bay Area.
ABC 7 Bay Area	(The email pitch was re-sent after speaking to the newsroom on the phone. MANY TV stations will never open your email and you have to call and re-send pitches with a cover email about the call.) I wanted to forward this pitch below for *ABC 7's* consideration for a Bay Area event tomorrow that is a Make-A-Wish type birthday party at George Mark Children's House in the East Bay hosted by philanthropist/Realtor Debbi DiMaggio,	An inspiring social good TV story on *ABC 7 San Francisco* with Debbi speaking at the event, the young adult blowing out the birthday candles, and the local fire and police singing happy birthday.

Publication	First Sentence in Email	Media Result
	where the local police and fire departments are going to sing happy birthday to a brave young adult XXX between 12:30 and 1:30pm (address, CA) at her Love Bravely Birthday Party.	

After this PR success, DiMaggio decided that she wanted to be part of a gifting suite in West Hollywood in celebration of the *Academy Awards*. Her goal was to set up an office in Los Angeles (along with San Francisco) with celebrity clients. For this event, we took a very different approach with an entertainment spin when pitching.

By partnering with the event host, Doris Bergman, we came up with the media hook that Debbi was the "Realtor to the Stars." As background, Debbi is a cousin of baseball legend Joe DiMaggio, who was married to Marilyn Monroe.

For this media hook, we highlighted her personal story and real estate client list that "reads like the credits of a Hollywood blockbuster, including celebrities such as Julianne Moore, Sally Field, Hugh Grant, Ted Danson, Tom Arnold, and Macaulay Culkin."

This celebration of Hollywood's biggest night also had a Valentine's Day theme. For the table display, we brainstormed ideas with Debbi to highlight her brand. Her table included a black-and-white poster-size photo of Joe DiMaggio kissing Marilyn Monroe. Debbi gifted both celebrity guests and media chocolate truffles in *Tiffany Blue* boxes with red ribbons.

Debbi also gave away copies of her new book, *Lights, Camera, Action!* that compares buying a home with going on an audition as an actor. This fun book was illustrated by *DreamWorks* animator Steve Hickner, and how they found each other for this book project was another entertainment industry media hook.

This "Realtor to the Stars" media angle and event display were so successful that Debbi used this theme for four different gifting suites connected to awards season in Los Angeles. Overall, she received mentions in about 40 earned media stories.

After this public relations strategy resulted in so much coverage and influencer awareness, DiMaggio achieved her goal to open a Beverly Hills office with a partner. (Debbi still has an office in San Francisco with her husband and travels back and forth.)

Step 4.3 Define the Star(s) in Each Story Pitch

A media story is rarely about a product. It's about how someone or something is positively impacting lives. To illustrate this point, you want to be really clear in every pitch who is the star or spokesperson who can share a moving story.

For the star or "WHO", always provide the personal WHY that connects them to your media hook. At the bottom of the pitch, include a short biography that clearly provides their name, title, career highlights, books, previous media and website to provide background and credibility.

Keep in mind that when a producer or reporter selects someone to interview, their reputation is on the line. They are always searching for a "sure bet" when booking experts on TV and radio, which is why the expert bio and personal story are a must.

For example, below is a comparison of two bios for a former client. Short bios are always better, and often used at the bottom of a column. When pitching experts to the media, it's ok to send a longer version (but still keep it to 1 paragraph).

Adding "fun facts" is also great information for expert bios because you are building "connectors" that can make your expert stand out as unique. In this case, Omar L. Harris started his first business at 7 years old, which shows his entrepreneurial drive goes way back to childhood.

A CASE STUDY EXAMPLE – AUTHOR AND EXPERT BIOS

SHORT BIO (2-3 sentences) - ABOUT: Omar L. Harris is a Former General Manager of *GSK* and *Allergan* with more than 20 years of experience as a global pharmaceutical executive. He is the Founder and managing partner at *Intent Consulting*, a firm dedicated to improving employee experience and organizational performance. He is the author of *"Be a J.E.D.I. Leader, Not a Boss"*, *"Leader Board: The DNA of High-Performance Teams"* and *"The Servant Leader's Manifesto."*

LONG BIO (1 paragraph) - ABOUT: Omar L. Harris (Charlotte, NC, born in Pittsburgh, PA) is a Former GM (GSK and Allergan), Intent Consulting Founder, Gallup Certified Strengths Coach, Speaker, and Award-Winning Bestselling Author of 5 books, including *"Be a J.E.D.I. Leader, Not a Boss: Leadership in the Era of Corporate Social Justice, Equity, Diversity, and Inclusion"* (2021), *"The Servant Leader's Manifesto"* (2020), and *"Leader Board: The DNA of High Performance Teams"* (2019). With 20+ years of global pharmaceutical executive experience building teams, Omar has worked on 4 continents (U.S., Middle East, Asia and Latin America) for *Pfizer, Merck, Schering-Plough* and more. His books and work have been featured by *CNN HLN Weekend Express, Black News Channel, WPXI-TV NBC News Pittsburgh, KPLC NBC/CW and, FOX/ABC Lake Charles, Fast Company, Real Leaders, Ladders, SHRM Blog, Thrive Global, CEO World Magazine, Human Capital Innovations (HCI) Podcast, VoiceAmerica Business Channel, Roland Martin Unfiltered* and 35+ leadership podcasts. **As fun facts, Omar speaks 5 languages, plays 7 instruments, and started his first company at the age of 7.**

Defining the spokesperson in story pitches is a must. If the pitch does not have a credible speaker and powerful backstory, it is going to be much harder to get earned media coverage.

Step 4.4 Define Why the Story is Relevant and Timely

Making a story relevant and timely in your media hook can significantly increase the chances of a reporter or producer calling you for an interview. If you are writing a column, connecting it to headline news can also improve the likelihood that your story will be published by the editor.

If you do not answer the "Why Now" question, your story hook may take months to get media attention. Let's take a closer look at PR tips for ways to move a reporter to cover your story.

RELEVANT MEDIA HOOK TIPS

The first thing you want to explain is how the story hook is relevant to the media outlet. The more specific you are in the pitch, the better.

Local News Connection – Was the spokesperson born in that city? Did they go to school there or nearby? Are they hosting a local event there? Do they work in that city?

National News Connection – Is your "Who" or "What" tied to a national headline, trending topic, new study, bestselling book, blockbuster film, or more with broad appeal and impact?

TIMELY MEDIA HOOK TIPS

Holiday Connections – Can your media hook be connected to a holiday (July 4, Small Business Week, Veterans Day, Thanksgiving, New Years, Memorial Day)?

Seasonal Themes – Does your media hook have anything to do with different seasons such as fall fashion, winter ski season, or New Year's resolutions?

Event Themes – Do you have an event (grand opening, book talk, charity event) happening that the media can cover? And how is this event helping other people?

> CASE STUDY EXAMPLE – GET A YES IN 5 MINUTES
> WITH A TIMELY MEDIA HOOK!

Getting a green light "Yes" for a national TV interview in 5 minutes almost never happens (unless you are a celebrity). Fortunately, it did happen for a national *CNN HLN Weekend Express* interview that I pitched via text for Omar L. Harris for Martin Luther King Day. We had been pitching the client to the same show for six months – with no luck.

In this case, the immediate "Yes" via text from the host was because Omar was the perfect spokesperson at the perfect time – with a timely and relevant media hook (You will find more insights on this pitch and interview later.)

NEWSJACK YOUR STORY PITCH

Newsjacking is the art of injecting your media hook into a news headline to generate coverage and social media engagement. This approach is one of the best ways to get your story covered, which is why our company constantly monitors breaking news.

Similar to the MLK Weekend example above, here are more case study examples of how this newsjacking worked so well:

GOODY PR NEWSJACK CASE STUDY 1 - HEADLINE NEWS – *BBC WORLD NEWS*

As an example of how to connect your expertise to headline news, let's go back to the very beginning of the COVID-19 pandemic in February 2020. No one was staying at home (yet), but there were many headlines and rumblings about the business impacts of a global outbreak.

At the same time, we were doing a PR campaign for Corporate Attorney and Asset Protection Expert Garrett Sutton, who's written many Rich Dad Advisor books about how to protect your personal and business assets.

To connect Garrett's work to this headline news that we saw growing momentum, we worked with our east coast PR team to write a pitch called, "How to Protect Your Assets during a Black Swan Event" (an unpredictable event like the pandemic). Fortunately, *BBC World News' Talking Business Show* invited Garrett to be interviewed on this timely topic via *Zoom*.

During the same week, the *Mobile World Congress Conference* in Barcelona (biggest wireless industry gathering in the world) announced their 2020 event was cancelled (which was the first major international business conference to be cancelled). As a result, the host asked Garrett to comment on how this cancellation may impact businesses who invested millions in this show, and whether they could get insurance for these type of unexpected events.

Overall, Garrett's TV interview was over 3 minutes, reached his ideal target audience on a global business show, and made his story and books very timely and relevant.

You should always be looking for ways to connect your story to what everyone is already talking about on the news. Here is another very different example of how this approach works.

GOODY PR NEWSJACK CASE STUDY 2 - NATIONAL HOLIDAY – MEMORIAL DAY

When asked to do last minute PR for a Memorial Day movie premiere in Los Angeles, the pitches resulted in two local TV interviews on major news stations, including *KCBS* and *KTLA*.

The pitch email included a powerful media hook (new documentary) with the 5 Ws:

- WHO - 95-year-old WWII veteran Leon Cooper produced the film.
- WHAT- New film premiere for "Return to the Philippines: The Leon Cooper Sequel" and special *Golden Goody Award* for Cooper who funded the film.
- WHY - The film was made to draw attention to the 80,000 Missing in Action.

- WHERE - The *Director's Guild of America*, Sunset Boulevard, Los Angeles.
- WHEN - Memorial Day, 5:00 p.m.

To magnify this story, we worked with our client, *Vanilla Fire Productions* Founder and Director Steven C. Barber. In less than ten days, we wrote a press release, secured event sponsors, and booked media to cover the event. Barber also invited over seventy Marines from the *Marine Corps Base Camp Pendleton* to attend in uniform, along with actors who actively support veterans, including John Savage (*The Deer Hunter*).

While we do NOT recommend these last minute publicity campaigns, they can work if you have the right story at the right time with a great spokesperson.

Newsjacking is one of the best ways to secure a media interview. The more you can tie a media hook to current events, the better your PR results will be.

Step 4.5 Define HOW You are Helping Others Improve Their Lives

You ALWAYS want to present how you are helping others and/or changing lives in your media hooks. Impact stories that make an emotional connection, provide helpful tips and inspire audiences can provide a compelling reason for reporters to cover your news.

A problem-solving approach to media hooks and pitches is so important because remember, "it's really not about you".

MEDIA HOOK TIP -
ANSWER HOW YOU CAN HELP OTHERS ?

Your story pitch will get a lot more attention if you can answer any of these questions:

1. Can your spokesperson offer unique insights as a credible expert for a story?

2. Can you comment or connect to a current headline news story?

3. Can you solve a problem and/or share how to make positive changes (diet, exercise, health, money)?

4. Can you help someone prevent getting the flu?

5. Can you help someone retire early (investments, cash flow)?

6. Are you saving lives, and if so, how?

7. Can you help someone rebuild their business after a crisis (economic, environmental)?

8. Can you reduce family feuds over the holidays? (improve relationships)

Remember, a story is rarely all about your "great company, product or book". Dig deep here and find ways to help others in all your media pitches.

GOODY BUSINESS BOOK AWARDS – UPLIFTING AUTHOR VOICES

Recognizing authors who are making a positive impact is the main reason that we launched the *Goody Business Book Awards*. People are looking for answers from credible experts who can improve their lives by saving money, living longer, increasing wealth, improving relationships, marketing smarter, and/or offering new solutions to a problem. It's the same thing for media interviews!

And to provide authors with the ability to shine in their niche, the *Goody Business Book Awards* is an annual awards program with 50 categories in the areas of Health, Self-Help, Leadership, Real Estate, Money/Wealth, Marketing and more.

Nominations can be submitted from January 1 – September 30, for any book published in the past five years. Winners will be announced November 15th, just-in-time for holiday promotions.

If you know an author whose words are making a difference, please nominate their book here: https://goodybusinessbookawards.com

Step 4.6 Define Three to Eight Talking Points to Support Your Story Hook

Whenever you pitch the media or schedule an interview, you want to provide potential talking points that your spokesperson can share. The best approach is to provide three to eight bullets that are simple one-liners and/or questions that the reporter can ask the expert.

Your job as a PR professional is to make the interview easy for both the media and the spokesperson. Remember, newsrooms are "crazy busy" and the producers are more overwhelmed than most people on the planet. They literally get thousands of email pitches a week and are constantly juggling breaking news stories.

The better your media hook, pitch, and talking points, the more likely the producer or reporter is to cover your story. It's also best to reduce the number of emails back and forth. Try to provide most of the information in your first email. Send limited follow-up emails to streamline the conversation. **Remember, the media is getting BOMBARDED with emails. The last thing they want is ten messages from you.**

We have also written the entire script for TV interviews in a question-and-answer format. It's important to note that a script should only be used as a guideline because you want an interview to be a more natural conversation. However, it would be rare not to have drafted talking points for your spokesperson.

As an example, here are the talking points that we sent to the host for the *KGO-AM* for their community affairs radio interview with Top Real Estate Agent Debbi DiMaggio and her husband Adam Betta about their new book, *The Art of Real Estate*.

GOODY PR CASE STUDY -
PITCH WITH TALKING POINTS - DEBBI DIMAGGIO

Email Subject – Bay Area Authors Launch New Book with DiMaggio Charisma

Potential Talking Points:

- How to win a bid on your dream house (they have won bids with lower offers).
- How to get your house ready to sell with professional imagery, no matter the price point.
- How to choose the right agent who understands marketing (social media and more), is a team player, and has a good reputation in the local market.
- How to stand out as a real estate agent.
- How hyper-local residential real estate is in the Bay Area, and how it differs state-to-state.
- How Debbi DiMaggio is related to baseball legend Joe DiMaggio.

These talking points were focused on how the authors could help educate a broad audience. Anyone interested in buying a home would find these insights helpful. Along with having great tips, the chemistry clicked with the radio host and guests.

Step 4.7 Provide Supporting Media For Your Story Pitch

In addition to booking an interview, the producer may ask you for supporting media. This request happens often before or after an interview is scheduled, and is most common for TV and podcasts. Hosts and Producers may ask for a book cover image, headshot, logo, and/or press kit documents.

IMPORTANT NOTE –
DO NOT SEND EMAIL ATTACHMENTS IN PITCH EMAILS

It's very important to emphasize that you should NEVER attach anything to an email when sending an initial pitch to a reporter - unless they specifically request it. You may be able to embed an image in a pitch using different email software tools, but simple text is best, in our opinion.

The media does NOT want to open your attachments unless they know you, and many will block emails with attachments. If you send a press release to reporters, do not attach a PDF of the release. Always copy the words within the body of the email or send a recognized source link (a well-known press release service, *Google Docs*, *Fortune* magazine, *YouTube*, etc.) versus attaching anything to a first email pitch.

For TV, many times the producer will ask for photos or b-roll video that they can use in the background during the interview. While they do not always use these digital assets, producers often say "send us as many as you can" because they want options. For example, several news outlets used b-roll from *Modern Family* EP Danny Zuker's *TEDx Talk* in the background during TV interviews about his book.

In all cases, make sure your file names include the people and places in the picture or video to make it very clear to the reporter. The more specific you are, the better. As another example, when our WWII Author/Son client Joseph Tachovsky went on his Hawaii Tribute Trip for Veterans Day 2021, we sent over 40 images to TV producers using a customized *Google Docs* folder and link. Every file name included the name of his book, an image number, and short image description.

Recently, we started creating Digital Press Kits for all *Goody PR* clients to provide assets to reporters because they have been doing so many podcast interviews. Every host wants a headshot, bio, website and social media links for the guest, and this digital format is a great solution that can save you tons of time.

BONUS CONTENT – DIGITAL PRESS KIT TEMPLATE

A Digital Press Kit can be easily created in *Google Docs* for you and/or your PR clients. The good news about *Google Docs* is that you can update it whenever you want. Anyone who has ever received the link will see the most current version when they open it. You can also post a Digital Press Kit on a website page. As a PR professional, we prefer to use *Google Docs* because we do not always have access to a client's website. Below is our template that you can use.

Goody PR's Digital Press Kit Template

LAST UPDATED - DATE (version control is important for everyone involved)

EXPERT NAME & TITLE

MEDIA CONTACT - Include the PR contact's information on top of the page.

MEDIA IMAGES - Headshots, Book Covers, Logos, Action Photos, Event Photos.

SHORT BIO – This should be 2-3 sentences maximum.

LONG BIO – This bio can be longer, but should still be only one paragraph.

TV/ RADIO INTERVIEW EXAMPLES - Reporters like to see how an expert comes across on camera and listen to their voice on the radio.

FUN FACTS ABOUT THE EXPERT – This trivia makes for great stories and personal connections with the reporter and audiences.

SOCIAL MEDIA LINKS FOR EXPERT – Reporters often want to tag you in their posts, so have this information ready for them!

DON'T FORGET - If you use *Google Docs*, make sure that you go into the Sharing menu, and make your files sharable to "anyone with the link."

After you complete your interview preparation steps, it is almost impossible to control what ends up in the final version of the story because, remember, it is earned media. You cannot ask a reporter to edit a story because they own it. For earned media, the final decisions are always made by the reporter and/or their editor. If you had complete control over the content, it would be a paid ad. Some outlets now let you buy a TV, print, radio or podcast segment, but we recommend seeking free media first. It is WAY more valuable and credible.

What is in your control is giving reporters options for visuals, sharing great soundbites and presenting your story in a clear, concise, and compelling way.

Step 4.8 Test Media Hook A, B, C and Repeat

As we have discussed, it is always best to test different media hooks and email subject lines. Ask a colleague to give their honest feedback before pitching. And do not send an email to everyone on your media list at once. Make time for A/B testing! And remember, personalized emails to warm contacts are always your best bet.

As an example, below are 3 media pitches for a client about the same topic with slightly different wording:

A/B TESTING FOR MEDIA PITCHES – 3 EXAMPLES

PITCH 1 - In Sync with Summer Olympics: 5 "Winning Tips" for Sports, Business and Life

PITCH 2 – In Sync with Summer Olympics: LA Native, Author, Mom and Mentor shares 5 "Winning Tips" for Sports, Business and Life

PITCH 3 - How Mom/Author taught Children to Be Champions with Business Success Tips - and then Backed Off (**this pitch got the best response**)

In this case, Pitch 3 worked best. The author Therese Allison did a timely 20-minute interview on *Girls on The Air 1590 KVTA (ABC Radio Affiliate)* in Ventura, California, in the spring of 2021 when students were just starting to play sports together again post-pandemic. As a prize, Allison also gave away a pair *Converse* sneakers to one lucky listener - the same shoes that she is wearing on the cover of her book, *Playing for Keeps*. And this interview was a big hit!

The timing of your email or call to a reporter is also important. For example, you do not want to pitch right before, during or after the show's airtime for TV or radio.

Similar to sending out press releases, it is better to pitch on a Tuesday, Wednesday, or Thursday. Mondays can be overwhelming for media with breaking news stories, and by Friday, many reporters are checking out for the weekend.

WHEN TO CALL A TV NEWSROOM - 8-SECOND BRANDING PODCAST TIP

When we interviewed Former TV Anchor/Reporter, *Girls on the Air 1590 KVTA* Show Co-Host and Real Estate Professional Traci Baldwin Mahone on our *8-Second Branding* Podcast, she explained that most newsrooms meet daily at 9:00 a.m. to discuss the stories for the day. She also emphasized that you want to avoid calling a TV reporter after 3:00 p.m. because they are in crunch mode for the evening news.

I've found that the best times to call a TV newsroom are around 8:00 a.m., 10:00-11:00 a.m. and 1:00-3:00 p.m. However, the best time really depends on the show. Do your research before calling!

Traci's extensive broadcasting career includes being an Anchor, Field Reporter, Assignment Desk Manager, and many radio industry roles. Traci shares many "media insider" examples based on her experience working for *KFMB* (*CBS San Diego*), *WOAI* (*NBC San Antonio*), and *KSPR ABC 33 News* (Springfield, Missouri) – which included interviewing celebrities, U.S. Presidents and covering major events such as Hurricane Katrina.

To learn more about what it's like to work in a newsroom and how to pitch them, you can listen to our eye-opening podcast interview with Traci Baldwin Mahone (dated May 20, 2021). Visit our podcast on *Apple Podcasts, VoiceAmerica, Spotify, Google Podcasts* or *Goody PR* website here: https://goodypr.com/8-second-branding.

And if you are looking for new ideas on the best topics to pitch, do not forget that you can go to *Facebook, Instagram, LinkedIn* or *Twitter* to see what is trending related to your keyword hashtags. Social media offers the best free focus group out there! You never know what a tweet or comment might inspire as a media hook!

CHAPTER 4 RECAP

Are you now ready to write media hooks that immediately connect with journalists? Do you have new ideas for how to pitch the right topic at the right time? All of these new skills for timely and relevant pitches are an important part of your Media Hook Superpower. Let's recap what we have covered in this chapter.

Step 4 Action Items – Write Powerful Pitches to Move Reporters to Cover Your Story

1. Write a timely and specific email subject with a moving story hook.
2. Define a clear and compelling hook in the first sentence of every pitch.
3. Define the star(s) in each story pitch.
4. Define why the story is relevant and timely.
5. Define HOW you are helping others improve their lives.
6. Define three to eight talking points to support your story hook.
7. Provide supporting media for your story pitch.
8. Test Media Hook A, B, C and repeat.

PR Superpower 4 - Media Hook Superpower

With adults having an attention span of less than a goldfish, your Media Hook Superpower will give you an advantage over thousands of other people pitching. If you are lucky enough to get a reporter on the phone, get to the point in one to two sentences. And if you are leaving a voicemail, write a short script that is under one minute. Are you ready?

Chapter 4 - 8-Second PR Challenges

As we close Chapter 4, here are your *8-Second PR* Challenges:

1. What are three compelling media hooks for each of your clients/projects?

Liz H Kelly

2. What will you write in your email subject line to get a reporter to open it?

3. How will the first sentence in your email or phone pitch grab their attention?

4. Who will be your spokesperson - and do they have a moving story?

5. How is your spokesperson/expert or organization positively impacting lives?

6. Does your story pitch include testimonials from customers, and are they willing to speak on camera about it?

7. What type of visuals can you provide to illustrate your media hook?

8. How are you going to use social media to research timely topics and trends?

While you may struggle writing powerful pitches at first, don't give up! Your Media Hook Superpower is an art that takes time to develop. The more you pitch, the easier it will become to develop a story hook that resonates with both the newsroom and your audience. This step is not easy. Resilience and creativity are a must for your long-term success.

In the next chapter, we will take a closer look at how to identify and find your target audience and reporters. You can fast-track your PR efforts by focusing on pitching reporters who are more interested in your topic.

Reminder:

"IF YOU CAN'T EXPLAIN IT SIMPLY, YOU DON'T UNDERSTAND IT WELL ENOUGH."

-ALBERT EINSTEIN

STEP 5

MEDIA VISION

Reach Your Audience by Laser Focusing on Niche Reporters

"WHERE FOCUS GOES, ENERGY FLOWS."

– Tony Robbins

How can you find the perfect media outlet for your story? How do you find the best contact who specializes in your topic? Now that you have your brand story and media hooks defined, your challenge is to inspire the right reporter to cover your story. With producers overwhelmed with daily email pitches, you need Media Vision to laser focus and see through walls. PR is a fine art with intense competition so it's important to do a lot of research before contacting a media outlet. You can do this!

PR SUPERPOWER 5 – MEDIA VISION SUPERPOWER

You want to use your Media Vision Superpower to connect with the right contact who is genuinely interested in your story. To reach your ideal media, fans, and influencers, laser focus your research to find reporters who cover your topics. For example, if you are a leadership expert, don't bother pitching your story to a beauty editor.

To enhance this PR superpower, *Google* to find out what your preferred reporters and media outlets are talking about online. Sure, most people would like to be in *TIME* magazine or on *CBS Sunday Morning*. However, media placements do not happen magically just because you asked for an interview with an outlet. You need to pitch the right media hook to the right person at the right time, to have a chance of your story being published to the world. It is critical to fine-tune this *8-Second PR* Superpower to achieve your publicity goals.

In this chapter, we will cover eight action items to enhance your Media Vision Superpower so your story is shared with a maximum number of eyeballs. One media interview can make or break your book, product, or service, so it is important to get this right.

STEP 5 ACTION ITEMS - REACH YOUR TARGET AUDIENCE BY LASER FOCUSING ON NICHE REPORTERS

1. Clearly identify your ideal target market.

2. Develop your marketing strategy for outreach and promotion.

3. Identify your target audience topics and sub-topics.

4. Research your ideal media outlets and influencers before pitches.

5. Reach your niche audience through podcasts (NEW!).

6. Identify ways you can work with brand influencers.

7. Build long-term relationships with media and influencers.

8. Send compelling pitches to your niche media using best practices.

PR SUPERPOWER 5 - MEDIA VISION SUPERPOWER

You can significantly increase your chances of getting media interviews if you are smart about who, how, and when you pitch. Along with reporters, you want to find influencers, family and friends who are excited to share your story 24/7 with their network.

Step 5.1 Clearly Identify Your Ideal Target Market

Before you even start reaching out to any media, research and document your brand's target audience. Many make the mistake of skipping this step. Research is one of the most important parts of any marketing and public relations strategy. Outlining the demographics for your ideal customer (age, gender, geography, and interests) will help you be much more successful in your media outreach.

Target Market Segment	Defining Your Audience and Media
Age and Gender	Are you targeting millennials, baby boomers, or everyone 18 to 69? Are you looking for outlets that focus on men or women? For example, a pitch for *Woman's Day* should speak to a different audience compared to a story idea for *Men's Health*.

Geography	We've spoken about the power of getting local media to cover your story first. Think about news outlets close to your home or office. Ask the spokesperson where they were born, went to school, and work to make connections based on geography.
Niche Interests	Look for media who focus on niche audiences. A niche may include women's interests, health, technology, or finance. For example, an entertainment reporter for *Variety* is not looking for the same things as a medical reporter for *Everyday Health* or finance columnist for *CNBC*. Pay attention to the niches for your media pitches!
Income	It is also helpful when pitching to identify the income range for your ideal target market. For example, if you are pitching a high-end retailer who wants to attract clients making over $250,000 per year, luxury lifestyle magazines such as the *Robb Report* may be perfect.
Profession	Identify media that write for the professions of your ideal customer. For example, if you are looking for successful small business clients with fewer than 500 employees, do your research first. Then, pitch reporters at leading publications such as *Entrepreneur* and *Inc.* who write for this audience.
Influencers	Identify influencers who are recognized experts with big social media followings related to your topic to increase ROI (Return on Investment). Working with trusted influencers in your niche can be gamechangers for your marketing and PR results.

Having the right strategy to connect with your ideal demographic and media are a must for anyone with a brand, business or book to promote.

Step 5.2 Develop Your Marketing Strategy for Outreach and Promotion

Before you get started with any media outreach, step back and ask questions. Take a walk, brainstorm, interview your clients, think about the timing of pitches for each outlet type, and determine the best strategies for each of your marketing campaigns. For example, a features reporter may only work on stories that are published in two months, while a TV news producer is primarily looking at topics for the next few days.

Let's take a closer look at a *Goody PR* case study with a client focused on reaching successful small business owners.

Target Market Case Study - Tom the Tax Expert – Successful Small Businesses

The first thing we did when working with Tax Expert Tom Wheelwright was to ask about his target market. As a CPA and CEO of *WealthAbility*, Wheelwright provides tax and wealth strategy services and education to a specific niche.

AUDIENCE – Wheelwright defines his target market as successful small business owners, entrepreneurs, and investors. The key word here is "successful" because his tax and wealth strategy services are not cheap. However, it is worth the investment for a sophisticated investor with a complex portfolio of assets.

GEOGRAPHY – For geography, I partnered with his team who identified seven major cities as key markets for clients, including New York, Chicago, Los Angeles, San Francisco, Washington D.C., Orlando, and Dallas. While Wheelwright has clients in over thirty countries, it was helpful to focus his PR campaigns more on these cities.

NICHE TOPICS – As a result, we primarily targeted finance, real estate, and wealth reporters focused on high-income, small business and investor audiences. For example, Tom can explain how to legally maximize tax savings by investing in businesses, real estate and oil and gas. His target media is reporters who cover tax and wealth advice tips. As a result of laser focused pitches, his work was featured in *The Washington Post, The Wall Street Journal, Investor's Business Daily, Forbes*, and many more.

Our public relations campaigns were a steady marathon for this client for over five years, averaging six unique media stories per month. While the topics, goals and priorities changed constantly, the target market and media focus remained steady. As a result, we were grateful to book this client on *FOX Business, CBS 5 News KPHO, FOX 10 KSAZ, 12 News NBC KPNX, ABC Radio*

News, NPR's Marketplace, 710 WOR, financial podcasts, and in *Accounting Today (25+* stories!) and hundreds of outlets.

Goody PR also pitched a column to the *Entrepreneur* magazine editor for Tom, and he has been writing for their audience for several years now. Overall, these PR campaigns resulted in over 700 media hits (print, radio, TV, podcasts, columns and syndicated pickups) and contributed to his *Tax-Free Wealth* book being a steady Amazon bestseller. And because Tom's book is the number one way that his company receives client leads, the continual interviews that mentioned his book in niche publications was a winning PR strategy.

Step 5.3 Identify Your Target Audience Topics and Sub-Topics.

When you develop your media outreach strategy, you also want to clearly identify your topics and sub-topics. While most experts want to be interviewed on *CNN,* thousands of reporters and producers work for *Turner Broadcasting.* In this scenario, your job is to clearly identify a client's expertise, find the right show and reporter, and then identify the Guest Booker to send timely pitches too.

Clients can have multiple topics and sub-topics, depending on their current campaign, product, service or book. Each time you reach out to the media or influencers, keep their core audience in mind. The more relevant the pitch is to the reporter, the better your chances are for getting an earned media story.

As an example, below is a comparison of two campaigns for the same client, using very different approaches for media and influencer outreach:

Client: Debbi DiMaggio, Top One Percent Realtor, author, and philanthropist	Campaign 1: Real Estate Book Launch	Campaign 2: Philanthropist Make-A-Wish Type Campaign
Campaign	Book Launch: *The Art of Real Estate*	Summer Birthday Make-A-Wish Type Campaign sponsored by local Philanthropist

Topics	Real Estate Success Tips	Philanthropy, Social Impact Tips
Sub-Topics	Real Estate Buyer Tips, Real Estate Seller Tips, Realtor Success Tips, Realtor Customer Service Tips	San Francisco Bay Area Charity, Charity Event, Make-A-Wish Type Campaign, Lady Diana (Debbi's role model)
Events	Book signings, real estate speaking events and real estate conferences	Event 1: Fashion Day for 25-yr-old with chronic illness who loved fashion, and Debbi loved fashion too. Event 2: Make-A-Wish Birthday Party at a local charity who helps children with terminal illnesses.
Geography	National and local	Focused PR pitches on local media with two Bay Area events and local charity.
Influencers	Realtors, real estate industry organizations	Social good influencers sent happy birthday video wishes. Local fashion retailers in San Francisco donated store space and new clothes for Fashion Day.
Media Results	*Unique Homes* profile, guest speaker at *Inman News* National Conference for Realtors, column in *Inman News*, *Real Estate Radio Live* (twice), local TV news stories, consumer advocate talk radio station interview and more.	*ABC 7 News* Bay Area story about Make-A-Wish type birthday party, *My Social Good News*, local paper coverage, birthday videos posted by key influencers, and local recognition by real estate clients for giving back to the community.

Step 5.4 Research Your Ideal Media Outlets and Influencers before Pitches

When you research your media outlets, reporters and influencers before pitching, you have endless ways to check their backgrounds with the internet (*LinkedIn, Muck Rack, Instagram, YouTube*, their website, podcast interviews, videos and more). While there are many sophisticated tools to find media quickly that you can purchase for big fees, this basic research is a must for connecting and customizing pitches.

To help you, below are our eight suggestions for researching reporters and fans:

8 MEDIA RESEARCH TIPS

1. *Google* the topic and desired media outlet to find the right reporter covering your topic. (This approach is how we initially found *PBS Postcards* for our WWII military history book client.)

2. Search the topic and click "News" on *Google* to see who has recently written about it, and then pitch them a related, but different story.

3. Search keywords using #hashtags on social media. For example, enter #SanFrancisco, #SocialGood, and #RealEstate on social media to find people interested in these topics.

4. Create a list of key influencers and reporters, and then start following them on *Twitter* and *LinkedIn*. Pay attention to topics they post to find connectors. You may also find a summary of their stories on websites such as *Muck Rack* for journalists.

5. Like, comment and share key media and influencer posts with compliments on social media. If you consistently engage with a reporter's stories (especially on *Twitter* where it is easier to reach someone you don't know), your support can help build media relationships.

6. Search on *LinkedIn* for a reporter's profile, read about their experience and join industry groups in your niche to meet thought leaders.

7. Attend conferences frequented by your core audience to meet reporters and influencers in that space.

8. Ask other PR professionals and clients for suggestions for outlets and reporters to contact about your niche topics. This step may sound obvious, but many skip it! Most PR professionals will guard their media contact list, and that is completely understandable. However, many will give you suggestions for outlets. You can also join a PR professionals group on *Facebook* or *LinkedIn* where industry leaders regularly share advice tips.

When you go to conferences, do not forget to engage with your ideal media and influencers. You can tweet and post on *Instagram* using @username and hashtags related to your media topics and sub-topics.

To reconnect in person with local reporters post-pandemic, I volunteered to tweet from the red carpet at *LA Press Club's* 2021 *Southern California Journalism Awards* in downtown Los Angeles. While I genuinely went to honor their work, it was exciting to see reporters we knew IRL again – and meet a few new contacts. You can bet that I will call these contacts with the next appropriate pitch for experts in the LA area.

To connect with reporters and influencers during live or online events, post photos on social media using multiple event hashtags before, during, and afterwards. You can also tag them, but don't go overboard with it.

You can also click on the most common hashtags for an event, and then comment on posts to connect with people with similar interests. For example, I went to the *National Publicity Summit* in New York City, and then again a few years later online via *Zoom* to pitch media one-on-one. Fortunately, I have also been able to connect with other attendees (reporters and authors) simply by researching the #NationalPublicitySummit hashtag on *Instagram*.

Step 5.5 Reach Your Niche Audience Through Podcasts (NEW!)

In the past three years since our first version of *8-Second PR* in 2019 was published, the popularity of podcasts has skyrocketed from 600,000 shows to now over 2 million with 48 million episodes (according to PodcastHosting dot org). Many radio shows are now also podcasts, and more business leaders, experts and authors are launching their own shows.

And what makes podcasts even more valuable is they offer the best opportunity to reach your niche audience. Whatever your specialty, you'll find many podcasts on that topic with active listeners interested in what you have to say.

PODCAST DEMOGRAPHICS – ARE THESE NUMBERS DRIVING THEIR POPULARITY?

If you just look at the podcast listener demographics, there are clear trends that support the rapid growth of this industry. Many businesses, leaders and experts want to reach this audience:

- 75% of the U.S. population is familiar with the term "podcasting"
- 50% of all U.S. homes are podcast fans
- 55% (155 million) of the U.S. population has listened to a podcast
- 37% (104 million) listen to podcasts at least every month
- 24% (68 million) listen to podcasts weekly
- 16 million people in the U.S. are "avid podcast fans"
- 51% of podcast listeners are male, 49% female
- 41% of monthly podcast listeners have household income over $75K (vs 29% for U.S. population)
- 25% of U.S. podcast listeners have a 4-year college degree (vs 19% of U.S. population)
- 51% are employed full-time
- Age of listeners:
  - 12-34: 48%
  - 35-54: 32%
  - 55+: 20%

Source: *PodcastHosting* dot org (as of April 2021)

What this surge in podcast shows offers is a huge opportunity for CEOs, small businesses and experts to reach their niche audience. If you're an author or expert with a specialized topic who can share tips for saving money, living a healthy lifestyle or better managing employees, or inspiring others to do anything, you want to be on podcasts!

The biggest challenge with podcasts is that most show hosts hide their contact information. They often don't do as many interviews as a TV or radio show, and just don't want to be found. As a result, it can literally take hours and days to find the right podcasts and contacts. However, once you get on a roll, this focused PR approach can positively impact your media and bottom line.

PODCAST CASE STUDY 1 – HOW TO GET 30+ PODCAST INTERVIEWS FOR 1 BOOK

As an example, when I worked with Former GM and Award-Winning Author Omar L. Harris, his goal was to be on 30 podcasts for the new book launch for "*Be a J.E.D.I. Leader, Not a Boss.*" While his previous 6-month PR campaign included only 8 podcast interviews, our team focused on supporting his goal. Fortunately, we were able to successfully schedule 32 podcast interviews on shows related to key topics in leadership that were in sync with his new D.E.I. (Diversity, Equity, Inclusion) book and leadership consulting services (Executive Coaching, Workshops, Apps and more).

In both the first and the second PR campaign, the media results included national TV, local TV, print, radio, podcasts and columns. While you want all types of media, the podcasts were able to steadily reach his core audience, which includes CEOs, business leaders, founders, managers and Human Resources professionals.

To support Omar's goal of 30 podcast interviews for one book, we literally spent hours researching the right shows, hired two interns to help us find the contact information, tested new tools to reach podcast hosts, and managed the follow-up to make sure the interview got published and promoted!

While this podcast success story is exciting, many don't realize the time involved in booking and getting one interview published. The hosts put a ton of time into each interview and often design custom graphics for a show. It's important for guests to show up ready, have an educational and entertaining conversation and always be grateful.

How to Manage a Podcast Interview and Get it Published with Success!

To help you better manage podcast interviews, here are your follow-up action items after an interview is scheduled to ensure success. It is similar to other media interviews:

1. Confirm the date, time and format for the podcast interview.
2. Provide assets to the host (send your Digital Press Kit and/or headshot and bio) .
3. Send out interview reminders using *Google Calendar* Alerts, Texts, Calls or Emails (You cannot afford to no-show or have a client forget, so send reminders!)
4. After the interview, send a sincere thank you to the host and ask when the interview will be published.
5. Set up a *Google Calendar* Alert reminder on the day that the interview is scheduled to be published.
6. Listen to the interview (yes, really listen!).
7. Congratulate yourself and/or your client on a great interview!
8. Share it on social media, tag everyone and use hashtags.
9. Genuinely thank the host for the interview - again - with specific details that show that you actually listened and care.

While it's a lot of work to find, pitch and secure interviews on the right podcasts, it's worth it to reach your target market.

PODCAST CASE STUDY 2 – HOW TO REACH A REAL ESTATE INVESTING NICHE

In another case for a very different topic and client, a similar process was used to research and schedule podcast interviews to reach a niche audience. From the beginning of her PR campaign, Former *Rich Dad Poor Dad* Advanced Trainer, Real Estate Educator and Investor Evie Brooks asked us to focus on booking her on real estate investment podcasts. Her goal was to reach potential investors interested in global real estate investments.

Evie's company, *My Panama Vacation Realty*, hosts VIP Tours for a maximum of 14 investors at a time. This trip is not for tourists. It is for people who genuinely want to learn about investing in real estate in Panama. While in Panama, it's a 3-day "boots on the ground" tour focused on learning and seeing hard-to-find real estate deals that include primarily oceanfront condos and organic agriculture. Yes, there are breaks, but it's mostly for gourmet meals or drinks at popular restaurants. Everyone has the option of staying a few days before or after to explore this tropical paradise.

As a result, podcasts are the perfect media for Brooks to connect with her core audience. While she won't reach a broad audience that watches cable news, people who are serious about investing in cashflow properties listen to experts on real estate investing and wealth building on podcasts. And yes, this podcast approach has attracted the right clients.

Keep in mind that the bigger the podcast, the harder it will be to find the right person and get an interview. And then once you get invited to be a guest, it can take months to get it published. For example, Evie Brooks* was a guest on *Joe Fairless' The Best Ever Real Estate Show*, which has 16 million real estate investment-minded listeners. While this interview was recorded in August, it was not published until November (5 months later) and required MANY follow-up emails before it went live.

As a disclaimer, Brooks and her employees and affiliates are not investment or tax advisors, and do not offer investment advice.

Being a guest on the right podcast can be even more valuable than being on national TV because their target audience is more interested in what you are selling.

How to Launch a Podcast to Reach Your Niche Market – 8 - Second Branding

In 2021, *Goody PR* launched the *8-Second Branding - Getting to Your PR Wow!* Show that is hosted on the *VoiceAmerica Business Channel*. It is syndicated on 10 major podcast platforms (*Apple Podcasts, Spotify, Google Podcasts* and more), and covers marketing, public relations and digital marketing topics to help brands, small businesses, authors and experts amplify their story.

Hosting our *8-Second Branding* Podcast is a great way to reach our target market for this book and potential *Goody PR* clients. It's also similar to writing a book. Hosting a podcast gives you increased credibility as an expert or media personality in your area of expertise. You also get to meet some really interesting people and learn their tips.

PODCAST CASE STUDY 3 - TOP 100 PODCAST HOST LAURA MICHELLE POWERS

Our very first *8-Second Branding* Podcast interview was with Top 100 Podcast Host Laura Michelle Powers about her new book: *Rock Your Podcast – How to Launch, Grow and Monetize Your Show* (2021). Along with being a well-known podcast host, Laura is a Celebrity Psychic, Creative Entrepreneur, Author, Speaker and Singer with many talents and stories about how her podcast has been instrumental in her success.

During this fun interview, Laura discusses her podcast success secrets for setup, equipment and promotion tips. She hosts six podcasts, including the Top 100 Podcast - *Healing Powers Podcast.* In addition, Laura highlights her publicity advice tips in *Rock Your Podcast's* Chapter 9: Leveraging Podcasts to Maximize PR.

If you want to host your own podcast, we highly recommend that you listen to this interview and/or purchase Laura's book. You can find this How-to Podcast pro interview titled: How Top 100 Podcast Host Laura Michelle Powers Leverages PR on *Goody PR's 8-Second Branding* podcast page, *Goody PR's YouTube* Channel and/or on all major podcast platforms: https://goodypr.com/8-second-branding.

Along with being a great podcast guest, I highly recommend that you consider hosting your own show. It will open many doors for you and your brand.

Step 5.6 Identify Ways You can work with Brand Influencers

How many times have you logged onto social media and asked your friends "What do you recommend for a great new [fill-in-the-blank]?" This Word-of-Mouth Marketing now plays a major role in any promotional plan. To be successful, you must target the right influencers in your marketing, PR and social media campaigns.

THE POWER OF WORD-OF-MOUTH MARKETING

- People are 90% more likely to trust a brand recommended by a friend.
- People are 4x more likely to buy if the product is recommended by a friend.

Source: *Nielsen Report* (2015)

There are many ways that you can partner with brand influencers to magnify your story on social media, at a conference, party, book signings, and family dinners. The Word-of-Mouth Marketing opportunities are endless. Let's look at some examples and suggestions for reaching influencers.

INFLUENCER MARKETING - PRODUCT GIVEAWAYS

One of the best marketing approaches can be product giveaways with the hope that the influencers will recommend your brand on social media, write an earned media story and/or post a photo or video showcasing it. In this case, no one is paid to talk about the product, making the results more genuine and authentic.

INFLUENCER MARKETING EXAMPLE -
SUNDANCE FILM FESTIVAL

Some of the best examples of product-giveaway marketing can be seen at the annual *Sundance Film Festival* in Utah. This event is hosted by the *Sundance Institute* and is known for defining "cool." Brands such as *Southwest*, *Chase Sapphire* and *Samsung* have spent huge budgets to rent space on Park City's Main Street during the festival that gets flooded with thousands of film fans, celebrities, entertainment industry professionals and reporters for ten days every January.

Companies spend a FORTUNE to rent space and participate in festival events to get celebrity and influencer photos with their products and/or recommendations.

For example, *Eddie Bauer* gifted their *MicroTherm® StormDown Jacket* at their *Adventure House* on Main Street for three years in a row, resulting in many celebrity and key influencer photos. This *Eddie Bauer Adventure House* lounge and gifting suite attracted *Academy Award* Winner Allison Janney (*I, Tonya*), Jeffrey Tambor (*Transparent*), John Legend (music legend), Molly Shannon (*SNL*), Gina Rodriguez (*Jane The Virgin*), *Golden Globe* Winner Alexander Skarsgard (*Big Little Lies*), James Marsden (*X-Men*), Ethan Hawke (*Training Day*), Jason Segel (*How I Met Your Mother*), Nikki Reed (*Sleepy Hollow*), Chris Pratt (*Guardians of the Galaxy*), Ron Livingtson (*Office Space*), Kristin Wiig (*Bridesmaids*), Jack Black (*School of Rock*), Kevin Smith (*Clerks*), Justin Long (*Dodgeball*) and many more.

Full disclosure, as an entertainment journalist, I received this *Eddie Bauer* jacket as a free gift. Because I truly loved this jacket, I posted it everywhere on social media and included it in my Top 10 Gifts at *Sundance* story recap.

Starting in 2017, the *Sundance Film Festival* cut way back on gifting suites to focus the festival more on film. However, you will still find major brands sponsoring festival events. For example, *DOVE® Chocolate* and *Refinery29* cosponsored a "Women at Sundance" brunch hosted by the *Sundance Institute*.

INFLUENCER CASE STUDY –
TRAVEL PR EXPERT - *SA/SB PUBLIC RELATIONS*

As another example, many travel influencers are given free trips to far-away places, resorts and cruises in return for their coverage and social media posts. These trips can be a complex negotiation that really needs to be handled by a public relations professional in the travel niche.

One of our public relations colleagues, Susan Bejeckian (*SA/SB Public Relations*) is a pro at travel media. Along with getting major media coverage for clients, Susan sets up trips for major media and key influencers to visit U.S. and international resorts in Fiji and the Solomon Islands. The reporters and influencers then write about their experience in travel publications.

In addition, SA/SB PR's has worked with resort clients who've gifted trips to major media outlets as a "give-away prize" in exchange for coverage on national shows, including *The View, TODAY Show, CBS This Morning, The Drew Barrymore Show* and more.

SA/SB PR's s media coverage for resorts has also been seen in the *Los Angeles Times, Travel and Leisure, The Chicago Tribune, San Francisco Chronicle, Boston Globe, Honolulu Star-Advertiser*, and hundreds of other publications – targeted to reach travelers.

INFLUENCER MARKETING AT INDUSTRY EVENTS - *CES* CONFERENCE

Many brands also incorporate influencer marketing into major industry conferences like *CES (Consumer Electronics Show)* in Las Vegas, Nevada. For example, Calvin Lee @MayhemStudios has 82,000+ *Twitter* followers and is recognized as a key influencer in the digital space. Calvin often posts gifts on social media that he receives (*Sony* cameras, new technology and more). Along with gifts, many influencers like Calvin may have their travel expenses paid by a sponsor.

What makes Calvin Lee so authentic is that he is a graphic artist by day and influencer 24/7 who openly shares his personal life online. Calvin posts regularly about everyday things that make him very relatable. For example, his *Twitter* feed has tweets about birthdays, dinners, family, photographs, and industry events.

Calvin also posts portrait photos that he takes regularly on social media. He has built a powerful influencer brand, and his photography has been seen on *ABC7 KABC News* in Los Angeles.

There are even social media management tools to help brands identify key influencers in their space based on geography, number of followers and key interests for this purpose. Brands will then reach out to influencers with special offers, invitations and "exclusive content."

PAID INFLUENCER MARKETING AND TALENT AGENCIES

There are also paid influencers for marketing campaigns now. Yes, there is currently a business where you can hire a *YouTube* star or social media influencer to create a video or piece of content about your brand for a fee.

8-SECOND BRANDING PODCAST - HOW INFLUENCER MARKETING HAS EVOLVED

During a recent interview on our *8-Second Branding* Podcast, Jessy Grossman shared her insights as an Influencer Talent Manager, CEO of *Tribe Monday*, Founder & President of *WIIM (Women In Influencer Marketing)* and Podcast Host at *WIIM* Radio.

Based on her influencer marketing experience, Jessy explains how brands should get started with a campaign, the difference between working with a celebrity with a TV show versus an influencer in a niche audience with a lot of followers, and why she built *WIIM* to create a professional network of women who support each other.

Grossman's clients have received fees that range between $500 and $200,000 for influencer marketing campaigns. To learn more, listen to our podcast interview with Jessy by visiting our *8-Second Branding* Podcast page on *Goody PR* here: https://goodypr.com/8-second-branding

In addition to influencers, many reporters will now offer to produce paid content for you. We usually run away from these offers because our goal is to find earned media for free for clients versus paid media. However, you may want to consider paying for a book review because of the time it takes to read and review your book.

For example, *Kirkus* is an example of a book review service that many authors use. The *Kirkus* traditional review now costs $425, and an expanded review costs $575, with a turnaround time of seven to nine weeks. You can also expedite a book review for an additional cost. (Check out their website: *kirkusreviews dot com* for the latest prices).

Step 5.7 Build Long-Term Relationships with Media and Influencers

Once you are fortunate enough to connect with a reporter or key influencer, you want to keep building upon that relationship. As in any long-term partnership, you have to find the right balance and right timing to keep in touch with each person.

CASE STUDY - LONG-TERM MEDIA RELATIONSHIP – *ESPN COVER YOUR ASSETS*

We have been fortunate to build a long-term relationship with Todd Rooker, who is the producer and host of *ESPN Cover Your Assets* show in Minneapolis, Minnesota. It's a one-hour 50,000-watt radio program on Saturday mornings that covers a wide range of financial advice topics.

As a result of building a long-term relationship with Todd, I have been fortunate to schedule all of the Rich Dad Advisors on his show, plus Robert Kiyosaki (Author of *Rich Dad Poor Dad*, the number one financial book of all time). And in several cases, I was able to book these guests multiple times.

Along with being a Radio Show Host, Todd's Rooker Financial Consulting business advises clients who are in a "financially challenged situation" to ensure it never happens again. I have enjoyed calls with Todd learning about how he has positively helped clients change their lives by investing in real estate.

In addition to these interviews, Rooker has graciously offered to record PSAs for clients and play them during his show. I cannot emphasize enough our gratitude to Todd for this extra support.

If you meet a reporter who is this passionate about your topic and helping others, go to great lengths to build a long-term relationship with them.

Switching gears to entertainment reporters, our PR colleague Doris Bergman has hosted awards' season events in celebration of the *Emmy Awards* and *Academy Awards* for years in West Hollywood. What she does most brilliantly is build long-term relationships with media, talent and influencers, who consistently attend.

To make her events a big hit, Bergman provides a relaxing experience with genuine people who don't have an "attitude", a gourmet lunch at the trendy *Fig and Olive* restaurant on Melrose Place in West Hollywood, and popular gifts for everyone invited to attend. And everyone there plays an important role in the success.

If you are trying to get media coverage for your product, always think about the reporter's point of view when pitching a story. Ask, why would their audience care?

For influencer marketing, step back and ask what public figures, celebrities, and trendsetters care about your topic – and see if you can connect them to your pitch?

CASE STUDY - INFLUENCER MARKETING FOR *JUKIN MEDIA* LAUNCH - AND SALE!

When we partnered with *Jukin Media* to develop their first PR campaign a decade ago, we identified a list of key digital influencers in Los Angeles to invite to their holiday launch party. Because *Jukin Media's* business was focused on acquiring viral video clips to sell to major TV shows (*Comedy Central, TODAY Show, MTV Ridiculousness,* and more), digital industry influencers were a perfect match to raise awareness.

To encourage them to attend, I sent out personalized VIP invitations to key influencers whom I knew from industry networking events in Los Angeles. Sponsors were also found to provide products for VIP gift bags. The majority showed up, tweeted about the new company, and posted photos of the event on *Facebook*. This influencer marketing approach contributed to putting *Jukin Media* on the map in the entertainment capital of the world!

For this event, *Jukin Media* also partnered with Rob Dyrdek, who was the star and Executive Producer of the *MTV Ridiculousness* show (232 episodes), to support his foundation. Dyrdek was busy shooting a Super Bowl commercial so he could not make the event. However, we received gifts to auction at the party and permission to promote his name, brand, and *Rob Dyrdek Foundation* in association with this launch.

Since then, it has been really fun to watch this company grow. Within 10 years (2011-2021), the company grew from 10 employees to 800 in 10 countries. And in 2021, *Jukin Media* was sold to *Trusted Media Brands*, the parent company of *Reader's Digest*. Cheers to CEO/Founder Jonathan Skogmo for his forward-thinking vision and awesome team for building this brand success story! We knew you when...

Step 5.8 Send Compelling Pitches to Your Niche Media using Best Practices

Once you have your Media Vision defined and contacts, start sending custom email pitches to reporters and influencers using our *8-Second PR* best practices. As a quick review, here is a summary of our top tips for your pitches:

BEST PRACTICES FOR MEDIA PITCHES FROM *GOODY PR*

- Keep It Simple.
- Pitch a timely Media Hook with your unique story or POV (Point of View.)
- Write a compelling email subject line or press release headline that is a teaser that makes the reader want to learn more.

- Include an active verb in your headline (launches, announces, changes, etc.)
- Use timely and specific keywords in your pitch.
- Get right to the point in your first sentence because you have only eight seconds to grab their attention (revise the first sentence several times to get this right).
- Provide the Who, What, and Why, plus How you are helping others in your pitch.
- Add When (date and time) and Where (the address) for events or contests.
- Provide three to seven bullet points as potential talking points to reporters.
- Include a short and/or long bio for each spokesperson and organization.
- Include media experience for a spokesperson to add credibility.
- Ask a question at the end of every pitch.

In addition to these best practices, pay attention to the title of the person receiving your email. You want to send pitches to Print Reporters (Writer, Columnist, Features Reporter, Blogger, Freelancer), Radio/Podcasts (Producer, Host, Podcast Host), and TV (Special Assignment Reporter, Features Producer, Guest Booker, Talent Booker, Assignment Editor, News Producer, Multimedia Journalist and/or newsroom).

Pitches that are emailed directly to a TV Host are often overlooked, especially if it is a major media outlet. Chances are really good that Jane Pauley (*CBS Sunday Morning*) is never going to open a pitch email, unless she knows you personally.

CASE STUDY EXAMPLE -
PITCHES FOR BUZZ PONCE CHARITY BIKE RIDE

We were fortunate to work on a PR campaign for Baby Boomer Buzz Ponce, who rode his bicycle cross-country in 2018 to raise awareness and money for *Warriors Heart Foundation*. Buzz rode his bike from California to Florida, and we got the best media response at his starting point in San Diego as a "hometown hero". Three local TV news stations requested interviews with Buzz within three days. To get this TV interview trifecta, we made the media hook timely, local, and inspiring.

In this case, Buzz's *ABC 10* News story reached a desired niche audience. San Diego is a military and veteran community whose residents would be even more interested in supporting his charity, *Warriors Heart Foundation,* that helps heal military, veterans and first responders with their peers in a unique program.

While pitching this story idea sounds easy, it was not. Remember, the newsrooms are overloaded with thousands of daily pitches competing for limited airtime. We pitched his trip launch several times in different markets, along with testing subject lines, pitch timing, and follow-up. As an example, here is the pitch subject line and first paragraph that got their attention:

WINNING PITCH - 3 TV INTERVIEW REQUESTS IN 3 DAYS

Email Subject: Pitch – Leaving May 1 – Why San Diego Author is Riding 3,100 Miles For *Warriors Heart Foundation*

Hi X,

As a potential timely story for X, 70-yr-old San Diego native and author Buzz Ponce (*A Long Ride*) is leaving in two days (May 1) from the Oceanside Pier and can discuss Why he is Bike Riding 3,100 Miles Coast-to-Coast to Support Military, Veteran & First Responder Healing and *Warriors Heart Foundation*. With *Marine Corps* Base *Camp Pendleton* nearby, the recent strain on San Diego Firefighters, and Buzz being born in San Diego, there are several great local connections here.

What was most surprising about this pitch response is that the email was sent on a Sunday. While our best practice guideline is to send pitches on Tuesday, Wednesday or Thursday, Buzz was leaving in two days so we could not wait. We had been pitching the San Diego media for a few weeks prior - with no reply. However, Buzz arrived in San Diego from Phoenix, Arizona, on Saturday night to prepare for the trip leaving Tuesday. Being physically there on Sunday and the urgent email subject line all contributed to getting this mega response from local TV stations.

Wait. Revise. Pitch Again.

As a wrap-up, once you have identified your topics, target market, best media, key influencers, and sent out your pitch, you are now waiting for feedback. Breathe in, breathe out, and let the reporter or influencer digest what you are saying.

You can always follow-up with phone calls and ask for feedback. While most reporters will not answer the phone, it is worth trying and leaving a short voicemail. Aim to leave a voice message that is about one-minute or less, and get to the point right away! If you make enough calls to your target market reporters, eventually, someone will answer the phone and give you feedback.

If you get really lucky, a reporter will get back to you soon after they receive the pitch. If they are serious about interviewing you or your client, trust me, they will call. It is always a good feeling to get a quick reply - but it is rare - unless you are a celebrity or have the perfect story at the perfect time!

It is much more likely that you have to send seven different pitches with a variety of media hooks to the same reporter before he or she actually opens the email, asks for an interview or says "No". Remember, getting media interviews is a marathon and a numbers game. The key to your media success is to research your niche media, identify the right reporter, write a great pitch and not get discouraged!

As a best practice, PR professionals should wait a few days or even a few weeks before pitching the same reporter via email or the phone again. You must be relentless, resilient and patient in your pursuit of public relations coverage. You can do this!

The key to your PR and brand's success is to never give up on pitching your top media! It could actually take years for you to get covered on your ideal show or in a top publication. One of our clients told us that they really wanted to be on *PBS*. It's primarily an educational outlet, and the author wrote a military history book about his dad's WWII platoon. After about 1.5 years, lightening finally struck with an interview request from *PBS Postcards* (more on this later). And when big interviews happen, remember to celebrate every media home run!

CHAPTER 5 RECAP

Are you ready now to pitch to your key media and influencers based on specialized topics, geography, and timing? Here is a quick summary of your key take-aways for this chapter:

Step 5 Action Items - Reach Your Target Audience by Laser Focusing on Niche Reporters

1. Clearly identify your ideal target market.
2. Develop your marketing strategy for outreach and promotion.
3. Identify your target audience topics and sub-topics.
4. Research your ideal media outlets and influencers before pitches.
5. Reach your niche audience through podcasts (NEW!).
6. Identify ways you can work with brand influencers.
7. Build long-term relationships with media and influencers.
8. Send compelling pitches to your niche media using best practices.

PR Superpower 5 - Media Vision Superpower

With your new Media Vision Superpower, you will now be able to find the right reporters, secure more interviews, reach your target market and build long-term relationships to increase your earned media and Word-of-Mouth Marketing.

Chapter 5 - 8-Second PR Challenges

As we close Chapter 5, here are your *8-Second PR* Challenges:

1. Who is your ideal target market for customers and media? Consider interests, income, geography, topics, and more.

2. What three publications are on the top of your media outlet wish list?

3. If you do PR, who are the top three preferred reporters for each client?

4. How can you build long-term relationships with your preferred media?

5. How can you research and reach podcast hosts for your niche audience?

6. Who are key influencers for your client's product or service?

7. How can you build long-term relationships with key influencers in your areas of expertise?

8. What are five different ways to pitch the same thing?

Your Media Vision Superpower will help you see through obstacles and find creative ways to stand out. A big part of your job is brainstorming ways to reach the media in different ways. Don't get discouraged if you get no response. It's just like being in sales. You have to keep going back, and never give up pitching until you get a "No".

In the next chapter, we will take a closer look at how you actually take a media request and turn it into a home run by getting a story published.

Reminder:

"I NEVER DREAMED ABOUT SUCCESS.
I WORKED FOR IT."

– ESTÉE LAUDER

STEP 6

MEDIA HITS

Make Your Interview Take Flight to Score Mega Media

"BE SO GOOD, THEY CAN'T IGNORE YOU."

– STEVE MARTIN

Are you ready to learn how to get your media interviews over the finish line? What are the PR secrets for booking an interview and getting it published? Most people have no idea what it takes to secure a TV, print, radio or podcast interview, and honestly, that is why many hire a public relations professional instead of doing it themselves. This book is meant to empower you with first-hand insights so that you can do your own public relations successfully – or be a better partner with your PR agency or team.

You've built your *8-Second PR* foundation with a Wow Story, Digital PR, Creative Content, Media Hooks, Media Vision, and now it's showtime!

> A MEDIA HIT IS ANY EARNED MEDIA FOR YOUR BRAND, BUSINESS OR BOOK WHERE SOMEONE ELSE PROMOTES YOU FOR FREE. A TV INTERVIEW, RADIO INTERVIEW, PODCAST INTERVIEW, PRINT STORIES, A FEATURE PROFILE, EXPERT QUOTES IN A STORY, BOOK REVIEW, SYNDICATIONS AND SOMEONE ELSE'S VIDEO ABOUT YOUR STORY ARE ALL MEDIA HITS.

Earned media coverage rarely happens by pure coincidence, unless you are a celebrity. In this chapter, we will provide the inside scoop for how to turn your media hooks, pitches and expertise into free publicity. It's a lot like playing baseball, and your Media Hits Superpower will help you score mega media in national outlets such as *CNN, PBS, Lifetime*, the *TODAY Show, NPR* and more.

PR SUPERPOWER 6 – MEDIA HITS SUPERPOWER

Many authors and experts do not realize that just because you get an interview request, it does not mean a story will become a published media hit. Your Media Hits Superpower can help you consistently secure interviews and get them published! When you receive an interview request from a reporter, you're up at bat.

However, even if you do the interview, it might not be published immediately – or ever. Just like scoring a run in baseball, getting in the headlines is a process that takes skill, endurance, and patience! Every time you get a media opportunity, you want to be prepared to advance your interview around the bases until it crosses home plate as a published story! If you stumble, get back up again until you score earned media using this *8-Second PR Superpower!*

In this chapter, we will cover eight action items to get your brand in the headlines.

STEP 6 ACTION ITEMS – MAKE YOUR INTERVIEW TAKE FLIGHT TO SCORE MEGA MEDIA

1. Get back to media within one hour of a TV interview request.
2. Make it really easy for the media.
3. Coach your PR client on what to expect and next steps.
4. Turn your talking points into a Q-and-A script for the producer.
5. Send the interviewer great visuals in support of your story.
6. Be available 24/7 if the media needs anything.
7. Follow-up to move your story around the bases and score.
8. Genuinely thank the reporter and their team.

PR SUPERPOWER 6 - MEDIA HITS SUPERPOWER

When a reporter calls or emails you to schedule an interview, it's then your job to actually get a story or mention published. You can make a media request take flight as long as you have a Wow Story, are responsive, and follow-up (this is one of the most important steps for a successful PR campaign). Once you get a request from a reporter, it is a baseball game of advancement until your story goes live! And then you should celebrate your media wins every time an interview is published!

Scoring media is truly a sport that requires skill, strategy and a lot of patience. Let's take you around the bases with our winning *8-Second PR* strategy that we have used over and over again.

Step 6.1 Get Back to Media Within One Hour of a TV Interview Request

If you are fortunate enough to get a TV interview request from a reporter, you should be dancing and cheering! Out of the hundreds, if not thousands, of emails, pitches and calls that they receive every day, you just won a Golden Media Ticket for a potential story.

To make sure that you own that opportunity, it is best to acknowledge the request by immediately replying with feedback. My goal is always to respond within one hour to a TV interview request, and sooner, if possible. Because many reporters send email requests rather than call, PR professionals need to be constantly checking email.

We are fortunate to have smartphones now that go with us everywhere. Being able to take this device with you makes it so much easier to monitor media requests remotely. However, you can still miss an opportunity if you are not paying attention.

To help our clients succeed with PR, I explain upfront that if there is a TV interview request for them, it's like a fire drill for us. We STOP everything, and start emailing, texting and calling until we get an answer about their interest and availability. And if they don't reply, we will start calling their team to find them. Unless you are a movie star or major household name (Elon Musk, Bill Gates), a producer may pick up the phone and fill that time slot with someone else. You don't want that to happen.

Based on your time zone, you may also need to adjust your media monitoring patterns because most major outlets are based in New York City and EST. Living in California, we often get requests from East Coast reporters early in the morning. And if you're based in Hawaii, you're getting up very early because you are 5-6 hours behind NYC.

If the interview request is for a radio show or print outlet, it is usually not as urgent and can actually wait a few hours. However, the bigger the media outlet, the more important it is to get back to the reporter ASAP! Sometimes print, radio and podcast reporters need a quick confirmation, so pay attention to the details in all requests.

And in some cases, if a TV or radio show producer gets a last minute cancellation, they may call you to be a substitute for a same-day interview. In these cases, the producer cannot wait if you don't reply right away, so please get back to them ASAP!

GOODY PR CASE STUDY EXAMPLES – 3 LAST MINUTE INTERVIEW REQUESTS

To help you understand this fast-track interview booking process, here are three examples:

NPR's Marketplace - We received a last-minute radio interview request from *NPR's Marketplace* for Tom the Tax Expert. The reporter wanted a soundbite for a nationally syndicated show that was being published later that day. Fortunately, we were able to reach the client in the airport before he flew overseas for a speaking engagement. While the producer only included a few sentences from Tom, this interview aired across the country on 800 radio stations with over 14.8 million unique listeners over a week (Source: *Marketplace*).

CBS Atlanta - For another client, we received a call at 6:30 a.m. PST from a *CBS Atlanta* TV producer, who wanted to interview our client that day by 1:30 p.m. EST (10:30 a.m. PST). We immediately called the client to work out the logistics. The spokesperson was in a very important annual budget meeting, and fortunately, his senior management team agreed to break for his TV interview. In the end, it was a home run for everyone involved! The segment ran four times with three promotional plugs. It featured our client's name, his charity's name, and the name of his company. The Calculated Publicity Value, according to a *Nielsen Media* Report, was over $28,000. (Note: This publicity value is very high for local news because Atlanta is a major media market - DMA 10 in U.S.). In many cases, a local TV interview is usually worth $3,000 to $10,000 for a 2-3 minute segment. The higher the DMA (Designated Market Area), the more viewers are watching your interview.

CNN - In a third scenario, I received a "maybe" interview request from *CNN Newsroom with Brooke Baldwin* for *Modern Family* EP and Author Danny Zuker. The pitch was that Zuker could talk about how politics and pop culture were overlapping, and the timing was perfect for his political humor book. With so much breaking news, the producer explained they would not be able to confirm until the morning of the show, which aired 11:00 a.m. - 1:00 p.m. PST. When we woke up at 7:00 a.m. PST, we got the "green light" for the interview. Our client was asked to go in person to the *CNN* Los Angeles office for a split screen interview with the host in New York City. Everyone scrambled to make this interview happen, and it resulted in a six minute segment on national TV!

To make it even easier to track interview requests and respond quickly, we set up a separate email for media only. This approach lets us easily monitor requests, so they do not get lost. If you are doing publicity for your product, business, book or a client, I highly recommend setting up a unique email for media requests. You should also include your cell phone number in the signature of your pitch email, so they can text or call you.

Step 6.2 Make It Really Easy for the Media

As shown in the *CNN Newsroom with Brooke Baldwin* interview example, you always want to make it really easy for the media to interview you or your client. While everyone has schedules and lives, you need to keep in mind that the media are constantly overwhelmed while juggling multiple interviews and breaking news. If you are fortunate to get a call from them, be as responsive and flexible as possible. Do not hesitate or delay getting back to them. Try to make it happen based on their schedule – not yours, unless you have a conflict that really cannot be moved. And please leave your attitude at the door because they are saying, "We want to tell your story to the world." You are so lucky, so be grateful!

While you may be saying, "Of course, I would reply immediately", you'd be surprised how many people mess this up. Yes, we are all busy, but remember, a TV interview request should be treated as a top priority. Stop everything and reply ASAP – if possible!

During a recent *National Publicity Summit* hosted by Steve Harrison, he asked reporters on a media panel to share their PR tips to authors and publicists pitching them potential stories. MANY said, "If we call you for an interview, please respond." And then they told PR disaster stories about how authors lost interviews because they made scheduling too darn complicated. Please, don't do that to a reporter! Re-arrange your calendar and just make it happen (unless of course you are traveling without *Internet* service, dealing with a health issue or faced with an emergency).

When a TV Producer gives you their best time for an interview, it's always best to just say, "YES, I am honored! I will be there!"

If you don't reply to a reporter enthusiastically right away, you'll not only miss the opportunity, they'll probably never invite you back!

While making TV interview requests a top priority sounds reasonable to most people, I cringed when a client declined a timely opportunity by saying; "I am going to pass because it is not convenient." In another case, when a TV crew was ready to go, the client told me, "I need to take a nap." OMG! Don't do this please!

In the first scenario, this TV interview "pass" was probably a loss of about $20,000 in Calculated Publicity Value because it was in a major media market. And yes, I wanted to scream because this statement not only hurt the client's relationship with the media outlet and reporter, it made *Goody PR* look horrible for recommending them. (Fortunately, I found a former client who was happy to do it. This substitute saved our relationship with this TV producer, and made the expert very happy!)

Yes, there are always exceptions where a "Pass" may make sense for your brand. If you get an interview request from an unknown media, do extensive research before saying "No". If it is a small outlet, there may still be a good reason to do the interview. Take the time to check out their *Muck Rack* page, look up their *LinkedIn* Profile and/or *Google* their name. If the reporter also writes for a major publication (*Forbes, The Hollywood Reporter, CNBC*) or hosts a relevant podcast, it may be worth doing the interview to build a long-term relationship with the reporter.

However, if you are truly not interested because you don't like the topic or media outlet, then it's a different story. Always be polite when passing if it's just not a good match. You are talking to a human being who has feelings. It's also important to keep in mind that many reporters do stories for multiple outlets and get paid very little.

A hard-copy press kit and book copy may also be requested by snail mail if you have enough time to send it before an interview. For a book launch, you always want to have a cover letter and press kit ready to go out. To ensure that this process is seamless, use *FedEx* or *UPS* service where you can track who signed for a package. I recommend using bright-color folders that include your business card, a one-sheet with potential talking points, book launch press release and recent media stories.

SNAIL MAIL PRESS KIT CHECKLIST – CUSTOMIZE WITH AUTOGRAPHED BOOK

If someone asks you to mail them a book, you can easily ship it via *Amazon* (this works great). However, if it's a big outlet and/or you want to make a lasting impression, send a customized press kit via snail mail with a personalized letter.

CONTENTS: In a bright-colored two-pocket folder, include a:

- Customized cover letter

- Business card with your contact information
- Book one-sheet with Potential Talking Points
- Author Q&A that highlights the author WHY and backstory
- Author bio with media experience
- Recent press release that summarizes the book on one page
- Recent news stories or book reviews that feature the author's key messages
- Autographed copy of the book

For a recent evening interview with *CNN International,* the producer initially said they did not need advance book copies. And then, they changed their mind the morning of the interview. Of course, we wanted to jump to make it easy for them, especially since this was a global TV interview. As a result, we scrambled to print hard copy press kits and drive them to Hollywood mid-day to avoid traffic so they had it in advance of a 9:30 pm PST interview. It really helped that we had an electronic press kit already prepared in a folder with the media assets on our computer that could be easily customized and printed.

After scrambling for this *CNN International* producer, *Goody PR* printed ten press kits for this author so they were ready to go the next time. The only things that needed customization were the cover letter and specific talking points.

Step 6.3 Coach Your PR Client on What to Expect and Next Steps

To be able to get back to the media quickly, you also need to coach your clients on this rapid-response approach and what to expect, especially for TV requests. Whenever you get a call or email for national media or local TV interviews, your job is to find out ASAP when the client is available, where the client is located (time zone and place), and then coordinate with the producer to make it happen. Fortunately, in a post-pandemic world, many TV interviews can be done via *Zoom* now, making the logistics much easier to coordinate.

To make sure your interview takes flight, work with the reporter, your client and/or their assistant to confirm the details. Recently, we had a last minute radio interview request from *KGO 810 AM* radio in San Francisco for a client about a timely pandemic topic. Because the interview was for a LIVE radio show that afternoon, we called, texted, and emailed the spokesperson until we connected. Fortunately, the interview was confirmed within about an hour and the producer held the timeslot.

To help you better manage interview requests, here is your checklist:

BEST PRACTICES - INTERVIEW CONFIRMATION CHECKLIST

- Confirm the topic and talking points with the reporter and the client.
- Confirm the interview date, time, and format (in person, remotely via phone or Zoom or written questions for print stories) with the media and the interviewee.
- Get specific instructions and/or directions for each party regarding the format (phone number, *Zoom* link, address if in person and/or deadline if it is a column.)
- Confirm the approximate length of the interview and/or word count for print stories.
- Provide media coaching for clients and/or your spokesperson before interviews (especially, if it's their first interview) based on the media type (TV, print, radio or podcast). (*Goody PR* provides media training and/or refers clients to coaches).
- Once the interview is scheduled, confirm everything again with both parties (interviewer and interviewee).
- Set up *Google Calendar* Alerts that are sent to both you and your client via email with multiple reminders.
- If it's for a big interview, set up planning calls with clients.
- If the interview is LIVE, listen live online and/or tape the interview for your client.

- If you are not with your client for a media interview, always ask them for feedback so you can manage the follow-up with the reporter.

- Other than live TV and radio, follow-up is key to getting it published. Ask clients, "How did it go?" and "Did they say when the story will be published?" Their feedback can save everyone time and reduces redundant questions with reporters.

It is also good to create a system for interview requests. Our preference is to have one main contact for each *Goody PR* client, even though most companies have multiple team members involved. If your client has an executive assistant, it's very important to work closely with him or her. Make sure you have everyone's cell phone numbers for last minute requests, and prepare the spokesperson for what to expect.

For our *Goody PR* clients, we now set up *Google Calendar* appointments and reminders for all interviews. For one client, they set up a specific *Google Calendar* just for their interviews, and gave us access. Because this system is not full-proof, we've still had clients no-show interviews (UGH!). If it's a really important interview, you should always text or call clients with a reminder about one hour before the interview. Yes, emergencies happen, but it's important for guests to show up and avoid rescheduling!

After booking thousands of media interviews, I've been fortunate to only have a few interviews get messed up. Yes, we are all human. I admit to making mistakes, and have had clients no-show interviews for various reasons.

We stress this interview preparation process because you want to avoid getting panic emails and calls from reporters saying, "Where is your client?" So extra reminders are a good thing, even if you think it's over-kill. And if you or a client misses an interview, send a heartfelt apology and ask when it can be rescheduled (this will work in most cases – but not all). So, while these planning steps may sound obvious, they are a must for your PR success.

Step 6.4 Turn Your Talking Points into a Q-and-A Script for the Producer

Another really important part of the media hits process is to write talking points that can be easily turned into questions or a script draft. We've talked about this action item previously, and it is so important that we want to emphasize it here with examples.

When you write potential talking points, they are meant to be teasers versus the whole answer. It is also helpful to include numbers (reporters love lists with numbers and statistics). For TV and major radio interviews, it is best to draft questions for the host. You have to use your best judgement based on everyone involved (the producer, reporter and your client) with what works best.

INTERVIEW TALKING POINT EXAMPLES – Q&A FORMAT

- Why did you write your book?
- Why did you start your company?
- Why did you create (fill-in-the-blank with whatever you are promoting)?
- What was your ah-ha moment that made you want to do this?
- How is dating different online during the pandemic?
- What are your top 3 secrets to retiring early?
- What are 3 ways to Thank a Firefighter?
- Why don't businesses need bosses in 2022?
- How can people help support your cause?
- What are your top success tips for (fill-in-the-blank)?

In a few cases, we have also written out the entire script for the client and the reporter. This extra preparation is rarely needed, but can make you a PR hero because reporters are so overwhelmed all the time that many appreciate the draft.

During a recent *KTLA Channel 5* News Los Angeles interview, we sent eight Questions and Answers to the producer for a timely book interview. Four anchors interviewed the author at their main desk, and the team used almost our exact list of questions. The more people involved in an interview, the more important a script can be.

For a *PBS Postcards* 30-minute segment for a different client, I emailed 30 suggested questions organized by category in advance to the producer. It was based on a brainstorming session with the co-authors one week prior to their in-person interviews. Because the producers planned to interview the co-authors for 3-4 hours, they were very grateful for this guidance!

Of course, any media interview never goes exactly as planned, but talking points and a script draft can provide focus for both the interviewee and the reporter.

The mistake that many authors make before an interview is assuming that a reporter will actually read their book. Yes, in an ideal world, the reporter reads a book (and yes, this does happen!). However, in our fast-track breaking news world, you can never count on it. For your publicity success, you must guide reporters with suggested topics!

GOODY PR CASE STUDY – WHY Q&A SCRIPTS MATTER

One of our biggest PR wins was a national TV story on *FOX and Friends* for four co-authors and Robert Kiyosaki (*Rich Dad Poor Dad*) for their book *More Important than Money – An Entrepreneur's Team*. The book was written by Robert, his wife Kim Kiyosaki (*Rich Woman*), and his eight Rich Dad Advisors. The spokespeople were in New York City to promote this book at the *Book Expo America (BEA)*, and this TV appearance all came together as a huge PR win - with a few hurdles.

We pitched the story with different angles for about three weeks, but the producers were very hesitant to have five guests on at the same time. Even though I knew the producers from a previous client interview, there was no guarantee of a TV interview happening.

When I finally wrote out the entire script, including an introduction by Robert

Kiyosaki of his team of advisors, followed by 1-2 entrepreneurial tips from each expert on the team, the producers agreed to proceed. They could finally visualize the interview with a script in front of them.

Coordinating with the *FOX and Friends* producers, Robert Kiyosaki, Rich Dad Advisors, the Rich Dad team and their guests resulted in many home runs for all!

Fortunately, this *More Important than Money* book panel interview ended up being six minutes on national TV (when most TV interviews are two to three minutes). And the Calculated Publicity Value, according to a *Nielsen Media Report*, was approximately $136,000.

You cannot buy that kind of publicity. Bottom line, you have to make it really easy for the media. Ask questions about what they need, send images, write potential talking points, and draft a script draft if you think it will help.

Step 6.5 Send the Interviewer Great Visuals in Support of Your Story

Along with writing meaningful talking points, you always want to send the reporter great visuals (images and/or video) that can add value to the coverage. We've covered this topic already, but it is so important that it is highlighted here again with examples.

When you say "Yes" to interviews, you always want to have your best media images ready to go, especially for TV and podcasts. We reviewed how to set up a Digital Press Kit in the last chapter.

As a case study example for a recent *CBS 17* Raleigh interview, we sent the producer about 20 visuals – as options – via a *Google Docs* link. This profile story was for a series called "Veterans Voices" featuring Former Special Forces and *Warriors Heart* Co-Founder Tom Spooner. These files included headshot photos, combat images, Warriors Heart logos, photographs of the three founders, and many action photos on-site at their 543-acre ranch in Bandera, Texas (near San Antonio). As a result, the producers used almost all of the photos and some video from the new *Warriors Heart – Warriors Healing Warriors* documentary trailer in this 2-minute primetime news story. Along with airing on the 5:00 p.m. local evening news, *CBS 17* posted a story online and the video on their *YouTube* Channel – resulting in three media hits for one story! In this scenario, the visuals added more emotional connections and context to Spooner's life in combat and his great work healing peers.

You may also get a custom request for digital assets that needs more planning and organization. Here's a great case study example that was complex:

CASE STUDY – HAVE DIGITAL ASSETS READY FOR REPORTERS – PBS POSTCARDS

If you're lucky enough to get a feature story on a mega TV outlet – for an entire 30-minute episode, you want to put extra energy **and** effort into the preparation phase.

For the *PBS Postcards* segment about our client's Award-Winning WWII book, *40 Thieves on Saipan*, the producer asked the authors to bring **one flash drive** to their 4-hour interview with all digital assets that could be used as visuals.

This segment covered the moving story-behind-the-story and military history book written by Joseph Tachovsky and Cynthia Kraack about Joseph's father, Lt. Frank Tachovsky, and his elite WWII U.S. Marines platoon, nicknamed the "40 Thieves."

As a backstory, Joseph's father never spoke about the war while alive. After his father passed in 2011 at age 96, he opened the "off limits" footlocker in the garage and found a treasure chest of WWII letters, photographs, medals, platoon rosters and more. This discovery was the beginning of 9-year coast-to-coast research and writing project for his award-winning book. Using the platoon roster and *Google*, Joseph was able to find six survivors and their loved ones who helped him uncover this mostly untold story of his dad's platoon.

To respond to the *PBS* producer's specific request for digital assets, I worked closely with the authors. In this case, I suggested that the digital files be organized in these folders:

1. BOOK (book cover, PDF copy of the book, social media)
2. CHILDHOOD / FAMILY PHOTOS (Joseph with his father and mother)
3. WWII LETTERS (Joseph found thousands of letters between his parents, who wrote daily. He also found letters to and from platoon members.)
4. WWII PHOTOS (Joseph found historic images from the platoon's training days in Hawaii, along with dramatic images from the Battle of Saipan.)
5. U.S. TRIBUTE TRIP PHOTOS (Joseph has visited most of the graves of the 40 men in his platoon to honor his father's men, including in Hawaii.)
6. WWII HAWAII TRIBUTE TRIP PHOTOS (The author made a special trip for Veterans Day 2021 to honor six men who served with his dad on Tarawa and Saipan. The men are in the book, and buried in the *National Memorial Cemetery* of the Pacific/ *Punchbowl*.)
7. WWII HAWAII TRIBUTE TRIP VIDEOS (The author filmed a few short videos on his Hawaii tribute trip.)
8. OTHER VIDEOS (There are a few videos of platoon members and book promo videos.)

As you can see, the more specific and organized you are when sending digital assets to reporters, the easier it will be for them to tell your story.

Remember, all interviews should "educate and entertain" because people want to feel like they are gaining valuable information. Visual learners like graphics, pictures, posters, and other visual aids. For this *PBS Postcards* interview, the old black and white photos and 1940s letters added so much value!

IMAGE QUALITY REQUIREMENTS - TV AND PRINT INTERVIEWS

Photographs and graphics should always be high-quality images for TV and print stories. What this means is the image should be at least 500KB or higher, and preferably 1-3 MB. If you do not know what this file size means, *Google* it or hire a marketing professional to help you.

High quality images are a must for most media interviews and your brand story! You can also hire a graphic artist or professional photographer to develop your digital assets. In a very visual world, it is really that important!

Step 6.6 Be Available 24x7 if the Media Needs Anything

Because the media never sleeps, you need to make yourself available 24/7 for last-minute changes or requests. While I try to avoid having my team work on weekends to maintain a life balance, you are never completely off when doing public relations.

To make sure a *CNN HLN Weekend Express* interview aired live without any issues, I set my alarm for a Sunday morning at 4:00 a.m. PST to support a client's 4:50 a.m. PST scheduled interview. It's always best to be available for both the media and PR clients to troubleshoot any last minute changes. And it was a good thing because they moved the interview time to the final segment of the hour around 4:57a.m. PST / 7:57a.m. EST and changed some of the questions. I was able to immediately update the client, and emphasize not to worry about the exact questions, and instead focus his answers on the key things we practiced the previous day during media training via *Zoom*. With so much breaking news, you can never be 100 percent sure that your story will actually happen when it is scheduled (or at all). You have to be standing by and flexible.

When I was promoting my dating book, I had a national TV interview cancelled two minutes before it was scheduled because of breaking news. It was like a scene out of the movie *Broadcast News*. I had asked a couple whom I helped to find love to be part of the interview. This couple took off work and were in the studio in Washington D.C. I was 3,000 miles away with a microphone and earpiece set up in the Los Angeles satellite studio for *FOX News Channel*. Then I heard someone in my earpiece say,

"Please pick up the phone." It was the NYC producer, who said, "Your segment just got cut due to breaking news out of Iraq."

Fortunately, I was able to reschedule the story within twelve hours, and the interview ran the next day. However, the happy couple in Washington D.C. were not willing to take another day off from work. I was relieved to find another couple in Los Angeles, and made the interview happen. This interview recovery process was not easy and required focus, patience, and a lot of emails and calls with producers and the other couple.

TV news never takes holidays either! And holidays can actually be a great time to book an interview because there is less competition for headline news. Thanks to smartphones and new technology, anyone can manage media interviews from anywhere and reach clients for last-minute requests.

Step 6.7 Follow-up to Move Your Story Around the Bases and Score

With all of the Media Hits Superpower tips in this chapter, here is the most important thing to remember. Getting a media interview aired is like playing baseball. Your job as a marketing and public relations professional is to get the earned media interview over home plate so the world can see your brand story.

You may run into obstacles in this *8-Second PR* Baseball Game. You could miss your turn at bat, strike out, or get stuck on one of the bases. It is important to navigate this process with confidence and patience. And yes, there is strategy and skill involved. To help you succeed, here is our analogy and tips:

> ## *8-SECOND PR* BASEBALL GAME - SCORING EARNED MEDIA (TV, PRINT, RADIO, PODCAST)

GET UP TO BAT – If you are lucky enough to get an interview request from a reporter who wants to share your story, congratulations, you are up at bat. If you do not get an interview request, keep reinventing your media hook until you get out of the dugout.

ADVANCE TO FIRST BASE – To get to first base, secure the interview by confirming a date, time and logistics. At any moment, your interview might get cancelled, so it is important to act quickly and get the timeslot booked on everyone's calendars.

ADVANCE TO SECOND BASE – When you actually have the interview, you have now advanced to second base. If your interview is LIVE, you will immediately score and advance to home plate! If the interview was pre-taped or was a phone or email interview, your primary job changes to follow-up.

ADVANCE TO THIRD BASE – If the interview was not live, the follow-up steps will advance your story to third base. At this point, it is all about follow-up and you want to avoid being stuck on third base forever. You want to avoid hurdles that can cause an interview to never be published!

SCORE AN EARNED MEDIA STORY– If you are lucky, the interview was live, and you immediately scored a TV, radio or podcast interview. If it was not live, your PR mission is to score by getting it published. To get there, it's a balancing act with the media. In all cases, don't burn bridges and know when to let go.

In our experience, 99% of interviews eventually get published, but many require a lot of follow-up, patience and persistence!

We've seen some interviews or columns take 6-12 months to get published. When an interview gets stuck during this follow-up process, it can be a big bummer for you and the client. Remember, it is earned media versus paid media, so the reporter decides whether and when to publish it. Be nice, stay calm, and don't give up - unless your gut instinct tells you that's it's not going to happen.

For example, we scheduled an in-person interview for a client at a major financial publication in New York City. A year after their face-to-face meeting and many follow-ups, no story has ever been published. The reporter kept changing the angle, and eventually stopped responding to our emails and calls. Yes, this can happen.

During the post-pandemic Zoom interview world, we've also seen a local TV station cancel airing a pre-taped interview because the client's internet connection and lighting was not good. Please take the time to check your internet connection using SpeedTest.net, connect laptops directly to your power cable, and get your home studio ready (good lighting, background and microphone) to avoid this scenario!

Sometimes things are just out of your control. A reporter may get a new job, the editor may not like the story, and/or the client's story does not work for them.

Your worst-case scenario is a client who is rude or has "an attitude that they are better than others" with a reporter. In this situation, the story will probably never be published, and you may not get another opportunity for them or any other clients. Big egos can kill a story fast. Remember, everyone plays an important role, including the expert, reporter, producers, executive assistant and the entire team at a radio or TV station. You want to emphasize to your clients that being grateful goes a long way with ensuring your PR success.

This *8-Second PR* Baseball Game process is just like dating. If you act too aggressive or desperate, your story might get cancelled. If you get a reporter on the phone, show empathy for their busy schedule, make personal connections (talk about mutual friends, a mutual hobby you discovered on the LinkedIn profile and/or how grateful you are to them for previous interviews), and then ask questions to learn more about the best next steps. In all cases, stay flexible to score more media hits!

Step 6.8 Genuinely Thank the Reporter and Their Team

No matter how big the media outlet, you always want to thank reporters before and after an interview. We've also talked about this point earlier in this book, but want to say it again because it is SO important! After you score an earned media story, it is easy to just move on and forget to say thank you.

We cannot emphasize enough the importance of giving specific and positive feedback to the reporter after an interview is published. Compliment their questions and graphics, praise their team for making it easy, and thank them for including a summary and/or your website link in their recap. A short and sincere email can go a long way and increase your chances of being invited back.

I worked with a PR mentor who used to write hand-written thank-you notes to journalists after every major interview. These thank-you notes repeatedly landed his clients on major national TV shows such as the *TODAY Show*, *Good Morning America*, *CNN*, and more. While this takes extra time, the snail mail approach can help you stand out in their avalanche of digital correspondence.

You also want to always share the story with your followers, tag the reporter and outlet, and add positive comments on a reporter's *Facebook, Instagram, LinkedIn* and/or *Twitter* posts to acknowledge their work. Your response shows that you care, reviewed their story, and cross-promoted their work.

Remember, many reporters are getting paid zero to almost nothing, and receive very little appreciation for working long hours. Journalists are human beings like you - so ALWAYS be courteous and say thank you! It's free and easy, so just do it!

CHAPTER 6 RECAP

Overall, this chapter is about scoring mega media interviews and building long-term relationships with reporters. Your goal should always be to get as many earned media stories published as possible, along with getting second interview requests.

Step 6 Action Items – Make Your Interview Take Flight To Score Mega Media

1. Get back to media within one hour of a TV interview request.
2. Make it really easy for the media.
3. Coach your PR client on what to expect and next steps.
4. Turn your talking points into a Q-and-A script for the producer.

5. Send the interviewer great visuals in support of your story.
6. Be available 24/7 if the media needs anything.
7. Follow-up to move your story around the bases and score.
8. Genuinely thank the reporter and their team.

PR Superpower 6 - Media Hits Superpower

With your new Media Hits Superpower, you will now be able to get your interview scheduled and published for the world to see.

Chapter 6 - 8-Second PR Challenges

As we close Chapter 6, here are your *8-Second PR* Challenges:

1. What tools or processes can you set up to ensure that you reply to a TV reporter within one hour of an interview request?
2. What items can you include in a Digital Press Kit for you or your clients?
3. How are you going to set expectations with your clients so they can help you reply to media requests with warp speed?
4. What talking points do you have ready for your clients to send TV producers?
5. How often are you going to contact the media if your story gets stuck on third base with continual follow-up?
6. When do you know it's time to give up on the story follow-up?
7. How can you show your appreciation and support for a reporter's story on social media?
8. How are you going to thank reporters after a story is published?

Your Media Hits Superpower skills can help you score hundreds of earned media for clients and/or yourself.

In the next chapter, we will talk about what you can say to make your interview hammer home with meaningful messages. Ready?

Reminder:

"THINK LIKE A PUBLISHER, NOT A MARKETER."

– DAVID MEERMAN SCOTT

MESSAGE IMPACT

Magnify Your Interviews with Meaningful Soundbites

> "PEOPLE HAVE AN INFINITE ATTENTION SPAN IF YOU'RE ENTERTAINING THEM."
>
> – JERRY SEINFELD

Do you know how to get to the point immediately? Do you know how to use emphasis statements when sharing your story? Do you know how to use the power of threes when making a key point? When you are given a media interview, you want to make every word count. Reporters want to talk to people who can deliver great soundbites, so add a little magic to your message!

It takes a lot of steps to get to an interview, so make the most out of every opportunity! Most reporters want their guests to keep it simple, deliver a compelling story with confidence, have a meaningful conversation with the reporter, and be camera-ready - especially if it's a live TV, radio or video interview. It all matters, so the spokesperson needs to be prepared.

If the person being interviewed thinks all they have to do is show up and deliver knowledge to their audience, think again. While there is some value to improv, hammering home messages in media interviews is much more complicated than it looks.

PR SUPERPOWER 7 – MESSAGE IMPACT SUPERPOWER

Presenting your brand story to the world is a PR art that you can master with the Message Impact Superpower. When you get the opportunity to do an interview with a reporter, make sure to be GRATEFUL and prepared to deliver moving messages from the heart.

For TV, print, radio and podcast interviews, you want to move your audience with powerful soundbites and stories. Use emphasis statements and examples of how your tips can help others to quickly draw attention to your brand, book or product. And always deliver your points in a meaningful versus promotional way.

Just as thunder can make you stop what you are doing and look up, you want people to stop multi-tasking and focus on what you are saying. Your publicity results will be impacted by your ability to deliver great content with a memorable delivery. For TV, your tone of voice, non-verbal expressions, props, what you wear and the lighting all matter in a very visual world. If you speak with confidence and conviction, you will make lasting impressions for your brand using this *8-Second PR* Superpower!

In this chapter, we will cover eight action items to enhance your Message Impact Superpower. By delivering your message with conviction, it can connect to your audience and receive a great response:

STEP 7 ACTION ITEMS -
MAGNIFY YOUR INTERVIEWS WITH MEANINFUL SOUNDBITES

1. Practice your talking points with 8-second messaging in mind.
2. Be grateful and a great guest.
3. Dress for success for TV and Podcast video interviews.
4. Speak from the heart with a genuine interest in others.
5. Speak with clarity and conviction, even if you get thrown off.
6. Be entertaining and interesting (tell me something I do not know).
7. Give real-life examples of how you helped others.
8. Smile. Breathe in. Breathe out.

PR SUPERPOWER 7 -
MESSAGE IMPACT SUPERPOWER

An interview is showtime for your brand story! Your audience will decide in the first eight to fifteen seconds if they will continue watching, listening, or reading your story. So get excited! Make some noise! And most importantly, make your audience fall in love with your brand story!

In this chapter, we will review How to be a Great Guest. All of these points are an expansion for your interview success. Ready? You can do this!

Step 7.1 Practice Your Talking Points with 8-Second Messaging in Mind

To secure a media interview, you have defined the brand story, sent out a press release, written a powerful media hook, and now you have a reporter who wants to interview you or your PR client. You made it to first base just by getting the interview scheduled. Now, you want to be ready to score big when the reporter starts asking questions.

To prepare, one of the best things you can do is practice saying your key talking points out loud with emphasis. Use your notes as a guide, and do not try to memorize it. A written script does not sound natural (which is why someone reading a speech can sound really awkward).

If you practice, your words will come out with more passion. You always want to deliver your message with a confident tone on the phone or on camera, so your audience focuses on your message. By saying the words out loud, you can make changes, so it sounds more natural based on your personal style.

For TV interviews, your preparation is a must. The interview will happen so fast that if you are not ready, you will be saying "could of, would of, should of " afterwards with regrets for a long time.

You can also practice saying your key talking points with a friend, your PR representative, and/or hire a professional media coach. The bigger the media, the shorter time you will probably be allotted to tell your story. Being clear, concise and compelling is not as easy as it looks. So avoid shortcuts on your preparation, especially for a TV interview.

CASE STUDY EXAMPLE – DON'T SKIP PRACTICE FOR MAJOR TV INTERVIEWS

As an example, we had a PR client who will remain anonymous here because we never want to make anyone look bad. However, this was their first TV interview, and the importance of practice and lessons learned can offer helpful insights.

Instead of getting rest, this individual decided to stay up all night before a 7:30 a.m. national TV interview because they were afraid they would not get up in time. No sleep was not a good idea because you always want to be rested, and be able to think without a script. Remember, the reporter will rarely ask exactly what was planned, so you have to be alert, ready to answer unexpected questions and treat it like a "conversation."

While I emailed them media coaching tips in advance, the client did not think it was necessary to practice with us via *Zoom*. Yes, I should have pushed them harder to practice. However, our clients are often CEOs who are very busy and don't think they need help. Our mistake – we should have insisted on media training and practice!

When it was time for the interview, this individual started sweating profusely. And then they picked up their hand-written notes and read them while they were LIVE on national TV – please do NOT do this – ever! You're the expert. You know your stuff, or they would not be interviewing you!

Afterwards, the client said to me, "I have a new respect for the people on TV." And yes, the next time, we practiced together via *Zoom* before a TV interview – and they did a fantastic job!

For all types of media interviews, we encourage our clients to start sentences with emphasis statements to gain the attention of the audience. If you watch cable TV news, look for the media pros who use these types of phrases:

GREAT EMPHASIS STATEMENTS

The most important thing is . . .

The number one thing is . . .

The top three things are . . .

Remember, the top two things about X are Number one . . .
and Number two . . .

If you only remember one thing, don't forget to. . .

To illustrate the importance of these emphasis statements, here are two TV interview soundbite examples from way back when I was promoting my dating book, *Smart Man Hunting*:

TV INTERVIEW EXAMPLES - EMPHASIS STATEMENT SOUNDBITES

TV Interview 1 – In a local TV news interview on *ABC 7* Los Angeles about internet dating profile tips, I emphasized, "The number one mistake is they write too much about themselves. They write something too general, and so I try to help them put some personality in the profile."

TV Interview 2 – During a national talk show interview about first dates on *NBC's The Other Half* (guys version of *The View* with Dick Clark, Mario Lopez and Danny Bonaduce), I used the word "biggest", "number one" and power of threes for emphasis. When asked by actor Dorian Gregory (*Charmed*); "Why do first date disasters happen?", our opening reply was, "Well I think the biggest cause of dating disasters is fear. People are anxious. Their fear of the unknown, fear of disappointment, and number one fear of rejection."

Think about your topic, and write notes about emphasis statements that you can use as great soundbites to share both knowledge and your story.

Step 7.2 Be Grateful and a Great Guest

To ensure media success, you always want to be early, grateful, and flexible for interviews. While we may sound like a broken record, you cannot afford to go through all the steps to get here and then blow the interview! To help you and others, below are our *Goody PR* best practice tips for How to be a Great Guest. These tips are based on booking thousands of earned media interviews for clients, and personally doing hundreds of interviews for our books – so take notes!

BEST PRACTICES CHECKLIST – HOW TO BE A GREAT GUEST!

To help you build rapport with reporters and increase your chances of media success, here are our best practice recommendations for your interviews:

- Review the interview notes at least 2 hours in advance (we add this information to our *Google Calendar* Alerts for clients).
- For TV interviews, watch the interviewer in advance to learn their style.
- Ask your publicist in advance for help if you don't have everything you need.
- Don't schedule other meetings right before your interview.
- Be ready and relaxed at showtime.
- Review the reporter's bio, media outlet and talking points before your interview.
- Review any references sent to you by your publicist (related stories, studies) so you can mention relevant studies and statistics.
- Make sure you have a great internet connection, lighting and microphone!
- Show up a few minutes early for the interview!
- Be grateful to reporters and their team from the very start!
- Consider an interview as a two-way conversation versus a monologue.
- Pause during an interview to give time for the host to ask you questions!
- Share great soundbites (1-2 impactful sentences) with tips for their audience.
- Compliment the host during and after the interview!
- Share helpful tips and stories with specific examples that interest their audience using only a few sentences (remember, it's not all about you!).
- Dress for success and smile during the interview!
- If you have a publicist, coordinate with them - every step of the way - as a team!
- Make any schedule changes by working with your publicist, who can navigate the process, manage the media relationship and minimize emails.
- Always cc your publicist when communicating directly with a reporter so you are all on the same page and reduce repeat questions!
- Don't cancel at the last minute, unless you really cannot avoid it!

To reinforce the most important points, here are our top three reminders for guests with more insights:

BE PROMPT – You also want to be prompt for media interviews. You do not need to show up early for a print interview phone call, but should always be on time. However, for a LIVE radio or television interview, you always want to be early. Most producers will request that you dial-in five minutes early for live radio. For TV, many producers ask guests to be in the studio 30 - 45 minutes before the scheduled interview.

BE GRATEFUL – As soon as you meet a reporter, the first thing you always want to say is THANK YOU for interviewing me! Get excited, and work with the reporter to make it their best interview ever!

BE FLEXIBLE – Always be flexible with the media. While you want to avoid rescheduling an interview, the media may ask you to move the date and time. The producer often cannot control breaking news, and things do come up.

For example, we were asked to reschedule a local TV interview twice over a two-month period for a *Goody PR* client in Los Angeles due to breaking news. In this case, we stayed flexible by working with the producer and client. Eventually, the story happened, was six minutes (which is long for TV interviews), and worth over $50,000 in Calculated Publicity Value. Being flexible definitely paid off in this case!

MAXIMIZE LIVE RADIO INTERVIEWS

The good news about radio is that you can usually do the interview from anywhere, as long as you are prepared. If you are a guest on a radio show or podcast, always review your notes and instructions again about 15-30 minutes in advance to avoid any delays and dial-in early. You do not want to be fumbling at the last minute trying to figure out the logistics and talking points because any stress may impact your tone and delivery.

The other important thing to know about remote radio interviews is that you need a high-quality phone or internet connection in a QUIET place. We cannot emphasize this enough! While it might sound so obvious, some clients may not take the sound quality seriously. We've seen clients do radio and podcast interviews from the car while driving, call-in using a cell phone outside, and/or do an interview from a public place. Please be considerate of the host, and don't do this!

As an example, when booking a client for a one-hour LIVE radio interview, it was a sound disaster. This show costs the host about $20,000 to produce one episode, and they spent a lot of time securing advertisers. Our client had a bad internet connection at a hotel, got disconnected several times, and had to dial back in during the LIVE show. Honestly, it is just inconsiderate not to plan ahead, test your internet or phone connection, and find a new location if needed. These sound quality challenges are bad news for the radio show host, your audience, your brand and the PR professional who booked it. We had to profusely apologize to the host, who was not happy. Please avoid this scenario!

CASE STUDY EXAMPLE – LIVE RADIO

On a positive note, here is a live radio interview success story. During a recent *Girls on the Air 1590 KVTA* talk radio interview, Successful Businesswoman, Bestselling Author (*Playing for Keeps – How a 21st century businesswoman beat the boys!*), Mom and Mentor Therese Allison called in early (and the producer let her listen to the show live while waiting, so she could hear the hosts). She also had a great phone connection in her home office.

Allison hit it out of the park when talking about how playing competitive sports taught her to succeed in business (this was the media hook for the interview). And the conversation flowed easily because she paused often to let the hosts talk and ask questions.

When asked about how sports helped her retire early at age 43, Allison explained, "As a young woman, it gives you confidence, particularly when you're playing a team sport, you're learning to win together and to lose together. And then with business, I took the same skills into the boardroom, and it worked."

In another radio interview example of what NOT to do, this is the opposite of being a great guest . When an *NPR* radio reporter called for a pre-scheduled interview, the client asked the host, "Can you call me back later?" When I asked the client how it went afterwards, they explained what happened, that the reporter said "no", and he agreed to do the interview. While they did record the interview, you can guess what happened next. This interview NEVER aired on this national radio program. The host would not reply to our MANY follow-up emails, phone calls, and apologies. And we could never get another interview scheduled again for other clients with this reporter! Please don't do this if you've agreed in advance to do an interview!

PR is a team sport. Remember, interviews are not all about you. It's about being a great guest, offering helpful advice tips for their audience, having a conversation with the hosts so they look good too, and promoting your product through stories.

NAIL YOUR LIVE TV INTERVIEWS

Through the process of doing PR for my first dating book, I learned that the top two rules for live TV interviews are 1) wake up at least two hours in advance so you have high energy and no puffy eyes and 2) arrive at the station at least 30 to 45 minutes early (fortunately, you can do many interviews now via *Zoom*). For in-studio interviews, most TV shows have a waiting room for guests to relax in until it's time for their segment. It might be the front lobby or a green room for bigger shows.

When our client was on the TODAY Show, we were in NYC with them. We worked together as a team to get there early. Fortunately, our hotel was only one block away from the studio. We also went to check out the entrance location the night before so we would know exactly where it was in the morning. Because the spokespeople had never done a TV interview, I also explained in advance that we would probably be sitting in the green room for an hour and they may do "hair and make-up" to help them understand what to expect. (We will talk more about this national TV interview success story in Chapter 8 – saving the best for last!)

In another scenario, I was fortunate to be invited to talk about my dating book on San Diego's *NBC 7 KNSD*. To get there on time, I booked a hotel room right across the street and got up at 3:30 a.m. for a 5:30 a.m. interview (ouch, but so worth it!).

DON'T TRY TO MOVE A TV INTERVIEW BECAUSE YOU ARE LATE!

In a rare case, a *Goody PR* client got stuck in traffic before a local morning TV news interview. It was a real challenge to try to move the time around with the producer who was busy running a LIVE news program. As a result, their interview almost got cut. While traffic snarls happen, you always want to plan way ahead so that you are early.

It IS a HUGE, BIG DEAL to move a TV interview because every second is scheduled in advance with questions, images and graphics! The producers are also busy on set and don't have time to take a call from you during a live show. Fortunately, our client made it in time, and their interview was a huge success!

Remember, this is the showtime you have been waiting for to share your story with the world. If you are late, you will be stressed, which will show in your delivery. If you mess up the producer's schedule, you may never be invited back. Yes, things happen in life that cannot be avoided. However, leave really early and make it a priority to always be on time for live TV and radio interviews. Enough said.

Step 7.3 Dress for Success for TV and Podcast Video Interviews

If you are fortunate enough to have a TV or podcast video interview, you always want to dress for success. Visuals are SO important for video, and along with images and other digital assets that you sent the producer in advance. While you can do print and some radio interviews in bed in your pajamas, you are the MAIN VISUAL in anything that involves video.

If you are a PR professional, it's important to coach your clients on what to wear and share tips on non-verbal communication. Media coaching tips, drafted scripts, role plays, talking points, and props are all your friends for TV and video interviews.

If you are the author or spokesperson, you cannot afford to show up without wearing your best look and positive energy. It is really that simple. There is no shortcut here. Get your hair done, get a manicure, wear your favorite color, choose business casual clothes, get sleep and smile!

If you are getting ready to launch a PR campaign for a new book, business, or event, consider getting a style consultant. These experts can review your best colors and styles to wear for your skin tone and hair. This honest advice can be a huge help and is highly recommended to anyone with on-camera interviews.

If it is the last minute and you have a low budget, go to a *Sephora* or a beauty expert to have a makeup artist help you. For my first TV interview, I remember my parents taking me to *Nordstrom's* makeup counter for advice tips. For women, they recommended going heavy on the makeup and wear eyeliner. Style consultants can also help you with what to wear. I also recommend taking a friend with you, and ask them for honest feedback, so you don't spend a fortune on makeup and new clothes.

Here are some of our Dress for Media Success Tips that we email our *Goody PR* clients in preparation for TV interviews:

GOODY PR'S DRESS FOR MEDIA SUCCESS COACHING TIPS

Based on our personal experience doing 30+TV interviews, producing hundreds of videos, working with three media coaches, and getting input from style consultants, here are our top Dress for Media Success tips:

- The most important thing to remember is to smile and speak with passion about the topic because you are the main visual (get sleep, eat well and drink water before an interview).

- Wear "business casual" in most cases (think about what you would wear to an important business meeting or networking event).

- Wear solid-color clothes versus patterns.

- Wear your favorite color or clothes that make you feel good inside. Your confidence will be naturally beaming as a result.

- Avoid wearing black, white, or red on TV or video. These colors are not good on camera. When I see these colors or detailed patterns on TV, it makes me cringe.

- **If you are a woman**, wear bright colors. Long sleeves are also much better on camera versus a sleeveless dress or blouse. Remember, you are going business casual (unless you are being interviewed on a red-carpet where everyone is wearing evening gowns). Great color options for women are hot pink, emerald-green, coral, royal blue or a purple/fuchsia.

- **If you are a man**, wear a navy jacket and light blue or neutral color shirt. Tan, light gray, avocado green, and pale blue are all great options. Avoid wearing a black or white shirt with a black jacket. A tie is always optional for men, and probably not needed today. However, you always want to watch the show in advance before making this decision.

- Relax, and look at the interviewer versus the camera.

- Speak with confidence and consider it a conversation with the reporter instead of memorizing a script.

- Avoid moving your hands around a lot, or banging on a table.

- Turn your off your cell phone ringer, alerts and computer notifications if the interview is via Zoom or video.

- Invest in a good selfie light so you look great on camera! (And please, don't put a window in back of you with bright sunlight that will wash out your face.)

What I often recommend to clients is to WATCH the show and/or any cable news program in advance when thinking about what to wear. Look at the different colors and styles to see what the hosts wear, and then think about what is best for you. What you wear is REALLY important on camera, so pay attention to this detail!

Step 7.4 Speak from the Heart with a Genuine Interest in Others

One of my first media coaches explained that it is very important to show empathy for others during interviews. For my dating book, my three media coaches gave me different advice. Be genuine, authentic and show gratitude were important tips that you should apply to all of your interviews.

If you come across as a "know-it-all" who has never made a mistake, you will lose some of your audience right away. Your best bet is to acknowledge the challenges and problems that you want to help people overcome.

For example, it was important to be relatable for my dating book, *Smart Man Hunting*. To connect with the audience, I would start off interviews by saying things like "dating is hard" or "it's not easy to find the right guy." Simply by acknowledging the audience's pain, you can win their attention and respect.

In another scenario, here is a PR campaign for a General Practitioner Doctor in Palm Beach, Florida, during the time of Ebola. To help others understand the virus, the doctor did many TV and radio interviews when the first cases were reported in the United States. His genuine interest in helping people came across on camera. As a result, he kept getting invited back to discuss this breaking news topic.

CASE STUDY EXAMPLE – GREAT TV INTERVIEW SOUNDBITES – EBOLA

While the Ebola virus outbreak was minor compared to the COVID-19 pandemic, below are great soundbite examples from a national TV interview with this GP doctor that shows empathy, compassion and helpful insights:

The reality is shocking for most of us.

It's an epidemic, and now it's here.

The healthcare workers are not trained, and cannot handle this disease.

This disease is a monster.

There are a number of reasons why temperature checks don't work, and to highlight this is a nurse who went to Cleveland and had an elevated temperature, and they let her go. (It's always great to tell stories with examples).

First of all, a forehead temperature check is about the third-least accurate in terms of taking temperatures. Number two, it has to be done accurately. It has to be placed on the forehead....And if that person has taken an Advil or Aleve, it may lower the temperature artificially.... (Notice how he uses three points and specific examples).

Fortunately, Ebola (2013-2016) did not have a major impact on the United States. The U.S. only had a handful of cases and two deaths. However, when the first "live" case was reported in the U.S. in 2014, the public and the media were looking for answers from medical professionals because the reports were horrible in other countries. The virus resulted in just over 11,300+ deaths globally. While this number is tragic, it is minimal compared to the COVID-19 losses worldwide.

In this interview, the doctor's tone showed a genuine concern for others with specific soundbite tips and examples. He also wore a doctor's lab jacket, and it was done via *Skype* from his medical office. As a result, this medical expert gained the trust of the audience and media as a credible source.

Step 7.5 Speak with Clarity and Conviction, Even if You Get Thrown Off

Along with looking and feeling great on camera, you want to share impactful messages. Speak with confidence. And even if you lose your train of thought, keep going. I usually advise clients to practice the top three things that they want to say over and over again, and then the other talking points will come out naturally.

TV STORY CASE STUDY - AMMA "THE HUGGING SAINT" HONORED

We were humbly honored to recognize Humanitarian and Spiritual Leader Mata Amritanandamayi, better known as Amma "The Hugging Saint" with our *Golden Goody Award* (or top humanitarian award), at the *LAX Hilton*, during her annual Los Angeles tour. When *KCBS-TV* showed up to cover the story, we lost the reporter with over 3,000 people there. We had to focus on the award presentation, and worked with her team to follow the proper guidelines for greeting a living saint.

To keep our speech simple and heartfelt, we decided to focus on thanking Amma for her *Embracing the World* charities and mention three of her widely recognized qualities.

When someone mentioned the next day that they saw us on TV, we were pleasantly surprised to learn *KCBS-TV* had done a 1-minute segment on Amma's work and award. The anchor told the story based on the press release and included our soundbite:

"This is for Amma for her worldwide humanitarian charities, selfless love, compassion and life of service." - Liz H Kelly, *Goody Awards* Founder

We share this soundbite example to highlight Amma's inspiring work, and emphasize the power of threes on TV. Producers are often looking for a short soundbite only, and this sentence worked for them.

If you are not familiar with Amma, Google her name to learn more. Her charities have contributed over $60 million in free medical care for the poor since 1998 (Source: *amma dot org*).

If you can deliver your top three points with emphasis statements, clarity, and conviction, you will master your *Message Impact Superpower*!

A TV producer is not going to risk putting someone on camera unless they are confident on camera and really know their stuff. When it comes to a live interview, they want experts who speak with confidence and can carry a conversation.

CASE STUDY: TODAY SHOW – *WARRIORS HEART* SPOKESPEOPLE SOUNDBITES

For another national TV interview, we were fortunate to work with Former Green Beret/ *Warriors Heart* Alumni Teddy Lanier, his counselor, *Warriors Heart* Manager and LCDC Vonnie Nealon, and the *Warriors Heart* team to secure and prepare for a *TODAY* Show segment about Lanier's long-term recovery success story.

While we provided media coaching to Teddy and Vonnie, both were naturally strong in their delivery during this interview and spoke with conviction. There were so many great soundbites that made this interview a media home run, including:

- Without *Warriors Heart*, Lanier explained, "I would be dead, make no mistake about it...They gave me the tools to live."
- Lanier later reflected, "I'll never forget the day I called. I had never heard the voice of an angel until I called *Warriors Heart*."
- Nealon, then commented, "When we welcome them back, we welcome them to a world they know."
- Towards the end of the interview, Lanier emphasized, "There is absolutely nothing I will not do to pass this on to the next person, and save as many lives as I can."

This mega media success example is covered more extensively in Chapter 8 about Story Reinvention because the interview was scheduled, cancelled, and then rescheduled.

NOTE: It's important to add that nothing was scripted for this interview. Instead, they spoke from the heart, which is always best. While we did practice hypothetical questions, we never wrote a script. We encourage you to watch their inspiring interview on the *Warriors Heart YouTube* Channel.

Most of the time you will walk away from a TV interview saying, "What did I just say?" You literally go into a zone, which is why practice and preparation are so important. Even if you cannot remember your talking points, you can remember to use emphasis and empathy statements upfront - and then focus on your top three points.

If you really lose your train of thought or are thrown off, simply say, "That is a really good question" or make another relevant comment to buy yourself time to think.

Always keep smiling. Never let it show if you are caught off guard. Media interviews are somewhat like a piano recital. Piano teachers will tell students that if you make a mistake, just keep playing because no one will really notice. It's the same thing in TV and radio interviews, just keep going with confidence, even if you say something that was not perfect in your mind.

As a quick recap, here are our Media Coaching Messaging Tips as reminders for all media interviews.

GOODY PR'S TOP 10 MEDIA COACHING MESSAGING TIPS

1. Draft 3-7 talking points or questions with key things you want to say. Use the list as a guideline rather than memorizing so you sound natural.

2. Focus on your top three points when practicing and say them out loud in front of a mirror before the interview to see if they sound natural.

3. Keep answers short (a few sentences) so you get to the point immediately rather than rambling, especially for live TV and radio.

4. Remember, take breaks so the host can comment and ask their questions.

5. It should be a two-way conversation versus a speech. (It's not all about you!)

6. If possible, use the power of 3s in one of your answers. For example, the top three things that you want to do are X, Y, and Z. These statements are much easier to follow, and you want your audience to pay attention.

7. Use sixth-grade vocabulary on TV because you are talking to the masses and want to use the same level that works best in most major newspapers.

8. Try to use the name of your company, book, or product one to two times naturally in your answers. For example, mention a product as an example of how it helped someone so that it does not sound like a commercial.

9. Be prepared for the unexpected. Reporters are not going to follow the talking points that you sent exactly, so be flexible and stay confident. Even if they ask something new, don't let it throw you for a loop. Remember, you know your stuff or would not have been selected for the interview. It's also ok to say you are not sure (which is much better than making up something that is not true).

10. Focus on looking at the interviewer rather than the camera. Leave it to the producer to get the right shots, unless you are told to look a certain direction.

Step 7.6 Be Entertaining and Interesting (Tell Me Something I Do Not Know)

Another must for media interviews is to be both entertaining and interesting. You want to tell the world something they do not know. To deliver great soundbites, it can take time and practice, unless you are a natural born comedian.

When I work with our *Goody PR* clients, we are always brainstorming media hooks, timely topics and stories that are unique. Reporters want to know how the spokesperson's message is different from others doing similar things.

THE MAGIC IN COMEDIC DELIVERY – *MODERN FAMILY* EP DANNY ZUKER

While doing PR for a political humor book by Emmy Winner, *Modern Family* EP and Comedian Danny Zuker, he was a pro at delivering funny lines during

TV interviews.

As a guest on the *KTLA* morning show in Los Angeles to discuss his "Rock the Vote" campaign for the midterms, Zuker incorporated these zingers:

- *It's great to be here with people I watch every morning.*
- *It's not enough to go out and vote, you have to drag your friends to vote.*
- *I went 53 years without ever calling a Senator or Congress person, and I have them on speed dial now.*

Using interesting and short soundbites is not easy when the cameras are rolling. With practice, you will get better each time you have a TV interview. Think about what makes you different, and then highlight this part of your story.

Step 7.7 Give Real-Life Examples of How You Helped Others

Along with being entertaining, it is critical that you can show how you have helped others. Remember, one of the best ways to get media coverage is by showing how you are making a positive social impact.

One of the main reasons we love working with *Warriors Heart* is the inspiring work they are doing to help warriors overcome their "War At Home." It is a very special team making a difference in many ways. For example, one of their top spokespeople is Former Special Forces / U.S. Army Veteran and *Warriors Heart* Co-Founder Tom Spooner. He served 21 years in the *U.S. Army,* including 12 deployments and 40 months in combat. After almost taking his own life and struggling with chemical dependencies, he understands first-hand the challenges many warriors face. During interviews, Spooner shares his inspiring story and powerful WHY. After retiring from the U.S. Army in 2011, Spooner chose to dedicate his life to helping his fellow warriors heal with their peers, reduce military, veteran and first responder suicide, and help them rebuild their lives as "Sober, Confident Warriors."

Switching gears to a very different social impact fundraiser, Kevin Costner and his *Modern West* band headlined a Thomas Fire Benefit to raise money to help people rebuild after the devastating 2017 fire in Ventura, California. This charity event attracted a lot of national and local media attention (Yes, this event had celebrities involved, so it got a lot of coverage).

In addition to Kevin, *GRAMMY* Winners, singers and songwriters Colbie Caillat and Olivia Newton-John performed to help this community rebuild after devastating fires. This fundraiser was supported by 180 sponsors (*Bank of Sierra, ACM Academy of Country Music Awards*) and 120 volunteers (including *Goody PR* who volunteered based on a request from AnnFlowerPR.com). Fortunately, the concert was sold out, and raised more than $730,000 (*Ventura County Star*) for the community to rebuild. Media coverage included *Entertainment Tonight, EXTRA, KCBS, KEYT, US Weekly,* and many more.

What many people do not understand is that a really great media story is never about your business or event. It is about how your story, brand or service can help others.

NOMINATE AUTHORS MAKING A DIFFERENCE – *GOODY BUSINESS BOOK AWARDS*

Because *Goody PR's* focus is magnifying stories, brands and authors who are making a positive social impact, we launched the *Goody Business Book Awards* to "Uplift Author Voices." Book awards can add great value to your marketing and PR campaigns. These awards were designed to draw attention to authors making a difference with words. You don't have to be donating millions to a cause. You just have to be an author who is helping others improve their lives with a book.

When submitting your book for these annual awards (January 1 – September 30), authors must answer two short questions (1. What is your WHY for writing the book? and 2. How is your book helping other people?) Nominate your book or someone else's book that is improving lives here https://goodybusinessbookawards.com

Step 7.8 Smile. Breathe In. Breathe Out.

For all media interviews, it is really important to smile, breathe in, and breathe out. Even if you are talking about a serious topic, please smile a few times on camera when speaking about something in a positive way (For example, you might smile while saying, "it was heartwarming to see….").

Does this mean that you will never get stage fright on camera? Absolutely not! What it means is that there are things you can do to help you relax and reduce your nerves.

USE A POSITIVE TONE

For all media interviews, use a self-assured tone for the best delivery. If you are confident and rested, this feeling will come across during both phone and on-camera interviews.

To boost your confidence, there many self-help books on this topic. You have heard many of these tips, including follow your passion, find work-life balance, do things that make you feel good, surround yourself with positive people, eat right, do yoga, and take walks on the beach. Whatever works best for you, make it a priority!

There are many reasons why your confidence on camera is important for your life, career and publicity success. If you do not like yourself (be honest here), start creating a plan to make your life better. **To help others as a media spokesperson, speaker or leader, your delivery, tone of voice and story all play a significant role in your message impact and results.**

Depending on your personality and priorities, you might want to read or listen to a self-help book by Jack Canfield (*The Success Principles*), Tim Ferriss (*The 4-Hour Work Week*) or Barbara Corcoran (*Shark Tales*). Whoever inspires you, watch and listen to their words to recharge and identify new ways to share your story.

USE INFLECTION TO VARY YOUR VOICE DURING INTERVIEWS

If you are interviewed on a longer radio show or podcast for 30-60 minutes, try using inflections in your delivery. Instead of talking in the same monotone level throughout a long interview, try laughing, smiling, speaking softly, speaking loudly, and pausing at important points for emphasis.

For a great example of the use of inflection in audio, listen to Ryan Treasure, VP of Operations and Host of the *Finding Your Frequency* show at *VoiceAmerica*. Ryan is also the producer for our *8-Second Branding* Podcast. You can listen to one of his shows, and/or hear his voice during the introduction and closing soundbites for our podcast here https://goodypr.com/8-second-branding.

BREATHE IN. BREATHE OUT.

Breathing in and out is also really important when you are preparing for media interviews. One of my media coaches recommended breathing exercises when I was nervous before TV interviews. Before going on-camera, it really did help to take a deep breath and then let it out to calm my nerves.

Another technique that I recommend is meditation. Your meditation can be in many different formats. You can try yoga, sit in a quiet meditative state, or simply close your eyes and visualize what you want in life.

Another way to meditate is called a walking meditation. Avoid talking on the phone or listening to music on your walk, and instead, just let your mind go where it wants too. You'd be surprised what soundbites and ideas may come to you on these walks.

If you are not relaxed, confident, and happy inside, your anxiety will show on camera. While I did thousands of training presentations early in my corporate career, speaking to a really large audience was nerve wracking. When I did my breathing exercises, it really helped for TV and speaking opportunities, especially when using props.

Liz H Kelly

OVERCOMING STAGE FRIGHT –
MEGA BOOK MARKETING CONFERENCE SPEECH

When I was asked to speak on stage as a testimonial in front of 700 people at the *Mega Book Marketing* conference with Mark Victor Hansen (*Chicken Soup for the Soul* series Co-Author) about how his program helped me book hundreds of media interviews, it was overwhelming. To calm my nerves, I used a prop. Inside the big hotel ballroom in Los Angeles, wearing sunglasses on stage made me more confident. With a big smile, I explained how grateful I was to Mark and the conference speakers for making me a "rock star author" with over 300 media interviews (at the time) - and emphasized that the authors there could do it too.

We met so many "media greats" at this conference, including Mark's *Chicken Soup for the Soul* series Co-Author Jack Canfield, bestselling author and Radio Interview Pro Alex Carroll, *New York Times* bestselling author Brendan Burchard (*Life's Golden Ticket*) and *National Publicity Summit* Co-Founder Steve Harrison. We are forever grateful for what we learned there, which really launched our public relations career.

Whatever you need to do to feel good inside for interviews, do it before, during, and after each opportunity. Dig deep into the emotions about whatever the interview topic may be. How does it make you feel? Are you proud, grateful, honored, happy, cheering and/or moved? And then let that emotion come out in your tone of voice and facial expressions.

BONUS CONTENT - SPEAKER COACH TONI CARUSO
TIPS ON *8-SECOND BRANDING*

For anyone interested in becoming a paid speaker, we highly recommend listening to our *8-Second Branding* Podcast interview with *Academy4Speakers* Founder Toni Caruso from September 30, 2021.

During this fun exchange, Toni explains how speakers can take their target audience through a journey with a powerful brand story that builds raving fans. She emphasizes the importance of identifying Your WHY - plus WHY people should care – and the importance of leaving your audience on a high note! Toni also shares her views on whether speakers should use a *PowerPoint*.

Plus, Toni uncovers 5 Things Every Speaker Needs in Place when a speaking opportunity comes up. And to help you get booked for more speaking gigs, Toni uncovers what to write in a pitch letter to an event chairperson. Plus, you'll learn how to be part of Toni's speakers community and upcoming events. For more tips, listen to this podcast on our *Goody PR podcast* page https://goodypr.com/8-second-branding.

CHAPTER 7 RECAP

When it comes to media interview showtime, this chapter is about presenting your magic clearly to reporters with confidence and conviction to maximize the response. Results may include more social media followers, increased sales or raising more money for a cause. By connecting with the audience with powerful messages, you are much more likely to achieve your media goals.

Step 7 Action Items -
Magnify Your Interviews with Meaningful Soundbites

1. Practice your talking points with 8-second messaging in mind.
2. Be grateful and a great guest.
3. Dress for success for TV interviews.
4. Speak from the heart with a genuine interest in others.
5. Speak with clarity and conviction, even if you get thrown off.
6. Be entertaining and interesting (tell me something I do not know).
7. Give real-life examples of how you helped others.
8. Smile. Breathe in. Breathe out.

PR Superpower 7 - Message Impact Superpower

With your Message Impact Superpower, you will now be able to get your point across in a way that is even more meaningful and memorable.

Chapter 7 - 8-Second PR Challenges

As we close Chapter 7, here are your *8-Second PR* Challenges:

1. What are the three to five key talking points for your story?
2. What are 3 things you can do to be a great guest for media interviews?
3. What styles and colors make you look great on camera?
4. What can you say if you get an unexpected question from a reporter?
5. What's different about your story versus others doing similar things?
6. How are you helping others?
7. What are you doing to create balance in your life?
8. How can you relax before interviews?

Your Message Impact Superpower will make people want to pay more attention to your brand and mission, so they stop multi-tasking and actually listen! By practicing your interview skills, your messages can go viral, sales will increase, and you will get invited back for repeat interviews.

In the next and final chapter, we will talk more about how to follow-up with reporters with new story ideas to increase your media hits. Reinventing your story can literally make your brand stay in the news for years (which is why we keep talking about it)!

Reminder:

"YOU WILL GET ALL YOU WANT IN LIFE, IF YOU HELP ENOUGH OTHER PEOPLE GET WHAT THEY WANT."

— ZIG ZEIGLER

STEP 8

STORY
REINVENTION

Reposition Your Story
and Extend Media Success

"YOU CANNOT USE UP CREATIVITY.
THE MORE YOU USE, THE MORE YOU HAVE."

– OSCAR WILDE

A re you ready to come up with 100 different ways to pitch your story to the media? Do you like brainstorming innovative ideas for your brand promotions based on the season, news or a launch? We're almost at the end of this *8-Second PR* book. Before we wrap-up, we saved the most important skill and case studies for this final chapter. Unless you only want to be in business for three months, your story reinvention skill is a must for long-term marketing and public relations success.

While many businesses and authors make the mistake of planning short-term publicity campaigns, the reality is PR is a marathon, not a sprint. To keep your company, product or service in the headlines, you need to be dedicated to your long-term publicity success. And with diligence, your new PR skills and a little luck, your stars will line up for mega media success. You just can't give up!

You want to continually follow-up with reporters by presenting a new story angle that may include new products/services, a new perspective on a timely topic, a new spokesperson's story, a new and relevant study with your unique perspective, and/or a new version of your book.

COMMIT TO LONG - TERM PR VERSUS BEING A "ONE-HIT WONDER" CAMPAIGN

PR repositioning means continually updating your Wow Story, media hooks, and pitches to stay relevant and timely - so you consistently raise awareness, attract loyal fans, and increase sales.

Many authors and businesses make the mistake of only planning for a 3-6 month public relations campaign. If a publication says "No" to a story pitch, some think that is the end of the conversation. Instead, it may be the beginning of an ongoing dialogue that gets you national publicity.

As an example, *Goody PR* originally pitched *Warriors Heart* residential treatment program to the *TODAY* Show 10+ months before this gamechanger interview happened. It was a process where we worked closely with the *Warriors Heart* team and the *TODAY* Show producers. And yes, there were bumps, every step of the way. The interview was actually scheduled, cancelled and then rescheduled two months later with a different angle (stand by for more on this mega media success story later in this chapter.)

If you are focused only on a short-term marketing plan, that might be okay for a hobby book. However, if you are promoting a brand that is central to a revenue-generating business, you must make a commitment of time and money for your PR.

PR SUPERPOWER 8 – STORY REINVENTION SUPERPOWER

To keep the interest of the media, influencers, and fans, you must master your Story Reinvention Superpower. This skill can help you reposition your story with new media hooks and powerful pitches that connect with reporters and your target audience - over and over and over again.

Asking questions, listening, and being able to change course are some of the most powerful PR tools for new and repeat interviews. You cannot sustain your business or a marketing campaign by doing the same thing over and over again. To have Ultimate Media Success, you must keep the creativity going - for years - using this *8-Second PR* Superpower!

STEP 8 ACTION ITEMS - REPOSITION YOUR STORY AND EXTEND MEDIA SUCCESS

1. Revise your media hooks so they are relevant and timely.
2. Build long-term media relationships to increase Follow-up Stories.
3. Prioritize media follow-up over everything.
4. Be patient, persistent, and never desperate in your follow-up.
5. Measure marketing results and Calculated Publicity Value.

6. Consistently reflect on lessons learned to improve your publicity approach.
7. Hold regular PR strategy meetings to reposition your story.
8. Revise your media hooks, and go back to Step 1.

PR SUPERPOWER 8 - STORY REINVENTION SUPERPOWER

The media is always looking for something new and different. A good PR professional and marketing team know how to consistently reposition your story to attract more media coverage. Great PR is a never-ending process that requires dedication, passion and creativity. By thinking differently, you can find ways to update your Wow Story and consistently stay in the headlines.

For example, I was fortunate to book over 700 media hits for Tom the Tax Expert over 5.5 years by constantly repositioning his tax saving tips based on the headline news. No matter who is President or in Congress, there are always new tax proposals and debates that need credible experts to explain it. To stay relevant and in the news, I regularly brainstormed with Tom and his team new media hooks. And because Tom LOVES taxes, speaks with enthusiasm, and uses a simplified approach to make taxes "fun, easy and understandable", it made him a great guest to continual pitch. The media hooks were constantly updated based on the latest tax proposals, tax season topics and legal ways to permanently reduce your taxes year-round.

Let's take a closer look at these winning PR Strategies for long-term publicity.

Step 8.1 Revise Your Media Hooks so they are Relevant and Timely

To stay in the headlines long-term, you must continually find ways to make your brand story relevant to the current news and/or timely. Every morning, we scan the latest news on apps and think about ways to connect headlines to our clients in pitches.

The fastest way to get an interview is to connect your story to what the media is already covering. Check out this example to see how this works:

CASE STUDY – CNN HLN WEEKEND EXPRESS – PERFECT PITCH!

As a story reinvention example, here is a case study about how patience and persistence paid off at last when the stars lined up for this Perfect Pitch for a *Goody PR* client!

In January 2021, I had previously pitched *CNN HLN Weekend Express* different media hooks for five different clients for almost 18 months before finally getting a YES for a national TV interview!

Because we pitched the perfect spokesperson at the perfect time with the perfect story, we got a YES within 5 minutes via a text! Let's look at how this happened!

For Martin Luther King Weekend, the spokesperson we pitched was Black Business Leader, Former GM, Executive Coach and Award-Winning Author Omar L. Harris who has written five leadership books. As a result of his work and unique POV (Point of View), below is our timely media hook:

Timely - For MLK Day/Weekend

PITCH - Why We Need more Servant Leaders like MLK – who showed us how to Lead with Love (especially at a time when our country is so divided - this was right after January 6, 2021.)

Harris wrote a relevant book called *The Servant Leaders Manifesto* that featured MLK Jr., and the importance of using "humility, will and empathy" as a leader. This book was featured by *CNN* during this interview, and added value to the story and PR.

To prepare Omar, I did media coaching on Saturday via *Zoom* before his early Sunday morning interview. The biggest tip that I shared was to get to the point immediately because TV interviews go so fast. Together, we practiced his first answer several times where he mentioned MLK's lessons about love and his book.

This national TV interview was a huge win for the author on many levels. It was about four minutes on Martin Luther King Weekend, promoted his book, and they incorporated images of MLK Jr. during the segment.

Step 8.2 Build Long-term Media Relationships to Increase Follow-up Stories

To extend your media success, you also need to build your "warm" relationships with media. Whether it is a producer, host, reporter, columnist, or blogger, meeting in person can go a long way towards building long-term relationships so you can regularly contact them with new pitches. If you cannot meet them face-to-face, schedule a Zoom call, follow them on social media and comment on their posts and/or find other ways to connect to build lasting connections!

For example, I've invested in our book PR and clients by attending the *National Publicity Summit (NPS)* in New York City several times to meet reporters IRL (in real life). This conference is one of the best opportunities to meet media in person and pitch ideas directly to them. Since the pandemic started, *NPS* Co-Founders Steve and Bill Harrison have offered this program online via *Zoom*. In 2021, we attended using this new format, and immediately saw the incredible value of virtual video connections. This conference is not cheap, but well-worth the investment. It also provides invaluable practice giving two minute pitches directly to reporters and getting their feedback. We cannot recommend this conference enough!

8 SECOND BRANDING PODCAST – STEVE HARRISON – NATIONAL PUBLICITY SUMMIT

To learn more about the how to get national media coverage, all authors should listen to our *8-Second Branding* podcast interview with *National Publicity Summit* Co-Founder Steve Harrison. During this fun conversation,

Steve shares tips for how to get booked on a national TV show. His summit has helped authors and experts get booked on the *TODAY Show, Good Morning America, CBS Mornings, CNN, MSNBC, The View, FOX News*, in the *New York Times* and many more media.

For the *National Publicity Summit*, Harrison and his team of experts provide attendees with training and coaching prior to the live Meet the Media sessions. During the pandemic, the *National Publicity Summit* shifted from in-person to Zoom, where authors are given two minutes to pitch the reporter and get immediate feedback!

I feel very fortunate to have met Steve in 2003 at the *Mega Book Marketing* Conference (Hosted by Mark Victor Hansen and Jack Canfield, *Chicken Soup for the Soul* series co-authors) while promoting my first book. His author training over the years, *RTIR (Radio-TV Interview Report)* Magazine and *National Publicity Summit* have been gamechangers for our career and business.

In addition, Steve is Co-Founder of Author Success and the *Quantum Leap Publicity and Marketing* Program. He is the chief instructor for most *Author Success* training programs, and is co-creator alongside Jack Canfield of *Bestseller Blueprint.*

Steve's dedicated the last 25 years to helping more than 15,000 non-fiction authors write and/or promote their books on TV, radio, print and podcasts. He's helped launch mega bestselling books such as *Chicken Soup for the Soul series* (Jack Canfield and Mark Victor Hansen), *Men are from Mars, Women are from Venus* (John Gray PhD), and *Rich Dad Poor Dad* (Robert Kiyosaki).

As part of his backstory, Steve was first bitten by the media bug in high school while working as a freelance writer for the local newspaper. A 2:44 marathoner in his younger days, today Steve's running around is mostly limited to the tennis court. Steve has been happily married for more than 30 years to his wife, Laura.

For more information visit https://nationalpublicitysummit.com (tell them I sent you!) and/or visit our *Goody PR* website podcast page to listen to this gamechanger interview here: https://goodypr.com/8-second-branding

If you cannot attend the *National Publicity Summit*, look for other local events and conferences where reporters offer media tips or a chance to meet them in person. For example, we attended the *LA Press Club Southern California Journalism Awards* in downtown Los Angeles – twice. During both events, we got to meet top journalists in a less formal setting. This event was also not cheap, but it was an investment in our company and clients.

Once you build rapport with a reporter over the phone or *Zoom*, you should keep in touch because it is much easier to pitch someone you know versus someone new.

If you are fortunate to meet IRL, be genuine and personable versus a pushy salesperson. You're interested in a long-term media relationship, and never know when the stars will line up for a story. For example, we booked an interview for our first client, Lee Ann Del Carpio (*Rich Dad Hawaii*) with Honolulu reporter Linda Dela Cruz from *MidWeek*. Linda wanted to do a profile story about Lee Ann for the top local newspaper that has a circulation of 800,000 readers. Because it was convenient, the three of us met at a local coffee shop on Oahu for this interview. The story was a home run for the client, who was a local business leader and consultant at the time.

Over ten years later, Linda is my friend on *Facebook*, and is now an Assignment Editor for a top local news station in Honolulu, Hawaii, called *KHON2* (FOX/CW). Fortunately, she has recently booked two TV interviews for our clients. It can be a very small world when doing PR, and your media relationships are gold.

You may also be able to meet reporters in-studio before or after live TV interviews. In all cases, take photos of the producers and hosts with you and the client for social media. Afterwards, always send a sincere thank you email, share their story everywhere and tag them to show you are grateful for their coverage.

Another way to build long-term relationships with reporters is to share their work all over your social media, and tag them. Always post interviews after they are published, and mention both the reporter and outlet in *Facebook, Twitter, Instagram,* and *LinkedIn* posts.

Remember, most reporters are underappreciated and working at warp speed. A genuine thank you can go a long way.

Step 8.3 Prioritize Media Follow-up over Everything

Another way to extend your media success is to build a reputation that you are helpful, provide great guests and follow-up. You've learned How to be a Great Guest, which includes follow-up. You always want to provide digital assets, offer assistance and sincerely thank them every step of the way. Stay on top of any interview request to build their trust that you are a reliable PR source who they can all anytime they need a source.

MANAGE INTERVIEW REQUESTS ACROSS TEAMS

As a reminder, when a reporter emails or calls with a question about a potential or scheduled interview, you should get back to them ASAP. If they are on a deadline, it is especially important to respond, or you may lose the media opportunity.

GOODY PR CASE STUDY - CBS HEALTH WATCH – BIG WIN!

As another example of a BIG media win, we worked on a *CBS Health Watch TV* interview that took about a month of back and forth follow-up emails, calls and filming. We originally pitched a story idea about the *Warriors Heart* Grand Opening on October 15, 2016, as the first private and accredited addiction treatment center exclusively for warriors (military, veterans, and first responders) in the United States.

We pitched the client's event in early October, and got a reply on October 16 from a producer saying they wanted to cover the story, but not the Grand Opening. After tons of follow-up, planning, identifying the best spokespeople and on-site interviews, this news segment aired a month later on November 11 (Veterans Day) on over 150 *CBS TV* stations across the country, which was a better date to reach their core audience.

The time between the early October pitch and the November 11 air date could be a short film about how to partner with your client and the media to produce a powerful news story. We worked closely with the *Warriors Heart* team, the *CBS* producer in New York City and the assigned reporter in Houston, Texas.

Fortunately, the client found great spokespeople, which included a veteran and Gold Star Mother, who was also their clinical director at the time. Both were willing to share their personal stories with the world to help others.

For this story, a *CBS News* crew flew from Houston to San Antonio for the day to film at the *Warriors Heart* ranch on November 2. Our client preferred to have the interviews on November 1 because of a previous business trip planned, but when the *CBS News* crew was unavailable, everyone was flexible and made November 2nd date work.

If you want to feel inspired, watch this *CBS Health Watch* story on *Warriors Heart*'s *YouTube* Channel or website.

(P.S. The Calculated Publicity Value was $394,000, according to a *Nielsen Media* Report.) And yes, *Goody PR* sent everyone involved thank you emails and cheers.

When you get a mega media story like this one, there are endless ways to extend your media success. For example, you can magnify your media by sending out a press release recap, post a video recap, feature it on your *LinkedIn* profile and/or post it as a news story on your website's Press page. You can also submit recaps with photographs to other outlets and reporters.

MANAGE FUTURE STORY REQUESTS

If a reporter says, we'd like to have you or your PR client back soon, follow-up within 24-48 hours. When we booked a doctor on a *KGO 810 AM* radio show in San Francisco, the host said he would like to have them back. We followed up the next day. As a result of continually reinventing the media hook, the same client was on this top radio station four times over four months.

Most reporters and clients are overwhelmed, and so continual follow-up with new ideas is a very important part of anyone's media success!

Step 8.3 Be Patient, Persistent, and Never Desperate in Your Follow-up

If you were dating, I would recommend "be patient, persistent, and never desperate," and the same advice holds true for your follow-up with reporters. While you want to get back to the media ASAP when they ask for an interview, there is a fine line to how much you should contact them afterwards to ensure a story gets published. Remember our *8-Second PR* Baseball Game analogy to getting a story published. Your job is to avoid getting stuck on third base doing endless follow-up because the interview is completed, but not published.

In another case, a client submitted a story to a health publication for review. After many follow-ups, the editor finally replied that they did not have the staff to review it and could not publish it. And then somehow, their story got magically published ten months later without any notice. We were happy to have it show up unexpectedly in our *Google Alerts*.

When submitting a column for publication, it is always a gamble whether it will be published (even if the editor requested it). To get it published, follow-up is key.

CASE STUDY EXAMPLE – MEDIA HIT MARATHON WITH OUT-OF-THE BOX FOLLOW-UP

In another case study example, I pitched a story to a women empowerment column editor called *Bizwomen* for *The Business Journals*. The story was written by Successful Businesswoman, Award-Winning Author and Mentor Therese Allison. For this column to get published, it was a media hit marathon that took months of follow-up and out-of-the-box thinking.

Based on the editor's specific request for a story submission on a unique topic pitched, we emailed Therese's story draft featuring her 3 "Pearls of Wisdom." It was based on her book, *Playing for Keeps – How a 21st century* *businesswoman beat the boys!*, that includes tips for how to become financially independent and retire early.

What I did not know was that the editor somehow (it's a still a mystery) was not getting any of our follow-up emails with the story draft. The email did not have attachments (remember, attachments can send your email into the junk folder, so don't attach anything, unless it is requested). Therese's story text was copied and pasted into the body of the email, but she still never got it?

Because this was the perfect column and business publication for Allison to reach her target market, I refused to give up. Since we did not have the editor's phone number (remember, most media hide their contact information), we connected and messaged her via *LinkedIn*. When she told us to re-send the draft to the same email, there was still no reply via email or *LinkedIn* – even though we kept following up every few weeks.

Instead of giving up at this point, we went to *Google* with our PR team and researched the editor's office address and phone number. During the pandemic, most reporters worked remotely, which made it even harder to get them on the phone. Eventually, we found the right phone number, left a voicemail, and she called us back (a connection at last!). While most reporters don't want calls about pitches, a voicemail may actually make you stand out. The majority of reporters will say they prefer email pitches only. If you are fortunate enough to find the right phone number, and they actually listen to it, you might just get a call back and a story.

When the editor explained that she was still not getting our client's story three months later, I had to think differently. In this scenario, I asked for her personal email to send it too – and Wow, Eureka, that worked! After 3 rounds of editing, she finally approved it. And then, it took another six weeks before it was published!

For this media hit marathon, the client's story was finally published almost 7 months and 20+ follow-ups after the original pitch and story request.

Lesson Learned: If it's an important publication to reach your core audience, don't give up until you get a "No, Never" reply. Instead, get creative with follow-up and remember our mantra, "Be Patient and Persistent, and Never Desperate."

You never know what else is pulling a producer, editor or reporter away from your story. It could be a personal issue, staffing shortage, or just an overwhelming day-to-day with non-stop breaking news. Remember, you are dealing with a person with a life, so be patient and understanding!

In another related scenario, I called the Kansas City, Missouri's *ABC News* newsroom to ask when a pre-recorded interview was scheduled to air. The newsroom contact who answered said, "I am doing two people's jobs right now and it's no offense to you, but I will just forward your email to the producer." My immediate reaction was to acknowledge his feelings, and just say thank you. And, yes this story aired, but it required relentless follow-ups for about a month.

MANAGE STORY EDITS SOFTLY

Once a story is published by a reporter, it is best not to request any changes. Remember, it's their story. You did not pay for their earned media coverage, so the reporter owns it – not you.

Our exception to this rule is if something is inaccurate, really important to fix and easy to update. For example, I contact reporters if a brand name or spokesperson is misspelled, a contact phone number is incorrect or they give the wrong address or website URL by mistake to ask for a correction. Fortunately, it is much easier to ask for changes today because most stories are posted online. However, you always want to walk softly with reporters and only ask for small edits that are important for SEO and accuracy such as a company's name.

Once a TV story has aired, it's impossible to fix the file once the video is published online. However, if the story runs again, the TV outlet may be able to update it. In a rare case, a client's name got fixed in a TV story banner. The segment ran on the 10:00 p.m. news, and then again the following morning at 7:00 a.m. The morning news piece had their name spelled correctly.

We are all human, and mistakes do happen. The key take-away is to ask nicely and understand the limitations reporters face when requesting edits. It is always best to send your edits in writing with "Current" and "Correct" headings and then the corrections below so they can easily copy and paste the right version. Whatever you do, make edits obvious for reporters.

And don't be afraid to keep calling back if it is an important edit such as your brand name, and it's not fixed after the first call.

Step 8.5 Measure Marketing Results and Calculated Publicity Value

Clients are always looking for ways to measure their marketing, PR and social media results. There are many ways to calculate the value for earned media.

You should discuss goals and document them at the beginning of any marketing contract or PR campaign so everyone is on the same page. You want to set expectations, and avoid misunderstandings across the team. Always ask your clients upfront about their desired outcomes when creating a marketing or publicity campaign. Goals may include raising brand awareness, increasing book sales, attracting more customers, getting a column in a niche publication, receiving more speaking invitations and/or being in a specific media outlet.

To provide you with insights, here are eight ways to measure the business impacts of earned media.

8 WAYS TO MEASURE BUSINESS IMPACTS OF EARNED MEDIA

For TV, print, radio and podcast interviews, you can measure media success using these numbers:

1. Increase in social media followers (it helps if the outlet has a lot of followers).
2. Increase in social engagement (likes, comments, shares.)
3. Increase in website traffic (a high UVPM – Unique Visitors Per Month - to a website helps).

4. Changes in donations to a cause (this number can give you a dollar value).
5. Invitations for speaking presentations (as a result of being in the news).
6. Increase in enrollments for a class or event (how many new people signed up?).
7. Increase in book sales and/or *Amazon* rank (did your book rank go up?).
8. Increase in sales and customers (did more people buy your product?).

We also make it very clear to potential clients that if their goal is to make enough money in book sales to pay our monthly retainer fee, they are not being realistic (unless they are a celebrity or well-known author with a major book deal). It's better to think of a book as a business card or lead-generator because it usually pays very little in royalties.

It important to understand that a "successful book" sells 10,000 copies. If you are only making fifty cents to a few dollars for each book sale from the publisher or *Amazon*, the earnings will probably never cover a six month minimum PR contract. Instead, public relations is a long-term investment in your business and brand.

As an example, my dating book resulted in a $10,000 royalty advance from *Kensington Books*. Because you have to sell enough books to cover the advance first, I never received any more money from the publisher. Overall, *Smart Man Hunting* sold about 11,000 copies. For the international rights, I did receive another $2,300 in royalty checks from Russian and Taiwan distributors. I also made some money selling additional services, which included Internet Dating Profile Makeovers and Dating Coaching. We are not doing dating coaching anymore, but it is important for you to sell services and packages if you want to make money from a book.

Overall, I estimate investing $100,000+ in time and money to promote the three versions of our dating book over five years. We took money out of our IRA to pay for two publicists, a web developer, event costs, travel, magazine ads, media coaching and

MANY how-to promote your book seminars, including the *National Publicity Summit* that we recommended earlier. However, the real return on investment did not happen until much later when I started my *Goody PR* company to promote primarily small businesses, CEOs, experts and authors.

If you have a consulting business and write a book about your area of expertise, a book can be a great lead-generator to attract clients. Along with helping others do their own PR, this business model is one of the main reasons for writing this *8-Second PR* book.

CASE STUDY EXAMPLE -
BOOKS ARE GREAT LEAD GENERATORS

The number one way our former client and Tax Expert Tom Wheelwright attains clients is through people who read his *Tax-Free Wealth* book. At one point, Tom discovered that he had 900 books on back-order on *Amazon*. Because this level of demand for a book is so rare unless you are a household name, his publisher asked how did this happen? The author's response was "Well, we hired a PR company!"

Of course, the backlog was a team effort, and *Goody PR* does not take full credit for this success. However, this backorder news was a GREAT PR RESULT for our client, who continued to invest in public relations as a long-term business expense.

For media interviews, there are several things to consider when measuring earned media for TV, print, radio and podcast stories. All of these points are important to consider when evaluating your ROI (Return on Investment) for public relations.

HOW TO MEASURE VALUE AND ROI FOR
EARNED MEDIA

Measuring Print Interviews

- UVPM – Unique Visitors Per Month (monthly website visitors).

- Is it a national or local publication?

- If local, what is the DMA (Designated Market Area) for the location? The DMA indicates the nationwide rank of the media market. The higher the DMA, the more people you are likely to reach. For example, NYC is DMA 1, Los Angeles is DMA 2, and Kansas City is DMA 32.

- Did the story get republished and/or syndicated (And, how many times)?

Measuring Radio Interviews

- Average number of listeners.

- Is it a national or local radio show?

- If local, what is the DMA for the market?

- Did the story get syndicated (picked up and shared by others)?

- What is the number of the station's watts?

- 10,000 watts is the minimum required for *Clear Channel* Stations.

- 50,000 watts is best because it is the highest power authorized for AM stations. The signal for a station with more watts will travel farther and reach a bigger audience.

Measuring Podcast Interviews

- What is the average number of monthly downloads?

- How many listeners do they usually reach?

- Who is their niche audience? (This question is very important for podcasts who can reach your target market. In this case, quality over quantity of listeners may be more important.)

- Is it a radio show and a podcast? (For example, *Girls on The Air 1590 KVTA* Ventura CA does both. The show is LIVE on Saturdays, and is later posted as a podcast on Mondays).

- How many major podcast platforms will republish your interview (*Apple Podcasts, Stitcher, iHeartRadio*, etc.)?

- How many podcast reviews have they received? And what is their overall rating?

- How many business referrals have you received as a result of podcasts? (Remember, this media type is the best way to reach your niche audience).

Measuring TV Interviews

- Average number of viewers during that time and day of the week.
- Is it national or local TV?
- If local, what is the DMA (Designated Market Area) for the market?
- Did the story get replayed and/or syndicated (picked up and shared by other outlets)?
- What time of day did the story run? (primetime gets the most viewers)
- What would it cost to run an ad for the same length in the same timeframe?
- What is the Calculated Publicity Value? (Earned media is often worth three times a paid ad played during the same hour. The publicity value is the ad value x3.)

While there are many ways to measure the success of your earned media, we are a huge fan of the *Nielsen Media* Research Reports that *Goody PR* orders with copies of TV interviews from our clipping service. These reports show the time, audience size, advertising cost, and gives a dollar value for the coverage. Sharing this value information with clients is very helpful for providing a ROI perspective. *Nielsen* is also a credible source for media data and measurement.

ROI CASE STUDY - CALCULATED PUBLICITY VALUE FOR TV INTERVIEW - $46,000+

For example, when our client was interviewed on *KTLA 5* Los Angeles for a book launch, it aired for 5.5 minutes, which is really long for local TV. The Calculated Publicity Value, according to a *Nielsen Media* Report, was over $46,000 because of the length and major market.

Because Los Angeles is DMA 2 (Designated Marketing Area), the Calculated Publicity Value is much higher than if the story ran in most U.S. cities.
It is very important to understand different ways to measure success. Another way to explain the ROI is that your earned media is worth 3x the value as paid media.

In this case, if you bought ads for the same amount of time on *KTLA*, the cost estimate is $15,540. If you multiply this cost x3, the Calculated Publicity Value = $46,620.

Social media marketing measurements are a completely different story. It is about exposure, engagement and Calls to Action. I could write a whole book about the strategies for valuing fan engagements (go back to Chapter 2 on Digital PR if you want a Refresher.)

8-SECOND PR – MARKETING AND PUBLIC RELATIONS CLASSES ON TEACHABLE

If you want to learn more, we now offer *8-Second PR* marketing and public relations classes online. Based on feedback from authors and experts, we offer this as an option with videos and workbooks for you to expand your knowledge.

For more information, visit our book website https://8SecondPR.com or *Teachable* page here: https://8-second-pr.teachable.com/.

If you are not getting the desired results from your marketing and PR campaigns, it is probably time to reposition your story. To develop new media hooks, consider a different spokesperson, look at how you can connect your story to headline news, schedule a special event and/or do a fundraiser for your charity.

It is hard to predict what media hook or angle will click with a reporter. Keep reminding yourself over and over again to "Never Give Up". Go for a walk or run when you need a break and/or want to recharge. Do A/B testing on social media posts to get feedback, ask for input at your favorite local coffee shop and/or hire a PR professional or agency.

Step 8.6 Consistently Reflect on Lessons Learned to Improve Your Approach

By now you may have started pitching ideas to the media, and gotten a few rejections. It's important to "fail forward" in your PR marathon and reflect on the lessons learned along the way. Mistakes will happen in your marketing and public relations campaigns. By taking time to reflect, they can make your PR even stronger.

"Everything you want is on the other side of fear," **explains** *Jack Canfield,* Author of *The Success Principles* and Co-Author of the *Chicken Soup for the Soul series.*

Using *Constant Contact* is a great way to test story ideas via email because it tells you what percent of reporters actually opened the pitch email – and when.

In some cases, the first email pitch may result in an immediate interview request. This result happened when *TMZ* asked to interview *Modern Family* Executive Producer Danny Zuker about his new political humor book. In this case, we sent a personalized pitch with the email subject line: Why Emmy Winner Danny Zuker Launches New Humor Book This Week – and got a quick reply asking for an interview. (Remember, Zuker is a celebrity, but this type of response can happen for a "perfect pitch" like the *CNN* MLK Weekend interview previously discussed.)

In most cases, you will be left wondering what will work best, which is why doing public relations takes practice. A pitch with a sense of urgency connected to a holiday or a local expert usually gets more interest. However, you may still find yourself baffled with no replies to your media hooks and pitches. Don't give up!

GOODY PR CASE STUDIES - PITCH EMAIL OPEN RATES - WHAT FINALLY WORKED!

As an example of a baffling email pitching experience with a happy ending, *Goody PR* pitched a local profile story for over one year to the Kansas City, Missouri, media.

The unique media hook was about a local WWII U.S. Marine Cpl. Don Evans, who is now featured in a WWII military history book called *40 Thieves on Saipan*. Evans story was pretty unknown and had not been covered in his hometown – despite having three nephews. The client really wanted to reach this market to honor Evans, who made the ultimate sacrifice in his dad's platoon during the Battle of Saipan.

Our PR team called and followed up MANY times with specifically targeted Kansas City media hooks and pitches. Other national outlets had covered Evans' story, but we could not break through in his hometown. We were stumped!

One year after our initial PR campaign for this book, we were fortunate to secure a feature story on *KMBC/ABC News* and *KCWE /CW* in Kansas City. This Veterans Day profile piece highlighted Evans as a local high school football star who was Mr. Kansas City twice, and gave up a football scholarship to *Kansas University* to become a U.S. Marine.

Because Evans remains are buried at the *Punchbowl* in Honolulu, Hawaii, and the author was going to visit his grave at the National Memorial Cemetery of the Pacific for Veterans Day 2021, that was the timely event that suddenly clicked - and made this story happen!

To illustrate our attempts, below are four pitches sent to Kansas City media reporters about Cpl Don Evans with the different email Open Rates:

22% Open Rate - 11/1/21 – This one WORKED! Local *ABC* & *CW* News at Last!

Veterans Day Story - MEDIA ALERT for KMBC-TV - Kansas City WWII US Marine to be honored on Hawaii Tribute Trip for Veterans Day

12% Open Rate - 5/19/21

Memorial Day Story - Timely Pitch for (Media Outlet) - Honoring 2 Kansas City WWII Marine Corps Heroes

(There were actually 2 U.S. Marines from Kansas City in the "40 Thieves" platoon.)

22% Open Rate - 4/19/21 – Resulted in a KC National Radio interview

Timely Pitch for (Media Outlet) - How **Kansas City WWII Veteran** wrote Moving **Letters** to **Gold Star Mother**

17% Open Rate – 9/22/20

MEDIA ALERT - Kansas City Story - Gold Star Mother's Day Sept 27th Book Talk Reading

Step 8.7 Hold Regular PR Strategy Meetings to Reinvent Your Story

As we have discussed, marketing and public relations campaigns should be an ongoing process with different initiatives that go way beyond a short-term PR blitz. If the company wants to stay in business (which most do, of course), you want to be always looking for new ways to promote products, services, books, and/or the expert spokespeople.

For example, we meet at least monthly with *Goody PR* clients to have a formal strategy meeting with report summaries. While we are constantly brainstorming new media hooks and opportunities with them, this scheduled meeting gives the team (*Goody PR* and the client) a chance to discuss updates on the most recent company updates, media hits, current interviews in progress, press releases, suggestions, action item notes – plus new pitch ideas.

To help you maximize PR results if you hire an agency or have an internal publicity team, here are our top 7 collaboration tips for CEOs, authors and business owners.

7 PR AGENCY COLLABORATION TIPS - FOR CEOS, AUTHORS, SMALL BUSINESS OWNERS

1. **Participate in Monthly PR Meetings** – Meet with your PR team a minimum of once a month to brainstorm new media hook ideas and newsworthy topics for your business, book, product or service. Pitching the same story about your "cool company" or "program" will not work long-term. Regular strategy meetings will help you plan, minimize surprises, and produce better media results.

2. **Find Great Spokespeople** – Regularly identify experts with unique stories and tips that can help educate audiences at your desired media outlets with a unique POV (Point of View). Your spokesperson will often vary depending on the topic.

3. **Provide Timely Responses to Interview Requests** - Get back to your PR team as soon as possible when there is an interview request. Try to respond within one hour for TV and one day for radio/podcasts/print.

4. **Complete Written Answers within 1 Week** - If you get a request to answer questions in writing and/or contribute a guest column, send it back within one week. We lost a story with a top magazine that a client requested to reach their target audience because the expert took over a month to reply to the reporter's questions. By that time, the reporter went on leave. Don't do this please!

5. **Do Your Homework before Interviews to be a Great Guest** – Being a great guest is not about just showing up. You need to research the reporter's background on *LinkedIn* or their website, check out their previous stories, listen to their podcast, and/or watch a video with them speaking. And when the record button starts, be ready to share educational and entertaining soundbites!

6. **Follow-up with your PR Team after Every Interview** – Remember, it took 20 emails/texts/calls and a lot of planning to get your interview scheduled. Always, follow-up with your PR team to tell them how the interview went and if the reporter said anything about next steps.

Liz H Kelly

7. **Thank and Share after Every Interview is Published** – Once a story is published, don't forget to thank EVERYONE who played a role (reporter, PR team, producers, executive assistants, etc.) and share the story online. The reporters are counting on you to promote your interview on social media – and you want to be invited back – right?

Your Story Reinvention Superpower should be used continuously if you want to stay in business! This PR collaboration process is what can keep your brand relevant and in the news. It is fun for me, and why I love brand storytelling. If you also like this brainstorming, you can enjoy repositioning your story – over and over again.

To illustrate this point, here's a case study that we love:

CASE STUDY -
ROCK THE VOTE CAMPAIGN FOR BOOK LAUNCH

When *Goody PR* first started working with *Modern Family* EP Danny Zuker's on a PR campaign for his new political humor book, *He Started It*, the 2018 Midterm Elections were just three months away. Because the book was about a "*Twitter* War" in 2013, we needed to make the story more current.

As a result, I recommended a #RockTheVote Campaign with the book dedicated to voters. The team loved the idea, and everyone worked with Zuker to add more PR tactics to the campaign, which, included:

Charitybuzz **Auction for Your Charity** – This platform is like an *eBay* for charity. You can post an auction item and select your charity. People then bid for two weeks, and the highest bidder wins. The prize was a *Modern Family* set tour in Los Angeles, an autographed script written and signed by the Emmy Winner Danny Zuker and the cast, along with four autographed books. The winning bid was $2,750.00, which was split 80/20 between the designated charity and *Charitybuzz*.

Digital Hollywood Producers Panel and Book Table – Because the author is a successful TV executive and writer, we pitched Zuker as a panelist and organized a book table during a happy hour at this digital media conference. We got the green light for both elements from the organizer, and about 150 people attended the panel.

#RockTheVote Book Talk and Signing – To reach more digital influencers, we worked with the *Social Media Club Los Angeles* to host a special #RockheVote book talk and signing two weeks before the midterms that was attended by digital influencers.

Pop Culture and Politics Media Hook – Because Zuker's current tweets about breaking news were regularly quoted in media stories, we repositioned him as a *"Twitter* Historian", who could weigh in on how pop culture and politics were colliding (Fortunately, this media hook resulted in a timely *CNN* interview.)

Media Interview Results – Based on continual brand story updates, events, charity auction, and team approach, the top media placements included *CNN, CNN International, TMZ Live, The Howard Stern Wrap-Up Show, The Adam Carolla Show* (huge podcast!), *Chicago Tribune, Los Angeles Times, Dr. Drew Midday Live with Lauren Sivan, FOX 11 Los Angeles* (3 interviews on different shows), *KTLA, AXS,* bloggers, podcasts, and more.

This repositioning exercise made the book even more relevant to current events with the election just weeks away. Simply by changing the book dedication and media hook angle, this #RocktheVote PR campaign turned into a much bigger story with an average of 15 unique media interviews per month. Ok, yes, Danny Zuker is like a celebrity as an Executive Producer for *Modern Family,* but his book was not about the show. Our goal is to secure 2-3 interviews per month, and *Goody PR* usually gets an average of 5 per client, so 15 unique interviews per month is really off-the-charts.

Step 8.8 Reinvent Your Story Hooks and Go Back to Step 1

Is your head now filled with new ideas to attract more media and build long-term relationships with reporters? The overall theme throughout this chapter (and really this book) has been the power of reinventing a brand story to get continual earned media - so more people are talking about your brand.

The *8-Second PR* process is actually a lot like writing a book. The first draft is horrible, and then you re-write it 20-30 times to shape a compelling story until it has an emotional connection and "wow factor". If you like doing this exercise over and over again, marketing and public relations can be a great career. It may feel like *Groundhog Day*. However, if you do it right, this process can be a lot more fun!

And now for the finale, here's the story-behind-the-story with how our client got on the TODAY Show. These PR insights are being shared to help you get mega media by pitching a new angle. And yes, you will need a lot of patience and persistence.

GOODY PR CASE STUDY – *TODAY* SHOW – *WARRIORS HEART* TAKE 2 EVEN BETTER!

Getting our long-term PR client, *Warriors Heart*, on the *TODAY* Show was a dream come true for pretty much everyone involved. As a reminder, *Warriors Heart* is the first and ONLY private and accredited treatment program in the U.S. that is exclusively for military, veterans and first responders struggling with drug and alcohol addiction, PTS (post-traumatic stress), mild TBI (traumatic brain injury) and co-occurring issues (depression, anxiety, and more).

This mega media hit journey had a lot of moving pieces and people involved, and is a great example of the power of revising a story to secure a media home run. It's also an important reminder that if you don't get a YES right way, there may be something even better on the horizon.

In July 2018, we were fortunate to have a fan of *Warriors Heart* introduce us to a *TODAY* Show producer. This email introduction was the beginning of a 10-month journey to the finish line to their live TV interview in Studio 1A in February 2019.

Two people had volunteered to be spokespeople, and their authentic and moving story is really what made this segment so impactful.

Former Green Beret and *Warriors Heart* Alumni Teddy Lanier volunteered to tell his powerful long-term recovery story about overcoming a 17-year opioid addiction. With confidence and conviction, Teddy explained how his counselor, *Warriors Heart* Clinical Manager and Licensed Chemical Dependency Counselor (LCDC), Vonnie Nealon "saved his life."

The *TODAY* Show is also very supportive of veterans. *The 3rd Hour of TODAY* had started a segment called GRIT, that likes to feature success stories. Fortunately, the producers felt that this story was perfect match for their audience.

To get to the finish line (where the segment actually aired), the *TODAY* Show did separate pre-interviews with Teddy and Vonnie, along with requesting videos of them. Because neither one had been on local or national TV, the producers wanted to see how they came across on camera. (A request for a video is very typical from a TV producer, so make sure you have a video of yourself ready to go!).

After many calls, emails and scheduling bumps, the "Take 1" interview was originally scheduled for December 2018 as a "Hope for the Holidays" segment where the *TODAY* Show planned to visit Teddy's hometown and interview his relatives as a Part 1 of the segment, and then Part 2 was going to be LIVE in the studio with Teddy and Vonnie.

After the flights were booked, one week before, we got the call that the interview was CANCELLED – but they still "loved their story" and "wanted to receive updates" if anything changed for a future potential interview.

Teddy and Vonnie were devastated (and so was everyone on the team), of course. They thought they did something wrong. When I called the producer to ask for honest feedback, she said, "No, they did nothing wrong and we are still interested. It just did not work for right now, and please keep us posted if anything changes with Teddy or Vonnie."

A few weeks later during our January 2019 monthly PR strategy call, I asked the team if there were any "updates" on either Teddy or Vonnie. *Warriors Heart* Co-Founder Lisa Lannon explained that Teddy was going to visit their residential treatment ranch in Texas in February for a "recharge". (These return visits are done by some *Warriors Heart* Alumni as part of their aftercare. During these trips, alumni often share their recovery story with the current clients in treatment to provide hope and inspiration).

So we went back to the *TODAY* Show to pitch a revised "Take 2" segment with this update about Teddy's "recharge" visit. The show LOVED the idea of a renewal and recovery story. As a result, the revised segment idea for the *3ʳᵈ Hour of TODAY* show turned out even better than the first "Hope for the Holidays" story idea.

For this Take 2, a *TODAY* Show crew flew to the *Warriors Heart's* 543-acre ranch in Bandera, Texas (near San Antonio) for Part 1 of the story (versus going to his hometown to interview family over the holidays). They did interviews with Teddy and Vonnie on-site about his "recharge", long-term recovery story, the importance of healing with peers, and how *Warriors Heart* and Vonnie "saved Teddy's life."

This Take 2 approach was 10x better because it really gave viewers a sense how *Warriors Heart's* ranch is a very healing place. It included b-roll video of Teddy fishing at the *Warriors Heart* lake, sitting by the fire pit where a lot of peer support happens, and walking around the residential treatment ranch with Vonnie.

For this Take 2, Part 2 of the interview was at *NBC Studios* in the historic 30 Rockefeller Plaza. Vonnie and Teddy flew to New York City for *President's Day* Weekend for this Monday morning interview. To better prepare them, I worked with Vonnie and Teddy doing media training the week prior, and flew to NYC to offer on-site support and coaching along the way.

When we went to the Green Room, the magic started to unfold. All the preparation, phone calls, emails, and TEAMWORK for the past ten months came together.

This *TODAY* Show segment was over 7.5 minutes with the first 2 minutes at the ranch, and then 5.5 minutes LIVE in their Studio 1A. Teddy and Vonnie shared a very moving story from the heart (no pun intended) with great soundbites (previously covered in this book) that came out naturally. (Remember, they did not memorize a script.)

And P.S., the shorter 2-minute segment filmed at the *Warriors Heart* ranch aired again on *MSNBC*. One of the *TODAY* Show interviewers, Craig Melvin, was anchoring there later that day. He re-introduced the story, and this part of the segment was replayed.

Because it was technically a holiday (*President's Day*), there was very little breaking news, which probably made it possible to get more air time on national TV. 7.5+ minutes is REALLY long for national TV because most segments are 2-3 minutes. We've seen up to 6 minutes, and this was a first for 7.5 minutes.

To truly understand the significant impact of this *TODAY* Show interview and story, we highly recommend that you watch it on the *Warriors Heart* website and/or *YouTube*.

And according to the *Nielsen Media* Research Report sent by our video clipping service, the Calculated Publicity Value was the highest we've ever seen. It reached 4.1 million people, and the total airtime was 9 minutes 52 seconds when you combine the *TODAY* Show story with the *MSNBC* replay.

To celebrate, *Warriors Heart* posted this story with gratitude on their social media. We also shared it everywhere, and gave thanks to everyone on the team involved. When someone asked about "the team", I explained that the team was *Goody PR* plus the client plus Teddy plus the *TODAY* Show producers and hosts, and everyone else involved. In this case, it went way beyond "just show up for an interview." And this example shows why working as a team on PR is so important. Everyone plays a key role in these big media wins!

Goody PR is truly grateful to have worked with teams to promote small businesses, brand experts CEOs/Founders and author clients for years on a monthly retainer. We prefer these long-term clients because we LOVE being part of their team. As a PR collaborator, we continually revise their message and media outreach strategies. It is also more powerful to be part of an overall business plan and see the long-term results versus a short-term PR campaign.

Because we are in the final chapter of this book, here's a quick recap of eight ways to reinvent your media story for public relations success!

8 WAYS TO MAKE YOUR STORY RELEVANT TODAY

1. Connect your story to a major news headline or trend.

2. Connect your story to a season (summer, fall, winter, spring, holidays).

3. Connect your story to a time of year related to your business (examples: small business week for entrepreneurs, tax season for CPAs, spring buying season for real estate experts.)

4. Connect your story to a holiday (there are so many holidays now, so always include references to back-up your pitch if it is not a highly recognized holiday.)

5. Connect your story to a major event (business launch, awards, premiere, elections).

6. Connect your story to a celebrity (connect to celebrity and/or influencer news).

7. Connect your story to a charity (all *Goody PR* clients are making a positive impact, and support a charity).

8. Connect your story to pop culture events (movies, concerts, what's trending).

CHAPTER 8 RECAP

When it comes to reinventing your story, this process should be something that you embrace every day. You don't want to have your media coverage to stop – ever – unless you are going out of business.

Step 8 Action Items – Reposition Your Story and Extend Media Success

1. Revise your media hooks so they are relevant and timely.

2. Build long-term media relationships to increase Follow-up Stories.

3. Prioritize media follow-up over everything.

4. Be patient, persistent, and never desperate in your follow-up.

5. Measure marketing results and Calculated Publicity Value.
6. Consistently reflect on lessons learned to improve your publicity approach.
7. Hold regular PR strategy meetings to reposition your story.
8. Revise your media hooks, and go back to Step 1.

PR Superpower 8 - Story Reinvention Superpower

With your new Story Reinvention Superpower, you will now be able to get your point across in a way that is even more meaningful, relevant and memorable.

Chapter 8 - 8-Second PR Challenges

As we close Chapter 8, here are your *8-Second PR* Challenges:

1. How are you going to meet and thank the media?
2. How are you going to build long-term media relationships?
3. How often are you going to follow-up with TV, print, radio and podcast reporters about when a story will be published?
4. How are you going to measure results for your media interviews for you or your clients?
5. How often are you going to launch new marketing campaigns?
6. How often are you going to hold PR strategy meetings?
7. How often are you going to review and reinvent your story for timely media interviews?
8. Are you still having fun?

Your *Story Reinvention Superpower* will help you expand media opportunities for brands for months and years to come.

In the Conclusion, I will recap all of the eight PR Superpowers that you have learned in this book, along with suggesting ways to celebrate your wins! Every media hit is a WIN, and it is important to give yourself cheers along this journey!

Reminder:

"THE DAY YOU STOP PROMOTING YOUR BOOK OR BUSINESS IS THE DAY THAT SALES STOP."

–LIZ H KELLY,
 Goody PR Founder and Author, 8-Second PR

CONCLUSION

"CREATE YOUR OWN STYLE...LET IT BE UNIQUE FOR YOURSELF AND YET IDENTIFIABLE FOR OTHERS."

– DAME ANNA WINTOUR,
  Editor in Chief, *Vogue*

Now that you have a new set of *8-Second PR* tools, skills and best practices that you can use to create a Wow Story and book hundreds of earned media interviews, let's wrap this book up with some encouraging words. You can now use your new expertise and 8 PR Superpowers as a roadmap for your long-term Public Relations Success.

By now you know that getting an interview published is not easy. Every time you get an earned media hit through traditional PR (TV, print, radio, podcast) or digital PR (video, photographs, and social media) with stories that shine a positive light on your brand, it's time to celebrate your WIN!

Remember, you are playing *8-Second PR* Baseball, and your job is to continually advance your story from an interview (if it is not Live) to being published to the world – no matter how long it takes. You want to avoid getting stuck on third base with never-ending interview follow-ups such as our 20+ emails/texts/calls to get *The Business Journals* story published for a client! If you score an earned media hit that promotes you and your work, share it in a humble way with the world!

As long as your content continues to entertain and educate your audience, your fans and media will keep coming back for more – for years. Your company, brand and book are not going away. Your challenge is to be relentless in developing new media hooks, send out new pitches, secure continual media coverage and make a positive impact.

I will be forever grateful to the many cheerleaders and marketing professionals who helped guide us through this publicity journey. The two public relations companies whom I hired to promote our first book, media coaches, reporters, producers, editors, family, friends, web developers, fans, and our *8-Second PR* book team have all played key roles in this PR success path that is still evolving.

Remember, PR is a team sport, and you cannot do it alone.

If you are just starting your PR process, celebrate your first wins! Let them inspire you to keep moving forward. Every positive story is a major milestone, and I wish you mega earned media and business success.

CELEBRATE YOUR FIRSTS and ALL MEDIA WINS!

Every time you get an earned interview story published (TV, print, radio or podcast), you should be dancing with a big smile like the people you see doing the "Fancy Like" dance in *TikTok* videos and the *Applebee's* commercial.

Your public relations wins may include:

1. First Print Story (featured in newspaper, magazine, and/or blog)
2. First National Newspaper Story!
3. Every Print Story afterwards! (feature story and/or expert quotes)
4. First Local Radio Interview!
5. First National Radio Interview!
6. Every Radio Interview afterwards!
7. First Podcast Interview!
8. First Major Podcast Interviews!
9. All Podcast Interviews!
10. First Book Review!
11. First Major Book Review!
12. First Book Event!
13. All Book Events!
14. First Speaking Gig!
15. All Speaking Gigs!
16. All future Interviews!
17. Plus, Celebrate, the positive impact of PR on your business, brand or book!
18. Plus, Celebrate the positive impact you are making on the world!

Below are some of our personal wins that remind us every day where we first got started. I have been in your shoes, and sat at many coffee meetings saying to a bestselling author, "How do you write a good book? How do you get an agent? How do you get published? How do you get media interviews?".

Your first is always important, so please do a dance and celebrate every PR milestone:

Major PR Milestone	What happened?
First Major Magazine Story – *Cosmopolitan*	I remember being so grateful to be in *Cosmopolitan Magazine* with a sidebar story, for the first time for my dating book audience.
First National Newspaper Story – *USA TODAY*	When my father called Los Angeles from Baltimore at 6am PST to say that the story featuring our dating book tips made it into the paper, I was ecstatic!
First Local TV Interview – *ABC2 WMAR-TV* Baltimore	For my first local TV news interview, I will be forever grateful to a high school friend named Dabney who helped me book it because she worked there.
First National TV Talk Show Interview – *NBC The Other Half*	For my first national TV talk show interview on *The Other Half* on *NBC* (guys' version of *The View*), I was fortunate to be on a panel as the dating expert with Hollywood legend Dick Clark, Danny Bonaduce (*The Partridge Family*), and Mario Lopez (*Extra, Access Hollywood*), along with Gretchen Frazier, who was seeking relationship advice about a long-term boyfriend who would not propose. Yes, I was nervous and barely remember it.
First Radio Interviews – *RTIR*	I will always be grateful to *RTIR* (*Radio-Television Interview Report*) for their promotional magazine that was sent to over 4,000 radio producers around the country (and is now done digitally). The result was over 175+ print, radio and podcast media hits! Thank you Bill and Steve Harrison.
First Paid Column – *Smart Woman*	I am also grateful for my first paid column published in *Smart Woman* magazine in Baltimore, Maryland, by editor Sabina Dana Plasse. It is always best to start PR in your hometown. Baltimore has been very kind to me as an author.

Major PR Milestone	What happened?
First National Column – *Yahoo!*	After writing for smaller blogs, I was so honored to receive our first national column with *Yahoo!* The editor Rad Dewey is now our friend on *Facebook* many years later. To build this media relationship, we flew to the *Yahoo!* Headquarters in Sunnyvale, California, to meet Rad and his team in person. And for years, I wore my *Yahoo!* baseball hat from their gift shop.

You can also achieve all of these media milestones and success while promoting a personal or business brand. Be your own cheerleader, and jump into your PR.

Look for the PR opportunities, follow the *8-Second PR* process, constantly reinvent your story to develop timely and relevant media hooks and pitches. Yes, it is a process and it's hard, but you can get continual media coverage if you work it!

So let's review what you've learned in this book as an *8-Second PR* Success Roadmap to your Ultimate Media Success. It's a lot of information to digest, and it's ok to be overwhelmed.

Make a commitment to do at least 1 thing for your public relations campaign EVERY DAY (create a media hook, write a pitch, write a press release, email a reporter, call a reporter, book an interview, do an interview, update your website Press page, share your stories on social media – just do something!).

You will increase your confidence, lessons learned, and results as you fine-tune your PR process. You have the information and PR Superpowers now to see through obstacles. You can do this!

8 ULTIMATE MEDIA SUCCESS GOALS

As an example, here are eight Ultimate Media Success Goals for public relations that should be customized by each individual, brand, or marketing professional. Dig deep and define what you aim to achieve from your PR.

And then remember to celebrate each milestone and media hit:

1. Get 2-3 monthly interviews published for TV, print, radio and podcasts.
2. Increase sales and/or gain clients based on earned media.
3. Increase email subscribers.
4. Increase social media followers.
5. Increase brand awareness.
6. Attract more speaking opportunities.
7. Raise funds for a charity.
8. Make a difference.

The combination of the *8-Second PR* Superpowers can turn these goals into reality with bottom line results. And remember, one media story can literally reach millions of potential clients and fans.

It's the combination of your marketing and PR engine and 8 PR Superpowers that will get you consistent earned media (TV, print, radio, and podcast interviews) to propel your brand forward. Together, these strengths can result in hundreds of media interviews for your personal and business brands, increase your SEO (Search Engine Optimization) and positively impact profits.

To make your brand unstoppable, use your new *8-Second PR* Superpowers and process. Go back to the eight steps in this book when needed for examples and suggestions. You can also help others magnify their good by sharing this book with friends who want to break through noise - especially in their niche online.

8-SECOND PR STORY ENERGIZER PROCESS

1. WOW STORY - Define Your Story Magic to Inspire Fans and Media.
2. DIGITAL PR - Dominate Your Digital Bank to Increase Word-of-Mouth Marketing.
3. CONTENT STRENGTH - Create Compelling Content that Emotionally Connects with Readers.

4. MEDIA HOOKS - Write Powerful Pitches to Move Reporters to Cover Your Story.

5. MEDIA VISION - Reach Your Target Audience by Laser Focusing on Niche Media.

6. MEDIA HITS - Make Your Interview Take Flight to Score Mega Media.

7. MESSAGE IMPACT - Magnify Your Interviews with Meaningful Soundbites.

8. STORY REINVENTION - Reposition Your Story and Extend Media Success.

It will take time and practice, but you can get your message and story published in your ideal media to reach your target audience! Remember, be relentless!

And please, always ask others for their HONEST feedback and advice. I am still learning and continue to seek advice from other PR professionals and regularly attend educational seminars/ events on marketing and public relations topics.

The most important thing is to keep promoting a story, especially if it is your true passion! Even if you are told "No" hundreds of times, commit to continual PR.

With your new *8-Second PR* Superpowers, you will energize your story with continual earned media!

8-SECOND PR SUPERPOWERS = ULTIMATE MEDIA SUCCESS

1. WOW Storytelling Superpower
2. Digital PR Superpower
3. Content Connector Superpower
4. Media Hook Superpower

5. Media Vision Superpower

6. Media Hits Superpower

7. Message Impact Superpower

8. Story Reinvention Superpower

As a quick reference, keep your new *8-Second PR* Process and Superpowers nearby to encourage you to continue moving forward.

To help you, this *8-Second PR* Success Roadmap Summary can help you plan and commit to working on one-two action items per day, for your long-term public relations. Use whatever organization tools work best for you (*Excel, Notes, Google Calendar Reminders, iCal, Outlook, Sales Force, Constant Contact, Google Docs*) to organize and jumpstart your PR marathon.

8-SECOND PR SUCCESS ROADMAP SUMMARY

Step 1 – Define Your Story Magic to Inspire Fans and Media

PR SUPERPOWER 1 - WOW STORYTELLING SUPERPOWER

You need to go way beyond telling a great brand story using the Wow Storytelling Superpower by defining your magic. By mastering your message, you can inspire fans, media and influencers to make your story go viral. You must make a lasting impression that moves the reader, reporter, or customer to share your brand story - over and over again.

Yes, you want to find an A-team, unique product, and powerful spokespeople, but ultimately, your media results go back to the brand story.

If you have the determination and dedication to edit your story more than 100 times to make it truly inspiring, you will have Ultimate Media Success. Use your first *8-Second PR* Superpower to stand out and be memorable. You've got this!

Chapter 1 - 8-Second PR Challenges

As a recap, here are your Chapter 1 *8-Second PR* Challenges:

1. How can you get someone's attention in eight seconds?
2. How can you tell your brand story in one to two sentences?
3. What were 3 game changers in your life that led you to your ideal job?
4. What work would you do for free?
5. What are three things that describe your brand in one sentence?
6. Can you share a mission statement with a powerful meaning in eight seconds?
7. What are your three to seven key selling points?
8. When are you going to schedule time to work on enhancing your Wow Story?

Step 2 - Dominate Your Digital Bank to Increase Word-of-Mouth Marketing

PR SUPERPOWER 2 – DIGITAL PR SUPERPOWER

Once you have a brand name idea, the next thing you want to do is dominate your digital bank. For Ultimate Media Success, you must enhance your Digital PR Superpower to increase your Word-of- Mouth Marketing. You want to own your digital assets with the same superhuman strength as a superhero. Your digital bank includes a dot com URL, mobile-friendly websites, social media channels, blog names, videos, photographs, graphics, and more. If you embrace digital marketing, your content will be listed all over the first page of *Google* results when someone searches on your product's name. To get everyone talking about you online and attract brand advocates, you must master this *8-Second PR* Superpower!

Chapter 2 - 8-Second PR Challenges

As a recap, here are your Chapter 2 *8-Second PR* Challenges:

Liz H Kelly

1. Are you able to secure your exact match .com and top three social media usernames for your brand?

2. What is your SEO (Search Engine Optimization) keyword strategy for your content?

3. How is your website content going to wow a fan in eight seconds?

4. What is your visual marketing strategy for photos to tell a story in eight seconds?

5. What are you going to include in the first eight seconds of your videos to engage your audience?

6. What is your 2-3 minute brand story video going to include?

7. Can you tell a powerful story in a tweet that is clear, concise and compelling?

8. What marketing elements will be in one of your digital marketing campaigns?

Step 3 - Create Compelling Content that Emotionally Connects with Readers

PR SUPERPOWER 3 – CONTENT CONNECTOR SUPERPOWER

Once you own your digital domain, it is time to magnify your brand story with clear, concise, and compelling content that will make a lasting impression. To move readers, use the Content Connector Superpower to write memorable story that is unstoppable. You can gain the undivided attention of your fans by creating press releases, columns, blogs, videos, emails and social media posts with timely, relevant, and/or evergreen content.

An evergreen story is a plus because it has a long shelf-life and can connect to your target market audience for years. Evergreen story examples include profile stories, how-to guides, product reviews, lists (top tips are always good), best practices, and success tips with case study examples. Get ready to dig deeper using this *8-Second PR* Superpower. You want to continually review your content strength by asking, does it work?

Chapter 3 - 8-Second PR Challenges

As we close Chapter 3, here are your *8-Second PR* Challenges:

1. What are five compelling headlines that you can write in eight words or less about your brand or advice tips?
2. What are 3 evergreen stories that you can pitch?
3. How will the first sentence for each story compel the reader to continue?
4. Whom can you quote to add value to the content?
5. What statistics can add strength to your story?
6. What is the high-level outline for your content?
7. Are you going to send out press releases, and which service will you use?
8. Who is going to proofread your content and/or provide feedback?

Step 4 - Write Powerful Pitches to Move Reporters to Cover Your Story

PR SUPERPOWER 4 – MEDIA HOOK SUPERPOWER

To help you get more earned media (TV, radio, print or digital stories – for free), use your Media Hook Superpower. You always want to pitch a timely topic that uniquely connects your brand to an event, launch, milestone, or headline news story in a way that moves the reporter to cover your it.

With an eight-second adult attention span, you need to immediately grab the reporter's interest in your email subject line, topic headline and/or first sentence. Once you have sold the right reporter on your story idea, their media coverage can give your brand way more credibility than any paid advertisement.

If you build a good relationship with the reporter and have a reputation that you are "easy to work with and provide great story ideas," they will keep coming back for more. Use this *8-Second PR* Superpower to make lasting impressions, and secure hundreds of media interviews!

Liz H Kelly

As we close Chapter 4, here are your *8-Second PR* Challenges:

1. What are three compelling media hooks for each of your clients/projects?
2. What will you write in your email subject line to get a reporter to open it?
3. How will the first sentence in your email or phone pitch grab their attention?
4. Who will be your spokesperson - and do they have a moving story?
5. How is your spokesperson/expert or organization positively impacting lives?
6. Does your story pitch include testimonials from customers, and are they willing to speak on camera about it?
7. What type of visuals can you provide to illustrate your media hook?
8. How are you going to use social media to research timely topics and trends?

Step 5 – Reach Your Target Audience by Laser Focusing On Niche Reporters

PR SUPERPOWER 5 – MEDIA VISION SUPERPOWER

You want to use your Media Vision Superpower to connect with the right contact who is genuinely interested in your story. To reach your ideal media, fans, and influencers, laser focus your research to see through obstacles.

To enhance this PR superpower, *Google* to find out what your preferred reporters and media outlets are talking about online. Sure, most people would like to be in TIME or on CBS Sunday Morning. However, media placements do not happen magically just because you asked for an interview. You need to pitch the right media hook to the right person at the right time, just to have a chance of your story being published to the public. It is critical to fine-tune this *8-Second PR* Superpower to achieve your PR goals.

Chapter 5 - 8-Second PR Challenges

As we close Chapter 5, here are your *8-Second PR* Challenges:

1. Who is your ideal target market for customers and media? Consider interests, income, geography, and more.
2. What three publications are on the top of your media outlet wish list?
3. If you do PR, who are the top three preferred reporters for each client?
4. How can you build long-term relationships with your preferred media?
5. How can you research and reach podcast hosts for your niche audience?
6. Who are key influencers for your client's product or service?
7. How can you build long-term relationships with key influencers in your areas of expertise?
8. What are five different ways to pitch the same thing?

Step 6 - Make Your Interview Take Flight to Score Mega Media

PR SUPERPOWER 6 – MEDIA HITS SUPERPOWER

Many authors and experts do not realize that just because you get an interview request, it does not mean a story will become a published media hit. Your Media Hits Superpower can help you consistently secure interviews and get them published! When you receive an interview request from a reporter, you're up at bat.

However, even if you do the interview, it might not be published immediately – or ever. Just like scoring a run in baseball, getting in the headlines is a process that takes skill, endurance, and patience! Every time you get a media opportunity, you want to be prepared to advance your interview around the bases until it crosses home plate as a published story! If you stumble, get back up again until you score earned media using this *8-Second PR* Superpower!

Chapter 6 — 8-Second PR Challenges

1. As a recap, here are your Chapter 6 *8-Second PR* Challenges:

2. What tools or processes can you set up to ensure you can reply to a TV reporter within 1 hour of a request?

3. What items are you going to include in a digital press kit for you or your clients?

4. How are you going to set expectations with your clients so they can help you reply to media requests with warp speed?

5. What Q-and-A scripts do you have ready for your clients to send TV producers?

6. How often are you going to contact the media if your story gets stuck on third base with continual follow-up?

7. When do you know it's time to give up on the story follow-up?

8. How can you show your appreciation and support for a reporter's story on social media?

9. How are you going to thank reporters after a story is published?

Step 7 - Magnify Your Interviews with Meaningful Soundbites

PR SUPERPOWER 7 – MESSAGE IMPACT SUPERPOWER

Presenting your brand story to the world is a PR art that you can master with the Message Impact Superpower. When you get the opportunity to do an interview with a reporter, make sure to be GRATEFUL and prepared to deliver moving messages from the heart.

For TV, print, radio and podcast interviews, you want to move your audience with powerful soundbites and stories. Use emphasis statements and examples of how your tips can help others to quickly draw attention to your brand, book or product. And always deliver your points in a meaningful versus promotional way.

Just as thunder can make you stop what you are doing and look up, you want people to stop multi-tasking and focus on what you are saying. Your PR results will be impacted by your ability to deliver great content with a memorable delivery. For TV, your tone of voice, non-verbal expressions, props, what you wear and the lighting all matter in a very visual world. If you speak with confidence and conviction, you will make lasting impressions for your brand using this *8-Second PR* Superpower!

Chapter 7 - 8-Second PR Challenges

As a recap, here are your Chapter 7 *8-Second PR* Challenges:

1. What are the three to five key talking points for your story?
2. What are the top three things you need to remember when being interviewed?
3. What styles and colors make you look great on camera?
4. What can you say if you get an unexpected question from a reporter?
5. What's different about your story versus others doing similar things?
6. How are you helping others?
7. What are you doing to create balance in your life?
8. How can you relax before interviews?

Step 8 – Reposition Your Story and Extend Media Success

PR SUPERPOWER 8 – STORY REINVENTION SUPERPOWER

All brands need to continually update their media hooks to stay relevant to the latest headline news, technology and trends. To keep the interest of the media, influencers, and fans, you must master your Story Reinvention Superpower. This skill can help you reposition your story with new pitches - over and over and over again.

Asking questions, listening, and being able to change course are some of the most powerful PR tools for repeat interviews. You cannot sustain your business or a marketing campaign by doing the same thing over and over again. To have Ultimate Media Success, you must keep the creativity going - for years - using this *8-Second PR* Superpower!

Chapter 8 - 8-Second PR Challenges

As we close Chapter 8, here are your *8-Second PR* Challenges:

1. How are you going to meet and thank the media?
2. How are you going to build long-term media relationships?
3. How often are you going to follow-up with TV, print, radio and podcast reporters about when a story will be published?
4. How are you going to measure results for your media interviews for you or your clients?
5. How often are you going to launch new marketing campaigns?
6. How often are you going to hold PR strategy meetings?
7. How often are you going to review and reinvent your story for timely media interviews?
8. Are you still having fun?

YOU CAN DO YOUR OWN PR! – JULIE SPIRA ON *8-SECOND BRANDING* PODCAST

If you don't think you can do your own PR after reading this *8-Second PR* book, think again. For encouragement, listen to one of our first *8-Second Branding* Podcast interviews called How Top Online Dating Expert Julie Spira got 1500 Media Hits – including the *TODAY* Show. You can find this interview on our *Goody PR* website podcast page here: https://goodypr.com/8-second-branding.

Are you now ready for your Ultimate Media Success?

You've got this! You have all the PR Superpowers you need.

Do not overthink this. Make a plan, and start learning from the process! Remember, it's a PR Marathon versus a sprint.

Just start.

The end. (Well, not really, it is just the beginning of your story).

ACKNOWLEDGEMENTS

Thank you, Mom, for your writing skills, encouragement, and quirky sense of humor!

Thank you, Dad, for being president of my first book's fan club, endless LOLs, and teaching us storytelling skills!

Thank you to our *Goody PR* Clients for your partnership, ideas, and gratitude over the past ten years. Your stories have inspired us to continue magnifying good!

Thank you to my first PR teams and media coaches who got me started on the right track, especially Jess Todtfeld, Jamie Feldstein, and Roberta Gale.

Thank you, Vicki Winters, for finding my first literary agent and for being SUCH a passionate cheerleader!

Thank you, Jane Turner, for getting me to write a journal again. It was very healing, and got us to write again.

BIG Cheers and gratitude to every producer, guest booker, assignment editor, radio or TV host, columnist, blogger, book reviewer, podcast host and their teams who interviewed me and/or our clients.

Thank you to PR and marketing pros who have been great sounding boards and advisors over the past fifteen years, especially Ann Flower, Susan Bejeckian, Wendy Guarisco, Dr. Jess Neren, Mary Rau, Laura Michelle Powers, Cynthia Lieberman, Tara DeWitt Coomans, Carol Starr Taylor, Michele Weisbart, Richard

Winfield Lewis – and special thanks to Bill and Steve Harrison (*National Publicity Summit* Co-Founders).

Thank you to Lee Ann Del Carpio for being our first ever client!!!! Sending you aloha love!

Special thanks to Lisa and Josh Lannon for being our PR partner on this journey as a VIP client during the past decade for *Warriors Heart* and *Journey Healing Centers*. Your businesses, financial education, philanthropic contributions and book (*The Social Capitalist*) continue to inspire us and millions around the world!

Thank you Former Special Forces and *Warriors Heart* Co-Founder Tom Spooner, Former Master Sergeant Teddy Lanier and *US Air Force* Col (ret) Chris Stricklin for your many sacrifices and service protecting our freedom.

Thank you, Tom Wheelwright and your *WealthAbility* team (Clarissa, Clint, Irene and Ann). It was a true honor to constantly brainstorm your story and continually promote your educational products and services for over five years! Your enthusiasm and passion are contagious!

Special shout out to everyone on *Modern Family* EP Danny Zuker's book team, including Liz Dubelman, Paul Slansky and Dan Vallancourt. It was an honor to work with each of you for so many reasons!

Big thanks to our many clients who wrote and published books fearlessly with a passion during the pandemic. Special shout out to: Therese Allison (*Playing for Keeps – How a 21ˢᵗ century businesswoman beat the boys!*), Omar L. Harris (*The Servant Leader's Manifesto* and *Be a J.E.D.I. Leader, Not a Boss*), and Co-Authors Joseph Tachovsky and Cynthia Kraack (*40 Thieves on Saipan*).

Thank you to our *8-Second Branding* Podcast team at *VoiceAmerica* (Ryan Treasure and his rock star sound engineers who make everyone sound great!)

Cheers to Joyce Chow, who taught us how to interview celebrities on the red carpet!

Thank you to my rock star book production team: Heidi North (Book Cover Designer), Bader Howar (*Bader Howar Photography*), Meriam Bouarrouji, Susan Bejeckian, Yvette Bowlin, Shabbir Hussain (Interior Book Designer) and former English Teacher mom (who taught me too).

And many thanks to our family and friends (you know who you are!) for listening, being there, and providing cheers throughout this marketing journey. We could not write this book and magnify good without your support.

RESOURCES

Because the focus of *8-Second PR* has been primarily on brand storytelling, here are a few recommended resources, tools, and reading for you. Please visit our GoodyPR.com website for more tips, tools and our *8-Second PR* online classes.

Media Outreach Resources

Cision – National database of reporters (access to 600,000 members for annual fee) *Haro* (*Help A Reporter Out*) – Press Queries posted by reporters

Qwoted – Another Press Query service where reporters post stories.

RTIR – *Radio Television Interview Report*

PodMatch – *A new podcast matching tool*

Email Marketing Resources

Constant Contact

Mailchimp

Sales Force

Press Releases

PR Newswire – most expensive and biggest reach Business Wire PR Web (cheaper, and owned now by PR Newswire)

Business Wire

Marketing Wire

Digital Marketing Tips Reading

Mashable

Social Media Examiner

Social Media Club Los Angeles

Social Media Management Resources

Hootsuite

Sprout Social

Hubspot

Buffer

Tailwind (Instagram post scheduling)

Photo Apps

Adobe Photo Apps

Canva

Live Collage

Camera+

Books

Media Secrets: A Media Training Crash Course (Jess Todtfeld)

How to Sell Books by the Truckload on Amazon (Penny C Sansevieri)

GOODY PR - CONTACT US - MARKETING, PR, AND SOCIAL MEDIA MARKETING SERVICES

If you do not have time to do everything in this book and prefer to hire a PR team, please contact us to set up an introductory call: info@goodypr.com.

Check out our *Goody PR* website Services page that includes a menu of ways that we may be able to help you: https://goodypr.com/services

CLIENT **TESTIMONIALS**

Kelly's PR efforts and innovative ideas have been an integral part of our marketing team's success for the past four years. After booking hundreds of media interviews, we had 900 Tax-Free Wealth books on backorder on Amazon. When our publisher asked, "what did you do," we said, well we hired a publicist. If you're looking for a great PR partner to promote your business, I highly recommend Liz Kelly.

–**Tom Wheelwright,** CPA, CEO of WealthAbility and Tax-Free Wealth Author

Liz Kelly partnered with our Journey Healing Centers team on the Public Relations for 4 years, which included writing monthly press releases, pitching to the media, booking interviews, media coaching, and editing contributing writer stories. Her work contributed to our increased brand awareness, 53 TV interviews and educating the public. Liz was also on top of breaking news stories, and was willing to always work no matter the day or time when we got interview requests. She has tremendous follow through and keeps on top of what is going on. I highly recommend Liz and Goody PR.

–**Lisa Lannon,** author, social entrepreneur, and RICH DAD ADVISOR

Liz Kelly's enthusiasm, creativity and teamwork approach all contributed to a PR campaign that went way beyond the goals set for my book launch. With over 40 media hits (interviews and syndicated stories), two speaking events and a Charitybuzz campaign for one of our book charities in 3 months, it was off the charts. If you want a PR pro who knows how to adapt and adjust to headline news to amplify your story, I highly recommend Goody PR and Liz Kelly.

–**Danny Zuker,** *MODERN FAMILY* Executive Producer, 5-time Emmy Winner and Author, *He Started It!: My Twitter War With Trump*

We are beyond grateful to Goody PR Founder Liz H Kelly for promoting our executive leadership coaching brand, books and apps with 2 public relations campaigns that resulted in 4 National TV interviews, local TV interviews, a column in Real Leaders to reach our core audience, feature stories (including in Fast Company), a total of 40 podcast interviews and many more media over 14 months. Kelly constantly brainstormed new ways to connect our books to headline news such as Martin Luther King Weekend and the Great Resignation Trend impacting business leaders today. Kelly also provided media coaching prior to our national TV interviews that offered helpful reminders and tips. And most importantly, she was truly passionate about promoting our personal and business brand, books and products using the power of story. We highly recommend Goody PR Founder Liz H Kelly.

–**Omar L. Harris,** Former GM (*GSK, Allergan*), Intent Consulting Founder, Executive Coach, Award-Winning and Bestselling Author and Speaker

We were lucky to be one of Goody PR's 5 VIP clients during this past year that made us look like pros in launching Autism Guardian Angels (AGA). Goody PR partnered with us to develop a brand story, mission, logo, custom website, compelling content and an integrated marketing campaign for Autism Awareness Month that put us on the map with peer recognition and media within a month. We're grateful for all their hard work and dedication to creating a fun AGA brand that matched our mission to "bring out the brilliance in exceptional children and adults with autism by investing in tools that increase their smiles, confidence and independence".

–**David Luber,** AUTISM GUARDIAN ANGELS and LCC Properties Group founder

Thank you Liz H Kelly and Goody PR for pushing our DGA Memorial Day Premiere forward with marketing, PR, social media and sponsorships at the last minute. Within 10 days, it was amazing that you secured 2 news segments on KCBS and KTLA, food sponsors that made dinner for the Marines from Camp Pendleton possible, 2 photographers, special Golden Goody Award for WWII veteran Leon Cooper, videos and social media marketing support. Your marketing campaign blitz has greatly contributed to Vanilla Fire Productions being in negotiations for funding a sequel, only one week after this event! We can't thank you enough!

—**Steven C Barber,** *VANILLA FIRE PRODUCTIONS* Co-Founder & Executive Producer

Goody PR has been a gamechanger for our WWII military history book "40 Thieves on Saipan" about my father's US Marines Corps platoon in the Pacific. As a result of 2 PR campaigns, we were fortunate to have 13 local TV interviews, a 30-minute segment on PBS Postcards, a feature story in the Minneapolis Star-Tribune, and many radio interviews (National Defense Radio, American Veterans Show). And our book reviews went through the roof on Amazon to over 600. We can't thank Liz H Kelly and her team enough!

—**Joseph Tachovsky,** Award-Winning and Bestselling Author, *40 Thieves on Saipan*

We're grateful to Liz H Kelly and her Goody PR team for helping us promote our self-help memoir, "Playing for Keeps - How a 21st century businesswoman beat the boys!" - in the middle of the pandemic. Together, we fine-tuned our brand story, revised our book cover, and launched a new website in sync with a public relations campaign. As another woman in business, Liz continued to come up with creative ideas to pitch our career success story and money tips for retiring early. We were fortunate to get coverage in GoBankingRates, MSN, The Business Journals, MarketWatch, Yahoo! Finance, ABC Radio, VoiceAmerica Business Channel, The Secrets of Supermom Show, Raising Financial Freedom, a column in SWAAY and many more media. If you are an author, CEO or expert looking for someone to be passionate about promoting your story, we highly recommend Liz and Goody PR!

—**Therese Allison,** Successful Businesswoman, Award-Winning and Bestselling Author and Mentor, *Playing for Keeps – How a 21st century businesswoman beat the boys!*

It was great to bring Liz back for a second social media training workshop at The Recording Academy (GRAMMYs) for local members and clients of MusiCares. There was a lot of positive

attendee feedback for her 2.0 class held June 2013 which focused on increasing individual social media presence using Facebook, Twitter, YouTube, and Instagram. Her branding, popular music and mySpace examples were a big hit with the audience! There were approximately 40 participants, and Liz did a great job answering ALL of their questions. Thanks Liz!

–**Brett Bryngelson**, program specialist for *MUSICARES/GRAMMYS*

If you're looking for a public relations agency that really cares about you and secures media interviews, we highly recommend Liz H Kelly and her Goody PR team. Kelly's innovative brand storytelling approach includes constantly connecting your topic to current events and headline news. As a result, we are grateful for an 8-minute timely TV interview about our Occupational Therapy tips and books that increased our reach.

–**Sarah Appleman,** Occupational Therapist, Consultant and Children's Book Author, "Paw Prints" series and "Playing With Your Food"

Liz helped Jukin Media with our initial launch party campaign, which included PR, social media and cause marketing for the Rob Dyrdek Foundation to reach our primarily 18-34 male demographic. This was a last minute campaign, and within 1 month, she helped us fine-tune our message, publish a press release, get key influencers to the launch party, and our social media fans increased on Facebook and Twitter by over 100%.

–**Jon Skogmo,** founder and CEO of *JUKIN MEDIA Inc.,* Los Angeles, CA

@LizHKelly @GoodyAwards strategically helped us from early on thru launch to develop a global marketing campaign including press releases, social media and photography for @ComedyGivesBack 24 Hours of Comedy benefiting Malaria No More that contributed to our 100 million impressions in 2 weeks resulting in winning the IAWTV Best Live Event Award. We were thrilled to leverage the Comedy Gives Back platform to honor Budd Friedman with the Golden Goody Award.

–@**AmberJLawson** @ComedyGivesBack, Los Angeles, CA

Liz's UCLA Extension New Media Marketing online class was tremendously useful to me professionally and personally, and I have already begun to deploy some of the learnings in my consulting practice.

–**Jim E. Schiefelbein,** Chicago, Illinois

Thank you Goody PR and Liz H Kelly for helping us take our brand story to the next level for our Personalogy Game! We appreciate the powerful storytelling process that you took us through to rethink our positioning in a more playful way that emotionally connects with the media, customers and retailers. As a result, we now have Walmart interested in putting our games in their stores for Christmas! We can't thank you enough!

–**Michelle Burke,** Creative Director and Co-Founder, *Personalogy Game*

BOOK ENDORSEMENTS

Kelly's booked thousands of media interviews for PR clients, including CNN, CBS Health Watch, FOX News, USA Today, The Wall Street Journal, NPR and more, making 8-Second PR a go-to guide for anyone with a brand story to promote.

–Bill Harrison, co-founder, RADIO-TV INTERVIEW REPORT (RTIR) and NATIONAL PUBLICITY SUMMIT

Liz Kelly's 8-Second PR book has great tips for how to get editors and reporters interested in your story. Journalists are always looking for a moving "story behind the story." The author's case studies show you what works best to hook editors and get your story into print.

–P.K. Daniel, veteran journalist, whose work has appeared in *The Washington Post, San Diego Union-Tribune, Baseball America* and *CBS Sports Digital*

Follow the advice in this book. It will not only help you become better at the PR game, but become a better writer and better marketer, as well.

–Jess Todtfeld, CSP, former TV producer at *ABC, NBC,* and *FOX*, media trainer, speaker, and author (*MEDIA SECRETS*)

We can't thank Liz H Kelly enough for giving away her PR secrets in 8-Second PR. When we first started our new business Roma Leaf, my company could not afford to hire her PR agency, so Liz recommended reading her book instead. As a marketer, we knew the importance of PR, and went through it with highlighters and sticky notes. As a result of her 8-Second PR tips and examples of media pitches, we were able to land a feature TV interview on FOX 11 Los Angeles that was worth approximately $40,000 in Calculated Publicity Value, and contributed to an additional $10,000 in product sales. Trust me, read this book, take notes and share it with friends - because it is a gamechanger for brands!

–Mariya Palanjian, Founder/CEO, *Roma Leaf* and *Globafly*

It was like Christmas morning waking up every day working with Liz Kelly on our PR. She partnered with us to develop new and innovative strategies for media stories, events and promotions! And now, you can find all of her secrets in this must-read book!

–**Debbi DiMaggio,** Realtor to the Stars, HIGHLAND PARTNERS co-founder, philanthropist, and author of three books, including THE ART OF REAL ESTATE.

Liz Kelly is a PR Rockstar, who worked for Levine Communications Office, one of the world's most prominent entertainment PR firms, as a contractor for over a year. She consistently hit home runs for our clients by booking TV, radio and print interviews. Read Liz's book, 8-Second PR, to learn her storytelling secrets and get your name in the headlines!

–**Michael Levine,** LCO-Levine Communications Founder, Media Expert, Speaker and Author of 19 Books, including Guerrilla P.R.

I've worked with Liz for a number of years and the digital marketing strategies in 8-Second PR will help you not only engage influencers online, but it can help build Worth-of-Mouth Marketing to reach more people every day. And the photo and video storytelling tips are invaluable for social media marketing.

–**Lindsay Mauch,** Founder of LTM Digital (a Social Media and Digital Marketing Agency), Social Media Instructor, and Chapter President, SOCIAL MEDIA CLUB LOS ANGELES

Working with Liz on the PR for her first book launch, she showed incredible insights on unique angles to pitch media outlets. And it's no surprise that she transitioned out of a corporate job into media and publicity because she intuitively understands the reporter's needs. This innovative how-to guide is a must read for anyone wanting to understand the method behind the madness of the PR world.

–**Jamie Feldstein,** former journalist and media relations expert, and now licensed marriage and family therapist

AUTHOR REQUEST-
WRITE A BOOK REVIEW

If you found this *8-Second PR* book helpful, we would beyond grateful if you post a book review on *Amazon,* your column and/or social media. A few sentences with your comments would mean so much to us!

Feedback is a "gift", and authors are especially appreciative of book reviews.

Your thoughts on what was most helpful in *8-Second PR* can provide valuable insights for how we can best help others do their own public relations!

If you post a review, please tweet it and/or post on *Instagram* and tag us **@LizHKelly** so we can thank you. We will be happy to follow you back too.

ABOUT
PODCAST

Listen to experts talk about the latest marketing, public relations and social media tips and trends on our *8-Second Branding* Podcast that is hosted by the *VoiceAmerica Business Channel*, and is available on all major podcast platforms (*Apple Podcasts, Spotify, Google Podcasts, Stitcher, iHeart Radio*, and more).

We launched this marketing/public relations tips podcast to help brands like you better define your Wow Story in a clear, concise and compelling way. Listen to our interviews with successful business leaders and authors who share their story-behind-the-story and marketing and promotion secrets.

Using the same superpowers of an unstoppable superhero, the *8-Second Branding Podcast* can help your brand be a force for good, build loyal fans and ultimately increase sales.

To listen, visit https://goodypr.com/8-second-branding

ABOUT
GOODY BUSINESS
BOOK AWARDS

If you wrote a great book, and/or know an author whose book is helping others, please nominate them for our *Goody Business Book Awards*. Join our mission to "Uplift Author Voices" by calling attention to their great work. This annual awards program honors books making a difference through words (helping others save money, start a business, live healthier, be happier, build wealth, be a great leader, be inspired and more.)

Anyone can nominate a book in 10 genres and 50 award categories for books published within the past 5 years. The ten areas include Business, Children's Books, Entrepreneur, Health, Leadership, Marketing/Sales, Money/Wealth, Real Estate, Self-Help and Technology. Authors, publicists and publishers can nominate books.

These unique awards can help authors increase awareness of their book, build credibility as a trustworthy source, increase sales, along with attracting more raving fans and business clients through the power of recognition.

Nominate your book between January 1 - September 30, and winners will be announced November 15 - just in time for holiday promotions. **https://GoodyBusinessBookAwards.com**

ABOUT THE AUTHOR

Liz H Kelly is the Goody PR Founder, Award-Winning Author (*8-Second PR*) and Podcast Host (*8-Second Branding*) with 15+ years of experience promoting authors and brands with a WOW Story who are making a positive impact. She loves connecting her client's stories to current headlines, and finding a story that moves audiences. As a published author, Kelly had over 500 media interviews (TV, radio, print and syndication) over 5 years for her first book about dating ("*Smart Man Hunting*"). Her work and books have been featured on *CNN, Lifetime, USA TODAY, The Chicago Tribune, Thrive Global, KTLA, KNBC News, KABC News, BBC Radio, ESPN Radio, NPR* and thousands of media outlets.

Kelly's *Goody PR* clients have been featured in thousands of mega media interviews – including on the *TODAY Show, CNN, BBC World News, CBS Health Watch, FOX Business, PBS Postcards, Black News Channel, TMZ,* and in *The Wall Street Journal, The Washington Post, The Chicago Tribune, TIME, USA TODAY, Psychology Today, WebMD, BBC Radio, WOR Radio,* and hundreds of local TV stations and podcasts.

Kelly also teaches digital marketing at *UCLA Extension*, developed *8-Second PR* classes online (available on *Teachable),* and is grateful that her *8-Second PR* book was selected as a textbook by Instructors at two California universities (*California State University San Bernardino* and *UCLA Extension*).

On a personal note, Kelly is a *Johns Hopkins University Carey School of Business* alumna from Baltimore, Maryland, and an Autism Advocate, who loves living near the mountains and ocean in Santa Monica, California, feels fortunate to have attended the *Sundance Film Festival* for over a decade, and had a darkroom for processing photographs in her basement at age 17.

Websites:

https://GoodyPR.com

https://8SecondPR.com

https://8-second-pr.teachable.com

https://GoodyBusinessBookAwards.com

Follow @LizHKelly @8SecondPR on *Facebook, Instagram* and *Twitter* (25k+ followers) and/or email us: info@goodypr.com